THE PASSAGE WEST

GIACOMO MARRAMAO is Professor of Political and Theoretical Philosophy at the University of Rome III and Director of the Fondazione Basso. His publications include Kairós: *Towards an Ontology of Due Time* and *La passione del presente*.

THE PASSAGE WEST

Philosophy and Globalisation

GIACOMO MARRAMAO

Translated by Matteo Mandarini
With an Afterword by Antonio Negri

VERSO

London • New York

This English-language edition published by Verso 2012
Translation © Matteo Mandarini 2012
Afterword © Antonio Negri
First published as *Passaggio a Occidente. Filosofia e globalizzazione*
© Bollati Boringhieri 2003

1 3 5 7 9 10 8 6 4 2

Verso
UK: 6 Meard Street, London W1F 0EG
US: 20 Jay Street, Suite 1010, Brooklyn, NY 11201
www.versobooks.com

Verso is the imprint of New Left Books

ISBN-13: 978-1-84467-852-5

British Library Cataloguing in Publication Data
A catalogue record for this book is available from the British Library

Library of Congress Cataloging-in-Publication Data
A catalog record for this book is available from the Library of Congress

Typeset in Sabon by Hewer UK Ltd, Edinburgh
Printed in the US by Maple Vail

To Gianni Carchia

in memoriam

CONTENTS

PREFACE TO THE ENGLISH EDITION

In Paul Valéry's *Regards sur le monde actuel*, there is a striking set of reflections on 'East and West'. The first edition of *The Passage West* set out from Valéry to attempt to conceptualise the phenomena of interdependence and time-space compression that are now summarised under the name of globalisation. These phenomena indicate a threshold of no return in the history of civilisation. The populations of the globe are drawn into ever closer reciprocal dependence and velocity of communications, such that they can no longer ignore one another and limit their relationships to simple utilitarian manoeuvres. Eventually, there will be room for something other than acts of exploitation, penetration, coercion and competition.

While highlighting the extraordinary foresight of Valéry's inter-war diagnosis-prognosis, *The Passage West* took on the difficult task of problematising its contents, taking as its theme the nature of the obstacles, contrasts and conflicts that to this day keep humanity on this threshold, preventing humanity from taking leave of its own point of departure towards a new time and a newly open future. The book's title, *The Passage West* – which follows the second Italian edition in devoting its final chapter to a new form of cosmopolitanism – contains the sense and direction of the thesis it develops, linking 'argumentation' and 'rhetoric', logical regime of analysis and symbolic dimension of figures and *exempla*. The set of heterogeneous phenomena (economic, technological, political, cultural, ideological, religious) that we are now accustomed to weave together under the term 'globalisation', seems less and less subsumable by the rival paradigms, on the one hand, of the 'end of history', i.e., the definite triumph of acquisitive individualism (according to the positive diagnosis/prognosis provided by Francis Fukuyama), of the hegemony of *la pensée unique*, understood as a 'Westernisation' of the world (as in the completely negative perspective of Serge Latouche); and, on the other hand, of the 'clash of civilisations' (according to Samuel Huntington's diagnostic scheme). To grasp the specific logic of this globalisation, to draw out the traits that distinguish it from earlier globalisations, we must understand it as a 'transit', as a passage westwards. The word 'passage' no longer has any of the past teleological or destinal connotations which saturated past theories of 'transition'. The term must be taken, instead, in the double meaning of travel and change, risk and opportunity. The dynamics of the global transformation and dislocation of powers that has taken place before our eyes since the fall of the Berlin Wall is nothing but a rough 'North-West Passage' of all cultures. We are confronted with a thrilling and perilous transit to modernity which is intended to produce radical changes in the economy and in societies, in lifestyles as well as in forms of behaviour, not only of the 'other' civilisations but of Western civilisation itself.

Thus, in the title, one can find the thesis that guides the multiple circumnavigations of a book that grew out of a set of investigations and reflections pursued in *Potere e secolarizzazione* (Power and Secularisation) and *Dopo il Leviatano* (After the Leviathan), and that precedes the developments of the thesis presented in *La passione del presente* (The Passion of the Present). The principal themes went from the exhaustion of the nexus of political theology, secularisation and globalisation to the overcoming of the duality between East and West; from the new forms of conflict in the ambivalent scenarios of world-modernity to the genealogical reconstruction of the concept of 'global era' (considering thinkers such as Spengler, Jünger, Schmitt and Heidegger) and the problems of a 'post-Hobbesian order'; from the disenchantment of the category of 'market' by Karl Polanyi to the criticism of the theory of comparative civilisation in the work of Max Weber; from the debate between liberalism and communitarianism to the proposed universalism of difference. I shall not attempt to summarise the numerous responses to the book in Italy and abroad in recent years, but shall instead outline a list of the perspectives it has tried to open up and the problems left open:

1) *'Mondialisation'* has revealed the flexible, chameleon-like nature of global capital, which is able to adapt and change, operating within very different cultural contexts, and that contrasts with the paradigm of a standard-modernity as well as with the thesis of Weber's elective affinity between capitalist development

and the ethics of ascetic Protestantism. In the global era, the great alternative seems to be not so much between 'the West' and 'Islam' as Huntington argued but between the individualistic-competitiveness of North America and the productivist-communitarianism of China. In this context, Europe can play an independent political and economic role only if it is able to build upon and redefine the most vital aspects of its cultural tradition: by offering a not merely competitive vision of singularity and a not merely hierarchical-paternalistic view of community.

2) The axis of conflict/cooperation between the U.S. and China, which tends to characterise the twenty-first century as a Sino-American Century, is not able to neutralise the triggers of the current crisis of global capital. The present crisis is not only a financial crisis but a crisis of the real economy. It should be mentioned here that the urgency for a new Bretton Woods – now proposed as a remedy by the Western political and economic elite – had already been raised in chapter 5 of this book, through a comparison with the arguments advanced, a decade before the crisis, by George Soros in *The Crisis of Global Capitalism*.

3) The structure of globalisation cannot be defined as 'postmodern', but on the contrary as a transition from nation-modernity, dominated by the principle of territoriality, to world-modernity, dominated by the principle of globality [*mondialità*].

4) The principles of territoriality and globality [*mondialità*] co-exist and cohabit in a conflictual manner in the structure of the Modern (with respect to which globalisation, the opening of spaces, not only represents a consequence, but also a premise; this is evident in the link between the genesis of modernity and the conquest of the New World).

5) World-modernity is marked not by a mono-logic, but by a bi-logic, by an interface of techno-economic interdependence (and standardisation), and a differentiation of identities, material conjunction and symbolic disjunction, compression and diaspora of the forms-of-life.

6) The phenomenon of globalisation, i.e., the short circuit between the global and local levels, is due, in political and institutional terms, to the decline in the effectiveness of the territorial

sovereignty of nation states (with the consequent emergence of hybrid entities, either national or global) and, in cultural terms, to the phenomenon of the *global production of the local* (with the consequent proliferation of imaginary identities).

7) The dominant form of conflict in modern, 'glocalised' world-modernity lies in the logic of identity (this logic, which in extreme cases may take the form of religious or ethnic fundamentalism, marks a shift from the interest-value couple to the preferences-identity couple).

8) In the post-ideological and biotechnological age, identity becomes the reference point of political conflict.

9) The restless complicity of techno-economic logic and the logic of identity leads to a neutralisation of politics and to a ban on or occlusion of the dynamics of the constitution of subjectivity.

10) The reconstruction of a cosmopolitan perspective (which is now caught in the grip of technological standardisation and by diasporic identity) must now pass through a radical redefinition of the universal: we need a universal dimension setting out from the criterion of difference.

Except for the last chapter, the analysis and the arguments of the book were developed in the climate of 9/11. It is still too early to say that we have turned the corner of the global 'state of exception' which was inaugurated by that traumatic event. We can only decipher some *signa prognostica*. The hope is that they could represent signs of a shift towards a stage that is perhaps not simple, which is certainly more conflictual and still marked by the passage from the deconstructive climate (insisting on 'deconstruction' today would serve merely to perpetuate a kind of defence of the status quo) to a new constructive climate. But to give form and power, effectiveness and reality to the 'signs of the times', it is necessary to reverse the perspective of the conformist depoliticisation founded on the disenchantment of politics and on the mythology (and obsession) of the politics of identity. Even for those who are still firmly convinced of the necessity of remaining faithful, in their analysis and critique, to the passion of disenchantment, the invitation to continue a practice of disenchanted technical-managerialism of life-spaces and of experience can only

appear sterile and tired. This narrow-minded form of disenchantment has come to weaken politics, taking away its proper symbolic
dimension, i.e., its capacity to provide a horizon of meaning to its
individual and collective forms of praxis.

If up until yesterday the watchwords of conformism were of a
disenchantment with politics and a mythologising of identity,
today we need a diametrical reversal of that perspective. In this
sense I feel myself authorised to formulate now the following
injunction: *demythologising identity, re-enchanting politics.*

G. M.

NOTE TO THE READER

The book is organised radially. The first chapter aims to furnish a theoretical *map* of the global that concludes, after a critique of the various positions in play, with the assertion of the thesis of the passage to the Occident. All other chapters form a 'circumnavigation' of specific thematic epicentres: identity/difference, politics/law, sovereignty/global era, gift/exchange, democracy/community, tolerance/recognition and Europe/post-national public sphere.

I have discussed some of the analyses and proposals outlined here in lectures or interventions in Italy and abroad over the course of recent years. Chapter 2, the core of which dates back to a book I wrote some years ago with Michel Maffesoli,[1] was developed in the course of seminars held between 1997 and 1998 at the University of Hong Kong and Columbia University in New York. A version of this chapter has appeared in German and in English.[2] Chapter 3, which grew out of a series of conferences in Spain (Barcelona, Madrid and La Coruña) and Brazil (Universidade de São Paulo) in 1998, appeared in Spanish with the title 'El crepúsculo de los soberanos'. Chapter 4 was initially written as a 'critical profile' of Carl Schmitt for an important work published by Marzorati. An expanded version was presented at an international conference on Schmitt organised by Columbia University.[3] Chapter 5 began as a conference lecture for the San Carlo Foundation in Modena and then successive versions of it appeared in the journal *Paradigmi* and, in Spanish, in the collection

---

1   Michel Maffesoli and Giacomo Marramao, *Le culture comunitarie. Zone di confine*, Rome: Il Mondo 3, 1996.

2   Giacomo Marramao, 'Apologie des Möglichen. Technik und Ethik an der Jahrtausendwende'; 'Globalisation, Conflict of Values and Contingent Identity'.

3   The papers from the conference have been published in a special issue of the *Cardozo Law Review*, 21:5–6 (May 2000).

Democracia y Ciudadanía en la Sociedad Global.[4] Chapter 8 takes its cue from a course of seminars organised by the Virginia Woolf Centre in Rome and from my subsequent participation in the conference 'La diversità in età moderna e contemporanea' (Diversity in the Modern and Contemporary Age), which took place in Mantua on 5–6 June 1999. Chapter 9 began as an internal report to the research group Sfera pubblica e costituzione europea (The Public Sphere and the European Constitution), coordinated by Jürgen Habermas, Elena Paciotti, Stefano Rodotà, Alain Touraine and myself. Successive versions of it were presented at an international conference at the Lelio Basso Foundation in Rome in December 2000 and, on invitation from Étienne Balibar, at the University of Paris X – Nanterre in December 2001. Chapter 7 consists of a reworking of the themes of my introduction to Voltaire's *Trattato sulla tolleranza.*[5] Finally, chapter 6 takes up again, in a different context, some of the theses I presented in *Dopo il Leviatano. The Passage West* constitutes, in every way, the natural development of that book.

G.M.
Rome, 21 February 2003

---

4   Giacomo Marramao, 'Dono, scambio, obbligazione', *Paradigmi* 48 (1998); '¿Es la edad global un dramatico, pero interesante capitulo de la Gran Transformación?', in María Cristina Camacho Ramos et al. (eds.), *Democracia y Ciudadanía en la Sociedad Global*, Mexico City: Universidad Nacional Autónoma de México – Aragón, 2001.

5   Giacomo Marramao, introduction to Voltaire, *Trattato sulla tolleranza*, Rome: Editori Riuniti, 1994.

NOSTALGIA FOR THE PRESENT

At that precise moment to himself the man said:
What would I not give
to be with you in Iceland
under the grand immobile daytime
and share this now
like sharing music
or the taste of fruit.
At that precise moment
the man was together with her in Iceland.

(J. L. Borges)

Mundus *and* Globus

The political phenomena of our time are accompanied and compli-
cated by an unprecedented *change of scale*, or rather by a *change
in the order of things*. The world to which we are beginning to
belong, both men and nations, is only *similar* to the world that
was once familiar to us. The system of causes controlling the fate
of every one of us, and now extending over the whole globe,
makes it reverberate throughout every shock; there are no more
questions that can be settled by being settled at one point.[1]

These comments, which could have been written at the beginning of the twenty-first century by a philosopher of the global era
in which we live, were in fact composed by Paul Valéry in 1928.
They were then collated with his other remarkable thoughts on
the great transformations of the interwar period in *Reflections on
the World Today*. It is here that we must begin if we hope to shed

---

1 Paul Valéry, 'On History', in *History and Politics*, pp. 114–15. *Translator's
note:* Where necessary, I have modified existing translations in line with
Marramao's rendering. I have not indicated this in the text.

any light on the complex of events, processes and experiences implicated in the term 'globalisation'. This term is ubiquitous and its meanings extend beyond the economic and technological spheres, to those of society and politics, religion and culture. Since its beginnings, Western philosophy has taught us to be suspicious of the deceptive clarity of language and of the power contained in the deceitful transparency of words. The warning is all the more pertinent in our media-based society. Thanks to an arcane thaumaturgy, the recourse to an allusive and polysemic expression enables one to avoid the 'effort of the Notion' and its indispensable correlates: analysis and synthesis, decomposition and reconstruction, differentiation and comparison.

Those sentences of Valéry's acquire today, in the near surgical precision of their vocabulary, a relevance that goes well beyond their character of historical testimony. Not only do they document the intensity achieved by reflection, within the ambit of the 'culture of crisis', in the interwar period, they also contain precious theoretical indications of the structural characteristics of the *Global Age*. The set of phenomena that we commonly gather under the term 'globalisation' (which commonly privileges the technological-financial aspects from which the new dimension of the world market is said to have emerged following the collapse of the bipolar system) are from Valéry's perspective linked to the new terms of the relationship of technology to politics and, in this sense, is allied to the diagnosis-prognosis of the 'global epoch' (*globale Zeit*) elaborated by Ernst Jünger and Carl Schmitt in the same period. From this perspective, the trends of the transformation and crisis of the 'political' that are induced by the projection of technology on a planetary scale – under the pressure of massification and 'total mobilisation'[2] – do not constitute a simple extension of the horizon (a mere 'change of scale') with respect to the preceding phases of colonial expansion and internationalisation, industrialisation and interdependency. They produce, instead, a 'change in the *order* of things,' a new structure and configuration of the world:

> We must expect such transformations to become the rule. The further we go the less simple and predictable the effects will be, and the less any political operations and even interventions of force – in a word, obvious and direct action – will turn out as they were expected to do.

---

2 As analysed by Ernst Jünger in his homonymous essay from 1930; see Jünger, 'Total Mobilization'.

The sizes, areas, and masses involved, their relations, the impossibility of localizing anything, the prompt repercussions, all will more and more impose a policy very different from the existing one.[3]

Valéry's radioscopic gaze compels us to supplement our investigation so as to shed some light on the ubiquitous term 'globalisation', which has become an all-purpose label for disparate, cumulative and juxtaposed phenomena. It is an illusory keyword, a *passepartout* that serves to affirm the 'new' at the same time as it radically denies it. Following the tragedy of 11 September 2001, diligent *ex post* prophets of the 'spiritual condition' of our time have hastily announced the end of the long strike of events (in Jean Baudrillard's suggestive phrase that he borrowed from the Argentine writer Macedonio Fernández) or, according to a diametrically opposite standpoint, the end of globalisation itself. But it is also true to say that such multi-use categories are also ambiguous. Independently of the (positive or negative) evaluation given or the side taken ('New Global' or 'No Global'), it is understood by some as a dynamic of unification of material conditions and integration of cultures – that is not at all new but of distant origin, and that ultimately coincides with the history of the world itself. Conversely, by others it is taken to mark a veritable epochal discontinuity or rupture.

In the first case, contemporary globalisation, despite its indisputable significance, is considered to be nothing but the latest (and provisional) chapter in a series of successive globalisations that characterise the process of civilisation:

Globalization is often seen as global Westernization. On this point, there is substantial agreement among many proponents and opponents. Those who take an upbeat view of globalization see it as a marvellous contribution of Western civilization to the world. From the opposite perspective, Western dominance – sometimes seen as a continuation of Western imperialism – is the devil of the piece. . . . But is globalization really a new Western curse? It is, in fact, neither new nor necessarily Western. And it is not a curse. Over thousands of years, globalization has contributed to the progress of the world through travel, trade, migration, spread of cultural influences and dissemination of knowledge and understanding (including that of science and technology). These global interrelations have often been very productive in the advancement of different countries. They have not necessarily taken the form of increased Western influence. Indeed, the active agents of globalization have often been located far from the

---

3   Valéry, 'On History', p. 116.

West. To illustrate, consider the world at the beginning of the last millennium rather than at its end. Around AD 1000, the global reach of science, technology and mathematics was changing the nature of the old world. But the dissemination then was, to a great extent, in the opposite direction from what we see today. . . . The agents of globalization are neither European nor exclusively Western, nor are they necessarily linked to Western dominance. Indeed, Europe would have been a lot poorer – economically, culturally and scientifically – had it resisted the globalization of mathematics, science and technology at that time. And today, the same principle applies, though in the reverse direction (from West to East).[4]

In the second case, globalisation is thought to represent a rupture so great as to render obsolete the classical categories of philosophical and political modernity (the state, the people, sovereignty, nation, centre/periphery, public/private, etc.). From this perspective, these categories are said to have become 'zombie-words' or, in Adorno's peremptory definition, 'conceptual corpses' (*Begriffsleichen*) *par excellence*, mere survivals and inertial resistances of a paradigm now irrevocably past. For those who hold to this 'discontinuity' thesis – Martin Albrow heads the list – properly speaking one should no longer speak of a *process* of globalisation so much as the *advent* of a Global Age that is structurally and qualitatively different from the Modern Age. The Global Age has arrived: and, 'Paradoxically . . . in the Global Age we jettison three centuries of assumptions about the direction of history'.[5]

It is difficult to forecast to what extent the arguments presented on one side and the other are able to give rise to truly distinct and competing theoretical paradigms. In their current state, they appear able only to express two half-truths. They leave open the possibility that an aspect of Sen's 'continuity' thesis – i.e., the critique of the equation globalisation = Westernisation that is decisive – might interact with the need, advanced by Albrow's 'discontinuity' thesis, of a differential characterisation of the 'Global Age'. On this basis, I propose – as we shall see subsequently – my philosophical reading of globalisation as a *passage to the Occident*, where 'passage' draws together the continuous and the discontinuous, the process and the turning point. A preliminary question arises for those not prepared to welcome the presumed self-evidence of the *idola fori* that inundate the media.

---

4 Amartya Sen, 'Does Globalization Equal Westernization?'.
5 Martin Albrow, *The Global Age*, p. 107.

In what sense and on what conditions is the term 'globalisation' able effectively to comprehend the plethora of phenomena for which it undoubtedly, more or less effectively, accounts? Moreover, does not the ambivalence underlying the use of this term – as *object of investigation* (the 'real' dynamic of events) or as *methodological criterion of interpretation* – betray its nature as mere slogan, as a 'word without a concept'?

We can usefully begin our discussion with some lexical analysis. What in Anglophone countries is called 'globalisation' and in German *Globalisierung*, becomes *mondializzazione, mondialisation, mundialización* and *mundialização* in the Romance languages. It is difficult to render these terms in English and German, beginning with the terms 'world' and 'Welt'. In English, this is because of the evident cacophony of solutions such as 'worldisation' or 'worldwidisation'. In German, because the term *Verweltlichung* (literally, 'worldification') is already used to denote – in works from the field of theology, philosophy of history and the social sciences over the last two centuries – the phenomena of 'secularisation'.[6] However, it so happens that the different roots of the terms '*mondializzazione*' and 'globalisation' are central to the symbolic horizons each evokes. The reference to the concept '*mundus*' is unavoidable for anyone using the former term; because – as Jacques Derrida has observed – 'this notion of world . . . is charged with a great deal of semantic history, notably a Christian history'.[7] Equally unavoidable, for those who adopt the latter, is the reference to the symbolism of the globe, of the sphere, to the idea of the totalisation and the planetary finitude of the processes at work. In short, whereas *mondializzazione* immediately evokes classical themes and queries of the philosophy of history, 'globalisation' appears above all to be the business of cartographers and navigators. Consequently, the lexical difference between these two presumed synonyms implies not only the reference to different disciplines but also differing choices of localisation and periodisation of the phenomenon. Let us try to clarify the distinction.

---

6 I have attempted a philosophical reconstruction and 'genealogical' compendium of this latter category in *Potere e secolarizzazione* and *Cielo e terra*.

7 Jacques Derrida, 'The University Without Condition', p. 224.

Mundus

If we adopt the term *mondializzazione*, the reference to the epochal change signalled by the emergence from the still descriptive and synoptic fabric of the *Universalgeschichte* of the concept of 'World-History' (*Welt-Geschichte*), of a history understood as a process that tends to the level of the world [*si mondializza*], becomes canonical. This is a crucial passage in Western universalism that begins with the Enlightenment modernity of Voltaire, Rousseau and Kant (and through Herder as the 'Romantic' counterpoint), and concludes with Hegel's philosophy of history. However, there are no lack of genealogies that hark back still further in search of antecedents as illustrious as they are remote. For example, the Augustinian theology of history, with its idea of *civitas peregrinans* – just to mention two of the most celebrated interpretations, those of Karl Löwith and Étienne Gilson, for whom modern ideologies and utopias are nothing but secular transpositions of the Judeo-Christian *éschaton* and the metamorphosis of the City of God; or, looking even further back in time, the idea of the unity of the *prágmata* set down, with reference to the power of Rome, in Polybius' *Histories*. In the latter case, Rome becomes the political-symbolic cipher for the plane of the worldwide interconnection of events, which we find at the basis of significant recent theoretical reappraisals of the concept of Empire.[8]

From the perspective of the completion of the process, the consequences for a philosophy of history hinging on the category of *Weltgeschichte* appear ambiguous and vary in accordance with the slant that one gives them. They are either dissolutive (as in the postmodern thesis of the weakening, the exhaustion of grand narratives); pacifying (as in the trite version of the Hegelian motif of the 'end of history' provided by Francis Fukuyama following Kojève's influential reading of Hegel); or catastrophic (as, for example, in the messianic transposition of historical time elaborated by Walter Benjamin – and, in his wake, Jacob Taubes – on the basis of Schmitt's notion of the state of exception, as well as in Günther Anders' 'principle of desperation' and in the late Adorno's negative dialectics). From a different perspective, the *mondialisation du monde* (see Derrida and Nancy) realised

---

8 See Michael Hardt and Antonio Negri, *Empire*; Massimo Cacciari, 'Digressioni su Impero e Tre Rome'; and Massimo Cacciari, 'Ancora sull'Idea di Impero'.

by the cosmopolitism of tele-technics represents a thought of the end, but in a sense that cannot be reconciled with the variety of eschatological or millenarian secular figures. 'End' stands, here, for 'completeness', the definitive completion of that process of *mondialisation* – that is to say, of symbolic investiture and of *donation-of-meaning* to the world – that coincides in each and every way with the History of the Occident. The 'end of the world', the salient event of our time, does not only mean the end of a specific epoch of the 'world' (and of 'sense') but marks, rather, 'the end of an epoch – as long as the "Occident" and as long as long as "history" itself – that has entirely determined the "world" and "meaning", and that has extended this determination to the entire *world*'.[9] Two distinct conceptions lie behind this conclusion. The first appears, in truth, to be the 'common sense' one. The world that has become '*mondialisé*', the '*mundus*' that has become '*mondiale*', subverts the classical division between external and internal and upsets all lines of demarcation between 'worlds' that, at one time, we thought were constitutive *of* the world. The second presents itself in a philosophically sophisticated guise. The breakdown of the division between inside and outside, the possibility of the relationship with the 'other' (with other 'worlds', with other forms-of-life or dimensions of the world) means that the world no longer *has* sense but *is* sense.

'World' is not the mere correlate of sense but is structured in the same way as sense and, conversely, sense is structured as world. Which is why, as Jean-Luc Nancy admits, the expression which provides the title for his book, 'the sense of the world', is tautological. As one can infer from Nancy's preceding works, the premise of this argument rests entirely upon the possibility of playing on the contrast within the semiological coupling of sense and signification in such a way as to effect a reciprocal transposition of the Heideggerian theme of the *bringing-to-completion of nihilism* and the Wittgensteinian one of the exhaustion of the *metaphysics of signification*. With the *exhaustion of the regime of significations*, the event of the sense-world marks not only *the* end of the (*nihilistic*) trajectory of metaphysics but also *the* end of the Western *logos*:

> The *logos* that has reached its end has enclosed the general space of signification by completing the history of nihilism. Yet this very

---

9 Jean-Luc Nancy, *The Sense of the World*, p. 6.

accomplishment is itself in no way nihilistic. Nihilism means that signification infinitely escapes itself, but the accomplishment as such accomplishes the meaning of signification, the entire signifiable meaning of *logos*. Without this accomplishment, the Occident would not have taken place, and the Occident is not an unfortunate accident – even though we are not in a position to understand its 'necessity' because our idea of necessity, just like our idea of freedom, is bound to signification. If we seek to grasp the signification of the West, we run up against the exhaustion of signification accomplished by the West. . . . the West in its accomplishment asks us neither to revive its significations nor to resign ourselves to their annulment, but rather to understand that *from now on the demand for meaning has to go through the exhaustion of significations.*[10]

In the last resort, *mondializzazione*, understood as the *finite thought of the end of the world*, departs from the logic of *Sinngebung* (of a *future-orientated* donation-of-meaning inherent in the concept of '*Weltgeschichte*' – in both 'progressive' and 'apocalyptical' senses of indefinite Kantian progress and eschatological interruption – that is entirely contained in the 'metaphysics of signification'); and it involves the identification of the 'ontologically worldly and world-wide trait' of the world in the completeness of meaning that, in Heideggerian fashion, coincides with *being-to* or *being-towards*, that is, with the opening of the relation, the sending of the inoperative and desubstantialised community of the gift.

Globus

If, however, we adopt the term 'globalisation', the reference to the First Act of modernity represented by the new image of the earth as the circumnavigable globe and 'wandering planet' is inevitable. Far from constituting a mere 'result' of the *mondializzazione* of history produced by Modern Reason (Hegel), a simple historical-material upshot of the unification of the world market (Marx), or a destinal coming-to-completion of Western nihilism under the all-homologating dominion of technology (Heidegger), globalisation is said to be at one with the prototypical act of the modern age. In a work that is as suggestive as it is explicitly provocative, Peter Sloterdijk argues that the task of producing the *Weltbild*, the 'world-picture' of the *Neu-Zeit*, is no longer (*pace* Heidegger) the responsibility of metaphysicians

---

10 Jean-Luc Nancy, *The Gravity of Thought*, p. 48.

but of geographers and mariners.[11] Certainly in this case the genealogical reconstruction can easily be shown to hark back to the classical antecedents of modernity as well, by showing how the global dimension was connected to Western culture from its very origins. The Greek mathematicians who 2,500 years ago were captivated by the irresistible formal intuition of the perfection of the sphere and of its geometrical constructability marked the beginning of the globalisation of the world. But it was only once the closed cosmos was broken open by modernity that the sphere could be circumnavigated. Indeed, the first circumnavigators of the globe were the *Conquistadores* who colonised the New World, the cartographers who furnished them with maps for navigation, the adventurers and the overseas merchants, the Christian missionaries and scholars who threw themselves into the discovery of new languages and unknown civilisations. It was thanks to them that – against the backdrop of Renaissance *magia naturalis*, the embryo and source of modern science – arose the new image of the Earth, the terrestrial globe, becoming the dominant world-picture of the *Neu-Zeit*. The new image of the world – from the Renaissance to Alexander von Humboldt, who Sloterdijk terms the 'last cosmographer'[12] – is accompanied by a revolution in the concept of space: from the time of the voyages of Columbus, Magellan and Francis Drake, all the points in the circumnavigable rotundity of the planet are given the same value. The cartographic convention of the globalised universe presupposes an infinite, quantifiable space that gives rise to continuous neutralising localisations, in the same way as the Renaissance theory of perspective that was analysed in such magisterial fashion by Erwin Panofsky (from both an aesthetic and an epistemological angle).

Nevertheless, notwithstanding Sloterdijk's programmatic statements, it is difficult to think of taking leave of metaphysics once one affirms that the effect of the new global spatiality is a catastrophe for the regional ontologies and a metamorphosis of the *Lebenswelte*, of the life-worlds, turning them into mere locations. It is equally illusory to maintain that one has freed oneself from the philosophy of history once, echoing a Hegelian adage repeated throughout the twentieth century, one equates globalisation with

---

11   Peter Sloterdijk, *Sphären*.

12   *Kosmos*, his most important work, appeared in five volumes between 1845 and 1862.

a *spatial revolution towards the Outside*, in the sense of Westernisation.

> With his choice of the West, [Christopher Columbus] initiated the emancipation of the 'Occident' [*Abendland*] from its concern with the Orient which can be traced back to times immemorial and that was drenched in the solar mythology. Instead, with the discovery of a Western continent it had been able to belie the mythical and metaphysical superiority of the Orient. From that time, we have never gone back to the 'Origin' [*Ursprung*] or to the point where the sun rises and instead we have followed without nostalgia and in a progressive way [*fortschrittlich*] the course of the sun.[13]

The claim that Columbus' ocean crossing transformed Europe into the Occident and that the 'universal compression of the Earth' determined by the great global metaphor had been produced 'under the aegis of the Atlantic tendency' forms the starting-point and not the solution for the crucial problems that invest our present.[14]

Beginning with the irrefutable fact of the process of 'Westernisation' (promptly noted by thinkers such as Hegel, Tocqueville, Marx and Weber in the 1800s–1900s), two sets of questions emerge today. First, the question of the *differences within the concept of the Occident* or, rather, of the problematic relationship between the *two halves of the Occident*: the Anglo-American *oceanic model* and the European *Continental model*. Second, the question of whether the couple Orient/Occident is still plausible once the notion of globalisation is taken seriously.

The differential analysis of the constellation of meanings of the terms *'mondialisation'* and *'globalisation'* (understood as derivatives of *mundus* and *globus*) allows for the different prototypical metaphysics lying behind their respective genealogies and 'narratives', including the inevitable reciprocal contamination of their prognoses, to emerge. Going to the root of both the one and the other, of the divergences and interferences, appears as a *conditio sine qua non* for leading the term 'globalisation' to its concept without thereby sacrificing the richness or polyvalence of its meanings.

A decisive turning point for whoever sets themselves such a task – a task ignored by the majority of interpreters of

---

13   Ibid., vol. 2, p. 832.
14   Ibid.

globalisation – is that of the great debate on *technische Zeit*, on the 'age of technology', between the Joint Chiefs of Staff of European culture which began in the course of the First World War (the first volume of Oswald Spengler's *Der Untergang des Abendlandes* [*The Decline of the West*] was published in 1918). From Georg Simmel to Edmund Husserl, from Max Weber to Karl Jaspers, from Benedetto Croce to José Ortega y Gasset, from Ernst Jünger to Carl Schmitt, from Martin Heidegger to Ludwig Wittgenstein. Wittgenstein's reflections on the technical-constructive character of Western civilisation and on the conflict between science and life are literally saturated in Spenglerian motifs. While Jünger, who along with Schmitt was an acute and prophetic interpreter of the '*globale Zeit*' in terms of a new *Raumordnung*, a new 'spatial order' marked by planetary technology, evokes that atmosphere in the course of a series of revealing conversations held in 1995.

> Like everyone else, I was deeply affected by the *Decline of the West*, which appeared in a time of profound crisis at the end of the First World War. It was a charismatic book, which perfectly captured that atmosphere that one could breathe all around one. That, moreover, explains the enormous success of the work that, despite being vast (composed of two volumes), found a host of impassioned readers and went through numerous editions. Although there was no lack of professors of history and philosophy who attacked him on this or that point, the book became a reference point particularly for the younger generations. At the time of the defeat of the Austro-Hungarian Empire, which was experienced by German culture as a catastrophe, *The Decline of the West* was received as a grandiose taking leave of the optimistic perception that had characterised the positivism of progress typical of the Belle Époque. Spengler's vision of history implied that it did have a linear and progressive development, characterised by the passage from one civilisation to the next. Instead, it held that there were different civilisations, each one similar to an organism, with its own life and development but without progress. That is, each civilisation is born, matures, flowers but, sooner or later, it declines and dies.[15]

Once again, it is from Spengler that the author of *Der Arbeiter* (The Worker) takes his cue for his suggestive prognosis. The twenty-first century will mark the advent of 'a new era of the Titans', in which the globe will be subjected to unprecedented

---

15   In Antonio Gnoli and Franco Volpi, *I prossimi Titani. Conversazioni con Ernst Jünger*, pp. 103 ff.

acceleration propelled by a technology characterised exclusively by exactitude and functionality, which will relegate all the forms of humanist thought considered now inefficient and 'superfluous' to the margins.[16]

However, at its most acute and perceptive points, the great debate on technology prompted by Spengler's work was not limited to recording the event constituted by the *spatial revolution*, by the irruption of a new world-wide [*mondiale*] dimension of spatiality. It tended, rather, to *assume the global within the crisis of* Verweltlichung (and of the philosophies of history hinging on the categories of 'Progress' and *Welt-Geschichte*, or World-History). The notes gathered together in Paul Valéry's *Regards sur le monde actuel* are, as already discussed, exemplary in their extraordinary capacity for anticipation. The salient feature of these reflections – and another circumstance one often skirts around – is the revelation of a bipolar tension between 'globality' and 'world' [*mondo*] and, so, the characterisation of the *global event* as the era of the *finite world* [*mondo finito*].[17] Once the 'essential facts of the history of modern times' have been located in the 'ever closer interdependence' between events and in the interweaving of *increase in clarity* and *increase in power* determined by a technology that tends to modify 'man himself',[18] then, Valéry concludes, the season of the Frontier, of the expansive dynamic of *mondialisation*, of World-History 'made up of events that could be *located*', has now irrevocably reached its end and completion.

> The entire inhabitable earth has in our day been reconnoitred, surveyed and divided amongst the nations. The era of uninhabited lands, of free territories, of places that belong to no one, that is, the era of free expansion, is over. There is no stone that does not have its flag. There are no more empty spaces on the map, nor regions without customs posts or laws; neither are there any unreported tribes, which depend, by the evils of writing, upon far-away humanists in their distant offices. *The era of the finite world* [monde fini] *has begun.*[19]

Examined in this light, Valéry's diagnosis bears the valuable intuition of a secret correspondence between the two symbolic reference

---

16 Ibid., p. 105.

17 *Translator's note:* The Italian word 'finito' means both 'finished' and/or 'completed' as well as 'finite'. All these meanings should be borne in mind.

18 Paul Valéry, 'Avant-Propos', p. 922.

19 Ibid., p. 923.

points of globalisation: *mundus* and *globus*, expansiveness and completeness. But, transposed onto the plane of the concept, that brilliant intuition appears to compel us in a particular direction, to make the semantic constellations underlying the categories of 'globalisation' and 'secularisation' interact by highlighting their interferences and fields of tension. In other words, it is a case of establishing an extremely delicate and complex theoretical assemblage. I hope this book will take the first step on this path. To begin with, the consideration of the secularising dynamic of *mondialisation* in relation to the new, global dimension, demands a radical reformulation of the 'secularisation-theorem'. If, in general, 'secularisation' denotes any process of desacralisation, such as that effected by the Greek philosophical *logos* in relation to myth or of Jewish prophesying in relation to the preceding, magical-ritualistic forms of religiosity, then, strictly speaking, it designates a characteristic feature of European modernity: the *separation of religion and politics* sanctioned, at the halfway point of the seventeenth century (with the Peace of Westphalia of 1648), by the end of the confessional civil wars and by the affirmation of the 'intraworldly' sovereignty of the state.

But what chain of effects, what circuit of actions and reactions, is produced in the passage from the international order of sovereign nation states – a specific achievement of European/Western civilisation from which stems directly the functional differentiation between law and morality – to the new global (dis)order? This question is unavoidable if we are to shift the centre of gravity of the globalisation controversy from the technological and economic terrain to the political and cultural one. It is no coincidence that the neologism 'globalisation' makes its first appearance in the 1960s. It served to indicate, in the field of international law, the new terms of the 'Hobbesian problem of order' (in the words of the celebrated definition by Talcott Parsons in his *Structure of Social Action* from 1937) once the 'Westphalian model' had ended.[20]

The crux of this passage is constituted by the possibility of

---

20 The Westphalian model was a framework of international relations orchestrated by the European powers and founded on the exclusion of 'non-sovereign' areas, countries and peoples or ones with 'limited sovereignty'. See Wolfgang Friedmann, *The Changing Structure of International Law*, London: Stevens & Sons, 1964; and B.V.A. Röling, 'The Role of Law in Conflict Resolution', in Anthony de Reuck and Julie Knight (eds.), *Conflict in Society*, London: J. & A. Churchill, 1966.

redefining the categories of 'world-modernity' [*modernità-mondo*] and 'world-society' [*società-mondo*][21] so as to qualify the paradox that underlies the logic and structure of a global reality that is at once uni-polar and multi-centred. More rigorously, this planetary reality is not only polycentric – despite the indisputable techno-logical, economic, strategic and military hegemony of the United States – but also multi-dimensional and multi-directional.[22] The importance and subtlety of this theoretical operation consists in making the two perspectives of globalisation and secularisation interact in order to avoid falling into two traps that oppose but also mirror one another:

a) the risk of forceful homologation and unification that is latent in the interpretations that take modernity as a given, pre-constituted, universal plane, rather than as an open and conflictual problematic field;

b) the risk of the separation and dissociation that is character-istic of those dualistic interpretive schemas that take up the idea of *mondialisation* as a function of the essentially dichotomous image of the global/local couple, understanding the latter term as a merely reactive phenomenon (on the socio-economic plane or on the cultural-identity plane) in comparison to the expansive dynamic of modernity.

These two traps are well represented in the antithetical readings of globalisation provided by Francis Fukuyama and Samuel Huntington.[23] To escape the specular unilateralism of these posi-tions we must elaborate a theoretical model of world-modernity [*modernità-mondo*] in which the aspects of the global and the local, technological and communicational uniformity, and the differentiation of culture and identity are not set against one another in a static alternative, but interpenetrate dynamically, as though forming an interface. In short, globalisation should not be understood as universal homologation produced through the omnipotent dominion of Technology and the Market (Fukuyama). It should rather be understood as an economic-financial and socio-cultural interdependence disclosed by 'real-time' digital technologies. By the same token, it should not be read, in the

---

21   These terms were introduced by the Brazilian sociologists Octavio Ianni and Renato Ortiz and by the German systems theorist Niklas Luhmann, respectively.

22   See J.N. Rosenau, *Turbulence in World Politics: A Theory of Change and Continuity.*

23   Francis Fukuyama, *The End of History and the Last Man*; Samuel P. Huntington, *The Clash of Civilizations and the Remaking of World Order.*

diametrically opposed and equally reductive perspective, as a 'clash of civilizations' (Huntington) but, instead, as a fabric of conflicting tensions that traverses all civilisations, cutting trans-versally across the global as well as the local. (In this respect, perhaps one could most easily understand the nature of the conflicts within world-modernity [*modernità-mondo*] – and which emerged most strikingly with the attacks on the Twin Towers and the Pentagon – in the significant terms of the wars of religion. Indeed, except in a few, very rare cases, religious conflicts cannot be identified *sic et simpliciter* with 'civilisations', understood as homogeneous and compact blocs. They tend, rather, to cross them, upsetting pre-constituted ethnic or cultural identities.)

Once we have left behind us the *discordia concors* between the individualist-market homologation thesis and that of the clash of civilisations, globalisation will reveal its true character. Not as the 'Westernisation of the world',[24] nor as 'de-Westernisation' and 'desecularisation', but as the *passage to the Occident* of all cultures. That is, as a passage to modernity destined to produce profound transformations in the economy, society, lifestyles and codes of behaviour not only of 'other' civilisations but of Western civilisation itself.

Thus, the dynamic constitution of world-modernity [*moder-nità-mondo*] is neither univocal nor one-way. It does not proceed along a one-way vector from 'the West' to 'the Rest'. But neither is it intelligible – despite the undoubted global relevance of the current confrontation between 'Western values' and 'Asiatic values' – if we remain within the philosophical (and geopolitical) horizon delimited by the dualism of 'Orient and Occident'. These terms indicate an originary hendiadys, which is constitutive of European identity and has no counterpart in Asia other than in recent years (as a reactive-polemical function contrasted with Western 'supremacism'). The more modernity expands, spreading the economics and aesthetics of the commodity on a global scale, the more Western society is permeated by cultural 'alterity'. Never before the advent of the stereoscopic optic of world-society had the *pluriversal nature of the process of civilisation* and the *plural-ity of the possible paths towards modernity* been so evident.

Unification and differentiation, expansion and contamination, order and conflict. Keeping to the descriptive focus, these are the two inextricable sides of the same coin of the global era. In

---

24 Serge Latouche, *The Westernization of the World*.

shifting the focus from the descriptive to the prescriptive terrain, the two-pronged optic underlying the thesis of the *passage to the Occident* will be translated, through the theoretical programme of a *universalism of difference*, into a revival and 'transvaluation' of the cosmopolitan paradigm of the Modern (as we shall see in the conclusion to this chapter). However, to arrive at such a conclusion, we must proceed via the conceptual articulation of the arguments summarised above.

Globalisation and Secularisation

What are the characteristics of world-modernity [*modernità-mondo*] that differentiate it from classical modernity? To answer this question in more than a merely typological or empirical-descriptive manner, it is necessary to go beyond the definition elaborated in the sphere of the social sciences, despite its significance. According to Octavio Ianni,[25] the formation of 'global society', far from remaining confined to the economic-financial dimension, 'opens up again the problem of modernity in its philosophical, scientific and artistic implications. In the area of the globalisation of commodities, persons and ideas, one witnesses a modification of the social and mental frames of reference. All that which is evidently local, national and regional reveals itself to also be global'.[26] The passage from the epoch of nation-modernity to the current epoch of world-modernity [*modernità-mondo*] could, according to Ianni, be explained by capitalism's dual character. As outlined by Marx, it is a mode of production based upon the universalising power of the commodity-form. As outlined by Max Weber, it is a 'civilising process' founded on the extension of the dominion of a specific standard of strategic-instrumental and social-technological rationality. The expansion of this bipolar structure to a planetary scale gives way to a 'world-wide civil society' [*società civile mondiale*], articulated spatially as a new geopolitical and 'geo-economic' order.[27] Following this analytical-descriptive path in the course of the 1990s, Renato Ortiz has turned to an examination of the impact of *modernidade-mundo* on culture, insisting also – following the classic works of Marshall

---

25   Ianni is the author of truly pioneering works almost entirely ignored by the Anglo-American and European literature on globalisation.

26   Octavio Ianni, *Teorias da globalização*, p. 163.

27   Octavio Ianni, *A sociedade global*, pp. 35 ff.

McLuhan and Saskia Sassen[28] – on the strategic relevance of identity conflicts to the determination of the specific curvatures and delimitations of global space.[29]

Writing from within a different theoretical context, Niklas Luhmann has – since the 1970s – developed the category of 'world-society' (*Weltgellschaft*). He understands this term not as a 'projection' but as a 'real unity of the horizon of the world (*reale Einheit des Welthorizonts)*'.[30] In the face of this new dimension, Luhmann censured the 'old European' social philosophy for persisting with a territorial paradigm structured in accordance with an ideal of a homogeneous and homologating society.

> The presumption is to continue founding the concept of society on the presupposition of a certain similarity between the different life-contexts. However, the fact is that such a criterion no longer works even in Manhattan.... If we are truly interested in seeing through which mechanisms differences are attenuated or sharpened on the terrestrial globe (*Erdball*), if we wish, for example, to discuss how limit-situations (*Grenzsituationen*) are determined in South America, we can no longer take our cue from the local unit. We must, rather, begin from world-society.[31]

The innovative and provocative aspect of the diagnosis consists in the characterisation of *Weltgesellschaft* as the final form of a powerful and precarious style of rationality that is characterised by the criterion of functional differentiation. It is precisely from such differences that new and unexpected dimensions of the conflict issue as from the cracks of an apparently sound building. In order to grasp the sense of this *co-presence of reticular all-pervasiveness and extreme fragility of world-society* [società-mondo], one must bear in mind the theoretical background to Luhmann's analysis.[32]

According to Luhmann's framework – which eludes all scholastic dichotomies, such as the one between the classical 'Aristotelian model' and the modern 'contract model' – the Western concept of

---

28   Marshall McLuhan, *The Gutenberg Galaxy*; Saskia Sassen, *The Global City*.

29   See Renato Ortiz, *Mundialização e cultura*; and *Um outro território*, particularly pp. 67–89.

30   Niklas Luhmann, 'Die Weltgessellschaft', pp. 8 ff.

31   Niklas Luhmann, 'Europa als Problem der Weltgesellschaft', in Ulrich Beck (ed.), *Politik der Globalisierung*, p. 29.

32   Giacomo Marramao, *Dopo il Leviatano*.

society exhibits, from its very beginnings (from Aristotle's *Politics*), a complex structure that includes a specific combination of difference and identity, of differentiation and reconstituted identity, or, in the language of the tradition, of the parts and the whole. In all traditional societies – ancient, medieval and proto-modern – the principle of differentiation, whose criterion is, first and foremost, hierarchical, is that of stratification. As hierarchy comes to be secularised at the turn of the seventeenth and eighteenth centuries, we observe a progressive *de*-naturalisation and artificialisation of the social marked by the passage from the principle of hierarchy to that of functional differentiation. In the course of this transition, the principle of unity ceases to act as the ontological or theological-political presupposition. It stops being a *fact* and becomes a secular *problem*. The consequences of this process strike at the heart of the logic underlying the couple difference/identity. Such a logic can no longer be related back to the paradigm of hierarchical and stratified differentiation, and is instead subsumed under the binary pairing of *inclusion/exclusion*. The secularisation dynamic outlined by Luhmann reaches its final stages in the *Weltgesellschaft* where the imperative of hierarchical subordination is replaced by the logic of delimitation of *inside* and *outside*, of the border [*confine*] and confinement [*confinamento*], of integration and marginalisation:[33] the compartmentalisation of the included and the excluded is carried out by a dual discrimination via external and internal boundaries [*confini*] that segment the subsystems of the forms-of-life.

The question concerning the future of the *Weltgesellschaft* must now be posed from two standpoints. First, from the *epistemological* standpoint, how can a global society survive that entrusts its stability to the incessant transformation of the devices of 'dual framing' to a 'catastrophe', in René Thom's sense: that is to say, to an anastrophe that evolves towards differential and ever more complex forms? Second, from a more properly *socio-political* standpoint, in what way can world-society [*società-mondo*] maintain its order in the face of the emergence of religious, ethnic or other fundamentalisms compared to which the conflicts of

---

33   *Translator's note:* Marramao's use of the Italian term 'confine' raises a number of difficulties for translation. 'Confine' is usually translated as 'border'. However, such a translation loses the etymological link to 'confinement', which will be particularly important in chapter 8 below. The inevitably unsatisfactory solution I have adopted is to indicate the Italian term in square brackets, so that the link is retained.

interests (to whose logic the Absolutist Leviathan-State apparatus conformed in its development into a Constitutional, Welfare State) will appear trifling when compared to what the future holds for us today? Both questions put in question the dominant ethical-political paradigm of European modernity. In conclusion we can ask ourselves 'whether the modern way to describe conflicts as conflicts of interests and values is still adequate in view of a global condition that suggests the emergence of fundamentalist identifications, that is 'against-identities' and not 'career-identities'.[34] Notwithstanding his proverbial eccentricity towards the ideological baggage of old Europe, Luhmann's ruthless diagnosis appears to locate the raw nerve of the global era in the cultural-identitarian nature of a fundamentalism that is only comprehensible in the light of the schema inclusion/exclusion and in the political void determined by the asynchronic development of world-society [società-mondo]. On the one hand, world-society [società-mondo] gives us a novel form of a society – irreducible to modernity – that is at once finite and deterritorialised, where the internal borders [confini] no longer coincide with geographical frontiers and where communication constitutes the fundamental unity of social systems. On the other hand, it appears furrowed by an unbridgeable gap between the global dimension – hegemonised by the operatives of the economy and finance, and by the epistemic communities of researchers and experts in new communication technologies – and the inertial and routinised practices of a politics still bound to the old territorial paradigm.

Building upon Luhmann's notion of *Weltgesellschaft*, and at the same time that Anthony Giddens was developing the thesis of globalisation as a dialectic of 'time-space distanciation',[35] Ulrich Beck locates the paradigm of the global in the phenomenon of the 'presence of the absent' (*Anwesenheit des Abwesenden*). Social space no longer coincides with localisation. It is no longer defined by physical presence in a determinate place. In the new dimension of world-society [società-mondo], physical and social proximity become detached. The 'cohabitation of absentees', at one time made possible by the 'imaginary community of the nation', is today realised thanks to the annulment of distances produced by

34 Niklas Luhmann, 'Globalization or World Society: How to Conceive of Modern Society?', p. 67.
35 Anthony Giddens, *Modernity and Self-Identity*, especially pp. 21 ff.

the new, 'real-time' multimedia technologies.[36] However, despite
the apparent radicalism of these statements, Beck does not follow
the strong discontinuity thesis of Martin Albrow and the later
Luhmann. The global era does not decree the end of the modern
but, rather, the passage from 'first' to 'second modernity'.[37]
Thanks to this framework, which brings Beck into proximity with
Giddens' moderate discontinuity thesis that sees globalisation as a
'consequence of modernity'[38] and keeps open a confrontation
with a problematic apologist of the Modern Project like Jürgen
Habermas, the theme of globalisation is expressly tied to a *taking
leave of Postmodernity*. If the success of philosophical postmodernism was entrusted (through Jean-François Lyotard's
hyper-renowned 1979 booklet) to the end of 'metanarratives',
how can one explain the vociferousness of the Great Story of the
Global that was heard following the fall of the Berlin Wall?

Beck introduces the category of the second modernity (*zweite
Moderne*) as the interpretive key to the complex of phenomena
that, today, are gathered together under the label of globalisation.
This has the undoubted merit of evading – in analogous fashion to
Alain Touraine's radical revision of the structuralist presuppositions of French sociology[39] – the drawbacks of postmodern
philosophical discourse, which interprets the exhaustion of some
of the cornerstones of the modern conception of the world (ideas
of the Subject, Centre, Foundation, Directional process, Progress,
etc.) as the kicking into touch of modernity as such. Beck's definition goes some way to responding to certain requirements that I
had formulated (in the already mentioned volume *Potere e secolarizzazione*) by introducing, in opposition to some versions of the
postmodern, the category of 'hyper-modernity'. Some years later,
in a different context but with analogous intentions, Marc Augé
proposed his notion of 'supermodernity' (*surmodernité*). I am still
convinced of the greater heuristic efficacy of this expression for
the simple but decisive reason that, before the progressive lists of
the type, 'first, second...' (and why not, 'third, fourth...')
modernity, we must bear in mind Augustine's old caution '*qui
incipit numerare incipit errare*'. It is important, nonetheless, to be

---

36   Ulrich Beck, 'Wie wird Demokratie im Zeitalter der Globalisierung
möglich? Eine Einleitung', p. 12.
37   See Ulrich Beck, *What Is Globalization?*.
38   Anthony Giddens, *The Consequences of Modernity*.
39   Alain Touraine, *Critique of Modernity*.

free of the artificial antithesis, modernity/postmodernity. Not because of its excessive radicalism; on the contrary, for its excessive indeterminacy and rhetorical nature. To pretend to tie the modern project to a substantially monistic and self-referential paradigmatic framework and, in contrast, to mechanically attribute to postmodernity only the thaumaturgical virtues of plurality, dissemination and eccentricity, is to close one's eyes or ignore the multiple (and conflicting) conceptions that are habitually assembled under the rubric of 'the Modern'. That said, when it is a case of developing the different qualities of the 'two' modernities, even Beck is unable to completely avoid being seduced by a certain schematic presentation. In his analyses, the successive epochs of modernity are distinguished by two sets of qualities:

a) A *socio-economic distinction*, which can be registered in the passage from the proto-modern era, polarised in the contrast between tradition and modernity, and *reflexive modernity*, dominated by the tension between imperatives internal to modernity itself (*in primis* by the conflict between industrial and post-industrial modernity).

b) A *socio-political distinction*, which can be detected in the transition from the protected order of the first modernity, shaped by the imperative of security, to the 'risk society' of the second modernity, permeated by the paradigm of insecurity.

Without the shadow of a doubt, these are valuable distinctions. But they cannot remove the suspicion that a partial perspective is at work. Only a one-sided perspective on the course of the Modern Project can prevent us from seeing that the ideas of risk, of the 'wager', of the unintentional nature and unpredictability of the effects of projected action, lie at the origin of an entire tradition of Western modernity; and, on the other hand, can blind us to the fact that the need for security and protection continue to play an important role in the heart of the *Zweite Moderne*.

The reason for such bias and for the optical illusions that it induces can, ultimately, be related to the conceptual deficit experienced by even the most sophisticated sociological interpretations. Even in the best cases, these end up as 'typological' systematisations of the *dóxai*, of the commonplaces and the widespread opinions regarding global phenomena. As Derrida has noted, something analogous happens to the notion of the 'end of work', which is directly associated with the problem of globalisation in a book by Jeremy Rifkin that had much success.[40] Even here, the emphasis falls upon the epochal turn: we are entering into a 'new phase in world history' in which, thanks to the technological innovations of tele-working and virtual work, 'fewer and fewer workers will be needed to produce the goods and services for the world population'.[41] Once again, what is at stake is revealed by the ability with which the typological differences with the preceding phases are presented. In Rifkin's case the magic number is not two but three. The new phase is that of the 'third technological revolution', which is said to mark a sea-change from the preceding ones. Whereas the first two revolutions – of coal, steel and textiles in the 1800s, and electricity, oil and the car in the 1900s – did not radically influence the history of work (since they required human labour-power that could not be replaced by the machine), Rifkin argues that the current cyberspace revolution, hinging on micro-computers and robotics, marks the end of the worker.

'End of *Der Arbeiter* and his age, as Jünger might have said,' replies Derrida to Rifkin's diagnosis-prognosis.[42] We should point out that the centenarian writer made a completely different prediction in the already cited conversation with Antonio Gnoli and Franco Volpi in 1995. Even when in the twenty-first century 'we enter a new era of the Titans' and 'the planet will be subjected to an acceleration to which humanity will have to adhere by transforming itself', even then, 'the Worker will be the form of man adequate to the new reality'.[43] In these words we must see a radical attempt to hold together a receptiveness to the new and the image of technology modified by the debate on the *globale Zeit* from the first half of the 1900s. Jünger continued to share with Schmitt and Heidegger, despite the notable differences of analysis and perspective, this modern, industrial and mechanical image of technology. To undo the discrepancy between Jünger's prognosis and that which Derrida, placing himself in the position of a hypothetical Jünger, erroneously utters, we will have to effect a break of great philosophical relevance. We must recognise that the 'dominion of Technology' (or, in Heidegger's terms, of the *Ge-stell*, 'Enframing'), as it was theorised by those great

---

40   Jeremy Rifkin, *The End of Work*.
41   Ibid., p. xvi.
42   Jacques Derrida, 'The University Without Condition', p. 226.
43   Gnoli and Volpi, *I prossimi Titani*, p. 105.

interpreters of European nihilism, has little to do with the global technological multiverse (as opposed to universe) of our time. That is, it stands in the same relation to it as a machine of the industrial age stands in relation to the micro-electronic network of the post-industrial era. But having elucidated this aspect, the problem – correctly raised by Derrida – of a philosophical consideration of the new pluriverse of *mondialisation*, poses itself in increasingly peremptory and compelling terms.

The action-at-a-distance of *techno-science* unquestionably brings about a virtualisation, a 'worldwide-izing delocalization of tele-work' that impacts upon the *forms of doing* inherited from the great Classical models decorporealising them.[44] Unmistakeably, we hear the echo of the diagnosis-prognosis of the modern condition elaborated by Marx and Engels in a crucial passage of the *Manifesto*: 'all that is solid melts into air . . .' The vertiginous velocity of commodity and information exchanges escapes the old logic of territorial confines rendering nation states increasingly porous. And yet, 'these phenomenal indices remain partial, heterogeneous, unequal in their development; they call for close analysis and no doubt new concepts'.[45] To start reflecting on the character of *dual contingency* of the new technologies, on the ambiguous nature of the global network (as all-pervasive as it is vulnerable), is perhaps the first way to answer Derrida's request. This is an entirely different thesis – as we have said – from that of the 'destinal' trajectory of Western nihilism outlined by Heidegger and, with an even more cogent ontological framework, by the Italian philosopher Emanuele Severino.[46] In this reconstruction, whose object is to fuse together Origin and Destiny, technology presents itself as a self-referential apparatus of means without ends: a functional apparatus as an end in itself, indifferent to any end that does not result in the reproduction, the optimisation and the growth of the apparatus itself. The nihilistic omnipotence of Technology was outlined in the same way in a celebrated work, composed in 1939 and published at the end of the war, by Ernst's brother, Friedrich Georg Jünger. In his view, even the politics of the more powerful sovereign states was destined to manifest its frailty before the rule imposed by the new global technology. 'The impotence of states in the face of explosive events that result from

---

44 Derrida, 'The University Without Condition', p. 226.
45 Ibid., p. 227.
46 See, for example, Emanuele Severino, *Il destino della tecnica*.

the evolution of technology is evident. There is no state that is able to dominate them, because the technology that excavates the state has insinuated itself in all areas of state organisation. Man no longer dominates the technological regularity he sets to work. Rather, it governs man'.[47]

However, as another Italian philosopher, Umberto Galimberti, has correctly noted,[48] the new technological pluriverse – in contrast to the technology of the industrial era – is not only a mechanical *dispositif* of means without ends. It is also, and above all, an environment. More precisely, a world-environment (*Um-welt*), a 'technocosm' that surrounds and constitutes us, imperiously dictating predetermined standards of rationality modelled, exclusively, on criteria of functionality and efficiency. We become aware of a significant theoretical effort directed to the recomposition of the ontological register of nihilism according to the approaches of philosophical anthropology to the subject of technology that we find in thinkers such as Hans Jonas and Günther Anders.[49] Anders' crucial theme of the anthropological gap or Promethean disproportion between human action and the world of technology, which tragically revolves around the 'destruction of life' (*Zerstörung des Lebens*) in the passage from the 'second' to the 'third industrial revolution', can, however, no longer be related exclusively to the menace exerted by atomic power. It must instead be extended to the point of embracing the power of the new biotechnologies. The *upsetting of the traditional confines between nature and artifice* puts on the agenda – beyond Jonas' 'imperative of responsibility' – a veritable anthropological leap in the direction that Nietzsche indicated of a 'transvaluation of all values' (*Umwertung aller Werte*). The new technologies not only retain a capacity for dominion over external nature but a power of manipulation of human nature, of the very sphere of the *bíos* as well. And yet it is precisely the themes of human engineering and of 'post-genomics' (of the scientific and biomedical inquiry that followed the laying out of the map of the human genome) that call upon a *dual contingency* rather than upon destiny – not, therefore, a

---

47   Friedrich Georg Jünger, *Die Perfektion der Technik*, p. 197.
48   Umberto Galimberti, *Psiche e techne: L'uomo nell'età della tecnica*, pp. 43 ff.
49   Hans Jonas, *The Imperative of Responsibility*; Günther Anders, *Die Antiquiertheit des Menschen*.

one-way but a two-way contingency that reverberates on the side of the 'sender' and the 'receiver' of codified messages.

To assert this is by no means to mollify or play down the 'question of technology'. It is, rather, to reconnect it to the terms in which it is actually posed in the face of a technological threshold that has imperiously given a new importance to biopolitical (as well as bioethical) themes. Not for nothing the paradigm emerging today is that of *uncertainty*, the authentic *trait d'union* of human and natural sciences, 'culture' and 'biology' – as demonstrated in a complex and rigorously argued work by Salvatore Veca.[50] In conclusion, the play of actions, reactions and multiple interdependences instituted by the technological pluriverse of the global network means that *science no longer enhances power but augments the coefficients of risk, of uncertainty and of contingency of decisions.*

Conjunctions and Disjunctions

Returning to the question of *mondialisation*, we must pose a further question. What consequences follow from the change of paradigm instigated by the new techno-cultural and biotechnological multiverse for the ordinary way of understanding the global dimension of problems? The first consequence is given by the 'gap' – upon which Derrida, with shades of Benjamin, has long insisted – between the unequivocal *signs of the times* connected to an ever more extended phenomenology of globalisation. And the *doxastic* use (not to speak of the ideological inflation and rhetorical and, frequently, inconsistent self-satisfaction) that lies at the basis of the proliferation of expressions such as 'the end of modernity', 'the end of work' and the like. Without doubt, to disregard such a gap is to forget entire areas of the globe, as well as individuals, groups and peoples that are, to a large extent, the excluded victims of the process commonly known as *mondialisation*. Above all, one must not give in to the temptation of disguising a situation of capitalist domination – where 'capital plays an essential role between the actual and the virtual' – which is 'more tragic in absolute figures than it has ever been in the history of humanity'.[51] No idea of the 'global' will justifiably be able to consider itself an insightful representation of our present, unless it

50   Salvatore Veca, *Dell'Incertezza: Tre meditazioni filosofiche.*
51   Derrida, 'The University Without Condition', p. 227.

is able to include, within its horizon, the *experience of this gap* as well as the awareness that humanity has, never so much as today, been 'from the worldwide-izing [*mondializzatrice*] or worldwide-ized [*mondializzata*] homogeneity of "work" and "without work" that is often alleged'.[52] Nevertheless, if we really want to get to the root of this literally *paradoxical* condition (in contrast to the *dóxa*, to the *communis opinio*), the preliminary task is to lead the current form of *globalisation* (as an *in fieri* process) and of *globality* (as structure of the *finite* world), beyond the specular opposition between globalist and anti-globalist ideologies, to the concept.

The first step is to conceive the relation global-local not only and not so much in terms of co-presence but also of *co-belonging*. That is, as something very close to the phenomenon defined by Ernst Bloch with the expressions 'contemporaneity of the non-contemporaneous' or 'synchrony of the asynchronic' (*Gleichzeitigkeit des Unglechzeitigen*).[53] To get to the bottom of the *paradox of globalisation*, these expressions – 'non-contemporaneity of the contemporaneous' or 'asynchrony of the synchronic' (*Ungleichzeitigkeit des Gleichzeitigen*) – should be understood in diametrically opposed terms. Therefore, we must begin to redefine the sociological notion of the 'glocal', which is assigned the meaning (with, true to say, questionable stylistic elegance) of the compulsive interpenetration of the global and the local. The term was introduced by Roland Robertson in a work, tracing the neologism 'glocalisation', which is rich in theoretical references and analyses. In Japan this term was employed to signify participation in the world market (the Japanese term *dochakuka* means 'global localisation', more or less) and became 'one of the main marketing buzzwords of the beginning of the nineties'.[54] Robertson's insight consists in his appeal to the mixture of elements within the term (itself formed by a telescoping of the global and the local so as to mix them up) in order to propose a non-linear reading of the process of globalisation. The key to doing so was provided by the phenomenon of 'spatio-temporal compression' that David Harvey had already identified[55] – in a work whose title is almost identical to Lyotard's

---

52 Ibid.
53 Ernst Bloch, *Heritage of Our Times*.
54 Sara Tulloch (ed.), *The Oxford Dictionary of New Words*, p. 134.
55 David Harvey, *The Condition of Postmodernity*.

famous text – as the fracture-line separating modernity from the global era. And it is precisely the theme of *asynchrony* that becomes the motivation for an interpretation that underlines the specifically cultural nature – ahead even of the economic – of that process. What we call 'globalisation' is nothing but the *form* on the basis of which the world has moved towards unity.[56] But the *new map of the world* is only theoretically comprehensible in the light of the complex and problematic character of the distinction between the global and the local, so much so that we must now, perhaps, speak of the global institutionalisation of the life-world and of the localisation of globality.[57] Considered as a whole, the global field is a multi-dimensional reality that springs from the compression of connected cultures and civilisations. Thus, the *world-system* is not guided by an exclusively economic dynamic (as Immanuel Wallerstein suggests it is) but also by the 'problematic status of the "culture factor"'. Consequently, not only is cultural pluralism 'itself a constitutive feature of the contemporary global circumstance ... [but] the very conceptions of the world-system, including the symbolic responses to ... globalization, are themselves important factors in determining the trajectories of that very process'.[58]

The *spatio-temporal compression* produced by global technologies through the implosion of the time necessary for communication to the zero degree of the instant, transforms the trend of unification into a general process of cultural differentiation that accelerates the development of *conflicting interpretations of world history*, thereby provoking the proliferation of the demand for identity based upon the search for *fundamentals* (in the dual sense of *totalising foundation* and of *anti-totalising fundamentalism*). These statements appear to be close to the antagonistic readings of globalisation as a 'clash of civilisations'. Indeed, even Huntington, who transposes to a global scale a typically communitarian argument (the question is not 'What do I want?' but 'Who am I?'), has maintained that in the post–Cold War world 'the most important distinctions among peoples are not ideological, political, or economic. They are cultural'.[59] It is

56 Roland Robertson, *Globalization: Social Theory and Global Culture*.
57 See ibid., chapters 3 and 11.
58 Ibid., p. 61.
59 Huntington, *The Clash of Civilizations and the Remaking of World Order*, p. 21.

for this reason that peoples and nations 'are attempting to answer the most basic question humans can face: Who are we?'.[60] But this is a mistake. For in his more recent works, Robertson warns against the dangers of an interpretation of the 'glocal' on the basis of dichotomous schema.[61]

This is the risk run by the reading of 'glocalisation' as an axial antithesis between *Jihad-World* and *McWorld* that is advanced by Benjamin Barber, and with which Robertson argues. Barber understands the former term as a cipher for the *local* and its tendencies towards tribalisation and balkanisation. The latter he takes as the logo for the *global* with its trends towards technological and advertising homogenisation.[62] However, there is an analogous observation in Zygmunt Bauman's albeit intellectually solid and attentive analyses. Although Bauman considers 'glocalisation' 'Roland Robertson's apt term, exposing the unbreakable unity between 'globalizing' and 'localizing' pressures – a phenomenon glossed over in the one-sided concept of globalization',[63] Bauman ends up treating the 'glocal' as a typological division with an 'active' side and a 'passive' one, with globalised classes on one side and settled localised classes on the other. 'What appears as globalization for some means localization for others; signalling a new freedom for some, upon many others it descends as an uninvited cruel fate'.[64]

The dichotomous standpoint overlooks a decisive element. To overcome the unilateral view of the process of globalisation, a doubling of it is insufficient. It is necessary, rather, to think through its paradoxical nucleus, which can be traced back precisely to the intimate belonging together and interaction of the two dimensions of the global and the local. If those two dimensions are reduced to locations, conditions or social areas that are topologically segregated, the one-sidedness of the concept will not be overcome but simply duplicated either in the re-presentation of the axial model of antagonism (Barber) or in the reproduction of the old stratified paradigm (Bauman). In this sense, the manner in which Bauman interprets the phenomenon of spatio-temporal compression implied by the term

---

60   Ibid.

61   See Roland Robertson, 'Glocalization Revisited and Elaborated'.

62   Benjamin Barber, 'Jihad vs. McWorld' and *Jihad vs. McWorld: How Globalism and Tribalism are Reshaping the World*.

63   Zygmunt Bauman, *Globalization: The Human Consequences*, p. 70.

64   Ibid., p. 2.

'glocal' is symptomatic. 'Globalization divides as much as it unites; it divides as it unites – the causes of division being identical with those which promote the uniformity of the globe'.[65] Such a statement fails to shed much light on the paradox of globalisation. In truth, *this* globalisation does not divide *while* it unifies but precisely *because* it unifies different life-worlds in the form of compression, i.e., in the form of a homologating indifferentiation and coercive juxtaposition. Thus, *glocalisation* should be understood as a dual process involving the *interpenetration of the universalisation of particularism and the particularisation of universalism.*[66] Not, therefore, as a mere contemporaneity–co-presence but rather as the mutual implication of homogenisation and heterogenisation: the inclusion of the locality of difference in the same *global organic composition.* In other words, glocalisation takes the shape of a diastolic-systolic movement, at once a circular and an intermittent motion that cannot be resolved according to scale (micro/ macro). The local is not a microcosm that reflects the global macrocosm. It is, rather, that the aporias of the world-system make way for the current form of polycentric and molecularly diffuse *world-conflict* [*conflitto-mondo*].

The *glocal* is configured as the conflictual cohabitation of two tendencies: the synergic trend of the global, represented by the techno-economic and financial complex; and the allergic local trend represented by the turbulence of cultural differences.[67] From this starting point, deep fault-lines, conflictual fracture-lines are produced that, *pace* Huntington, do not separate 'civilisations' as if they were homogeneous, unified blocks closed in upon themselves. Instead, they traverse all the societies of the planet along internal vectors – from Western democracies to the Islamic world. However, transferring the category of *glocalisation* from the descriptive to the conceptual plane, a further move is necessary. The phenomenon should not be understood as an inertial resistance of traditional communitarian forms to the expansive trend of modernity (according to the schema of the theories of modernisation which took root during the 1950s and 1960s). On the contrary, it should be understood as a veritable *production of locality.* It would be too easy if the global represented the 'new',

---

65 Ibid.
66 Robertson, *Globalization: Social Theory and Global Culture.*
67 See Angelo Bolaffi and Giacomo Marramao, *Frammento e sistema.*

the *Gesellschaft*, and the local the 'old', the *Gemeinschaft*. The demand for community, even in the extreme fundamentalist forms, is a strictly modern phenomenon.[68]

The paradox of globalisation is that, in it, the 'location' of difference is constructed, tradition invented and the community imagined. For this crucial reason, the paradox ends up being literally incomprehensible, unless one leaves behind that presupposition of Western social theory (from Hegel to Marx, from Tönnies to Weber, from Comte to Durkheim) which postulated a singular and dramatic break between tradition and modernity, in accordance with the typology of 'traditional' and 'modern' society. In the world in which we live, where modernity has 'turned to dust' once and for all,[69] the combined effect of media communications and mass migrations gives way to a mobile and unpredictable relation between globalisation and modernity out of which the phenomenon of 'diasporic public spheres' is catalysed by the collective creation of community.[70] Thus, the focus of the analysis shifts to the logic that presides over the *global production of locality* in an ever more trans-national and 'deterritorialised' world.[71] On the cultural plane today, the proliferation of diasporic communities constitutes 'one special diacritic of the global modern'.[72] However, it is precisely this that leads 'locality' to change its nature and means that it is no longer 'what it once was'. Immersed in a new relationality, determined by the new global electronic mediation, the local 'appears to have lost its ontological moorings' to become a *social practice of the imagination*.[73]

Post-electronic communication, crossing the path of deterritorialised and uprooted subjects, confers a novel extension and intensity to a phenomenon familiar to modernity (despite the academic separation between discursive and institutional forms) since the appearance of the 'Guttenberg galaxy' and of 'print-capitalism' (analysed, respectively, by Marshall McLuhan and Benedict Anderson): namely, the phenomenon of the 'invention of tradition'[74] and the narrative construction – in a public sphere

---

68   See Samuel N. Eisenstadt, *Fondamentalismo e modernitá*, p. 3.

69   *Translator's note*: Appadurai's *Modernity at Large* was translated into Italian as *Modernità in polvere*, or 'Modernity Turned to Dust'.

70   Arjun Appadurai, *Modernity at Large*, p. 4.

71   Gilles Deleuze and Félix Guattari, *A Thousand Plateaus*.

72   Appadurai, *Modernity at Large*, p. 11.

73   Ibid., p. 178.

74   Eric Hobsbawm and Terence Ranger (eds.), *The Invention of Tradition*.

shaped by the new typographical technology – of the 'imagined community' of the nation.[75] Today, the influence of the 'move-ment-images' (whether cinematographic, televisual or web) of the global media multiverse on the individuals and groups caught up in the experience of universal uprooting produces the para-dox of the 'invention of primordialism' by imagined communities that have lost their 'sense of place'. In the global imaginary of the Origin, the past idolised by the local practices of self-identi-fication is no longer a ground to which to return through a 'politics of memory'. It has become, instead, a sort of 'temporal central casting',[76] a synchronic deposit of cultural scenarios to draw upon from time to time 'depending on the film to be made, the scene to be enacted, the hostages to be rescued'.[77] But the crucial point of this trans-cultural dynamic is constituted by a second-order paradox. In the disjunctive flow of 'glocal' interde-pendence, the hegemonic society itself is sucked inexorably back into the localistic vortex of its own presumed 'universal' imagi-nary. The United States is progressively losing that cultural monopoly over the imagination that legitimised the characterisa-tion of the 1900s as the 'American century'. It is no longer the 'puppeteer of a world system of images' but simply one of the crossroads and nodes of a complex construction of culturally differentiated 'imaginary panoramas'.[78] So globalisation 'does not necessarily or even frequently imply homogenization or Americanization'; rather, 'to the extent that different societies appropriate the materials of modernity differently, there is still ample room for the deep study of specific geographies, histories and languages'.[79]

The theme of 'difference' emerges from the fabric of the global production of locality. It is a theme that, in the current debate on globalisation, we usually find associated with the term 'culture'. However, I think it worth noting that a sharp trans-cultural analyst of the present such as Arjun Appadurai, despite detecting

75 Benedict Anderson, *Imagined Communities*; Homi K. Bhabha, *Nation and Narration*.

76 *Translator's note:* the Italian translation of this phrase is somewhat differ-ent: '*archivio centrale del tempo*' or 'central archive of time'. Arjun Appadurai, *Modernità in Polvere*, p. 49.

77 Appadurai, *Modernity at Large*, p. 30.

78 Ibid., p. 31.

79 Ibid., p. 17.

in anthropology an indispensable 'archive of lived actualities',[80] feels the need to warn against the indiscriminate recourse to that association. While it is true that the notion of difference constitutes the 'most valuable feature of the concept of culture',[81] the current use and abuse of this noun (especially by non-anthropologists or extempore anthropologists) has contributed markedly to the diffusion of the preconception that culture is a type of object, a physical or metaphysical entity, which results in it being related back to the 'discursive space of race'[82] or of a biologically understood *ethos* (in the 'superorganic' manner of Alfred Kroeber). Instead of taking the term 'culture' as a noun, it should be taken in its adjectival form: 'cultural'. In this way, it can be related to the more fertile soil of contextualisations, contrasts and comparisons.

Despite this, we must admit that the characterisation of the *global age* from the perspective of *cultural* differences fails to exhaust the theoretical questions implied by the category of 'difference'. For this reason, even the sophisticated and complex discursive framework used by Appadurai stops short of actually crossing the threshold of the paradox of *glocalisation*. Certainly, in comparison to most contributions from the social sciences, a work such as *Modernity at Large* stands out. It does so for two reasons: first, because of the precision with which it identifies the privileged 'heuristic device'[83] for the analysis and definition of the global age in the 'idea of situated difference'.[84] That is to say, 'difference in relation to something local, embodied, and significant'.[85] Second, because of the clear recognition that many types of differences exist in the world and only some of these are, strictly speaking, cultural: i.e., those differences that express or form the basis for the 'mobilization of group identities'.[86] Thus, strictly speaking, the term 'culture' is limited to the demarcation of that 'subset of these differences that has been mobilized to articulate the boundary of difference'; coinciding, *de facto*, with 'a matter of group identity as constituted by some differences among

---

80   Ibid., p. 11.
81   Ibid., p. 12.
82   Ibid.
83   Ibid., p. 13.
84   Ibid., p. 12.
85   Ibid.
86   Ibid., p. 13.

others'.[87] Notwithstanding such a lucid awareness, the map delineated in the work ends up – taking a twist that is typical of the
approach of the social sciences to the question of the global –
orbiting the notion of cultural differences. It is not my intention
here to belittle the results that follow from such a method, from
the theory of cultural interactions based upon disjunctive flows to
the analysis of 'globally variable synaesthesia';[88] from the category
of 'postblurring' to the return of the idea of the 'religious' in a
global hypermodernity articulated by the 'dialectic of implosion
and explosion'.[89]

These are significant results, which have the unquestionable
merit of liquidating those schematic simplifications which maintain that the global stands in the same relation to space as
modernity stood to time. Nonetheless, in Appadurai the kaleido-
scope of cultural differences, ensnared by the flow of the
imagination, is unable to pass from the regime of the imaginary
(with its rituals of invention and community) to the sphere of the
symbolic. The passage to the 'global production of differences',
auspicated in this book, remains barred and the argument
concludes at the point where it should begin: on the threshold of
a *metacultural redefinition of differences as the perspectival point,
the criterion of destructuring and reconversion of the political
categories of Modernity*. Appadurai's stereoscopic vision suggestively delineates the scenarios of the glocal in relation to culture
and mass communication – *not* with respect to politics. But it is
precisely in the political void expressed in the conjunctive-disjunc-
tive hyphen between the global and the local that one finds the key
to interpreting the proliferation of fundamentalisms and the politics of identity.

To get to the bottom of the paradox of the global production
of locality and of the resulting inflation of logics and imaginar-
ies of identity that assume the semblance of 'cultural differences',
one must solder together, in a dynamic and unitary vision, the
categories of globalisation and secularisation. Only along this
path – as arduous as it is necessary – will it be possible to
escape from the misty indistinctness of 'imaginary' and
'symbolic' that, in the final analysis, lies at the root of the
conceptual and practical, the philosophical and political deficit

---

87 Ibid.
88 Ibid., p. 37.
89 Ibid., p. 51.

of the disputes between apologists and critics (and of the contrasting sectarianism of the 'global' or the 'anti-global'). For this very reason, it is difficult to comprehend the position of those who, like Robertson, declare secularisation to be an obsolete category, at the same time that they assume the perspective of a *global culture* as an *a priori* datum rather than as a result (a problematic one at that) of a determinate logical and historical process. Robertson's critique of Wallerstein's world-system theory is symptomatic. The unacceptability of this theory, he argues, is based upon the fallacious presupposition of the submission of all the great cultures of the planet (from Islam to India to China) to the *pensé unique* represented by the principles and standards of Western civilisation.[90] While in the *pars destruens* of his argument Roberston successfully demonstrates that the economic expansion of the world-system 'has not involved . . . a symmetrical . . . expansion of world culture to the point where all major actors on the global scene share the same presuppositions',[91] in the *pars construens* he ends up setting against Wallerstein's thesis the equally *a priori* assumption of the plurality of global culture. Until the core dynamic of the glocal paradox is understood (both genetically and structurally), the game of mirrors in which the antithesis between the unifying assumption of the economic perspective and the differentiating one of culture remains caught is destined inexorably to persist. By contrast, the impossibility of leading 'glocalisation' to the concept is confirmed if the question of the 'fundamental principles' and of identity-conflict is not linked to the category of world-modernity [*modernità-mondo*] and, thereby, to the theorem of secularisation. This impossibility is confirmed if one does not pose the question of the destiny of secularisation once the dynamic of modernity has left its place of origin in the 'Occident' and spread to other cultures.

Theatrum Orbis

At this point it is necessary to make a crucial theoretical move. The term 'glocal' does not only designate the phenomenon of interdependence but also that of 'short-circuit', of the contrastive-compulsive 'interpenetration' of the two dimensions, the

---

90   See Immanuel Wallerstein, *The Modern World-System*.
91   Robertson, *Globalization: Social Theory and Global Culture*, p. 69.

global and the local. That is, it designates the fusing together of the two, intimately interwoven movements of the globalisation of the local and the localisation of the global. But – and now we come to the crux of the problem – what do we mean by 'short-circuit'? The short-circuit occurs because the intermediate ring of the international order of modernity, the one represented by the nation state and the structure that had hereto sustained it (the isomorphism between 'a people', 'territory' and 'sovereignty') has broken down.

The paradox of the global production of locality is one of the characteristic features that distinguish *this* globalisation from all the phases that preceded it. Its principle characteristic can be found in the new political framework of the world, defined by Habermas as 'post-national constellation' and by Philippe Schmitter as the 'post-Hobbesian order' (whose semantic connotations are, to some extent, analogous to my expression 'after the Leviathan'). The current *mondializzazione* consists neither in a generic interdependence, nor in the pure and simple trans-continental parting of the seas. Both of these conditions had already been realised in the preceding 'waves', with the discovery of the New World and with the creation of the modern market. The originality of today's globalisation must be sought elsewhere: in the breakdown of the 'Westphalian model', i.e., of the system of international relations that, since the end of the religious civil wars of the sixteenth and seventeenth centuries, hinged on the sovereign, territorially enclosed nation state. From this standpoint, contemporary globalisation triggers, if not the end – since, structurally, the state-form appears destined to continue for now and, quantitatively, the planet has seen a veritable boom in the birth of national or sub-national states – certainly a decline of the Leviathan and a continuous erosion of its sovereign prerogatives. This process has advanced exponentially since 1989, following the fall of the dividing wall upon which the fortunes of the bipolar system rested.[92] But the critical mass of effects determined by this break, far from triggering a trend of unification and standardisation in the direction of a 'world state' (in accordance with Jünger's prognosis) or of a 'cosmopolitan republic' (as Kant had hoped), has given way to a sort of contracted hyperspace that is internally unbalanced and constitutionally refractory to any *reductio ad unum* by the exclusive logic of sovereignty. How, then, does the

---

92 Kenichi Ohmae, *The End of the Nation State*.

oxymoronic 'glocal' behave *after the Leviathan*, i.e., in the new, post-Hobbesian order (or disorder)?

The end of the Westphalian model initially manifests itself in the upsetting of an Order: the breaking down of a specific historical form of international relations structured by a clear line of demarcation between the 'inside' and the 'outside', between the dimensions internal to and external to states. The 1648 Peace of Westphalia signalled a veritable watershed in the course of modernity, 'between different historical times'.[93] With the end of the religious civil wars, the complex of *regna* that were already emerging along the lines of the state-form, broke the envelope of the *respublica Christiana* of the medieval Holy Roman Empire. They gave way to a system structurally different from the 'dualistic religious constitution of Europe', which turned on a sovereignty that was divided between a political *potestas* and a religious *auctoritas*. With the affirmation of the principle of the *cujus regio ejus religio*, new relationships were established between politics and religion,[94] in which the individual acquired full responsibility in the 'inner cavity' of his own conscience. Setting out from social contract theory and leading on to the doctrine of sovereignty by way of the liberation of individual conscience from the external strictures of theological morality, 'this is the course that (inaugurated perhaps by Hobbes and codified for the first time in the Peace of Westphalia and then put into practice in Enlightenment state-societies) enabled the extension of the problem and the need for a constitution throughout Europe'.[95] By arrogating to itself the 'monopoly of legitimate physical violence'[96] and exclusivity in the exercise of secular sovereignty (beginning with the power to create law and impose bureaucratic-administrative procedures), the secular state neutralised political and religious fundamentalisms and incorporated more efficient 'reasons' as well as more technical 'forms of knowledge' in order to delimit the internal and external areas of its operations. That is, it maintained peace within and defended the 'Commonwealth' from the menace of external states without. The constructivist logic of the *ius publicum europæum*, underlying the new system of inter-state relations, had

---

93   Pierangelo Schiera, 'Seicento e Novecento. Le categorie moderne della politica', p. 32.
94   See Paolo Prodi, *Una storia della giustizia*.
95   Schiera, 'Seicento e Novecento', p. 33.
96   Max Weber, 'Politics as a Vocation', p. 33.

two central implications. First, the strict complementariness between the two poles of the modern dyad, state/civil society: the administrative and policing practices of the territorial state and the competitive mercantile state of *bürgerliche Gesellschaft* were characterised as two out-and-out pillars of order and the two principal motors of discipline that would accompany secularisation. Second, it implied a clear reciprocity between internal order and external disorder. This is to be understood in the Hobbesian sense of the relationship between the peace internal to single states and the persistence of the 'state of nature' and, hence in this case, of the war between Leviathans; it is also to be understood in the historical and structural sense of the relationship between European space, 'civilised' and 'peaceful', and non-European space, characterised as a space without rules which could be subject to hegemonic acts of conquest or imperialist ones of colonisation and exploitation.

Today, the 'Hobbesian' paradigm of order, sanctioned by the Peace of Westphalia, is not only problematic in its single aspects or implications but in its very principle of construction. We do not suggest adding yet another chapter to the endless tale of the 'crisis of the state' that traverses the entire juridical and political debate of the twentieth century. The destiny of the 'mortal god', that is, of that 'jewel' of the *ius publicum europæum* represented by the modern state-form is, in reality, inscribed in its very genesis. This is something Carl Schmitt had clearly seen and tried desperately to combat. The entropy of the Leviathan has its distant origin in the eternal contest between Earth and Sea: the opening up of the oceans determined by the process of insulating England in the Elizabethan era. Embracing the maritime imperial model, Britain separated itself from the events of the continent by turning itself into the greatest global power. *General and Rare Memorials Pertaining to the Perfect Art of Navigation* by John Dee, Elizabeth's mathematician and astrologer, was emblematic of the new course. It marked the natural end of Shakespeare's *theatrum orbis*, not coincidentally baptised The Globe.[97] The panorama that opens up before us, however much it assumes the semblance of *another scene* from the theatre of the world, is comprehensible only as the result of a modernity that, through successive globalisations, escaped from its area of origin to spread to all areas and cultural

---

97 On this see Frances A. Yates' fundamental essays in *Astraea: The Imperial Theme in the Sixteenth Century* and *Theatre of the World*.

contexts of the planet. But the consequence of this expansion is the falling away of that border [*confine*] between the *inside* and the *outside* that constituted the essential presupposition of the logic and the function of the state. In the era of the 'finite world' (Valéry) and the planetary 'spatial revolution' (Schmitt), there is no *katechon* that appears able to check the inexorable decline of the Leviathan. Indeed, the modern state-form has always been characterised by its relation to an 'outside' and, therefore, is unthinkable outside of this relationship. The principle of construction of the state is not that of the all-or-nothing but that of the internal and external. 'The State is sovereignty. But sovereignty only reigns over what it is capable of interiorizing, of appropriating locally'.[98]

The idea of a *Weltstaat*, of a world-wide [*mondiale*] state, of a world-state [*Stato-mondo*] deprived of the possibility of reference to an *outside* (i.e., to a plurality of other states or understood as an anomic, 'outlaw' space, with arbitrary uses) is, therefore, a veritable *theorem of impossibility*. It is in contradiction with the constitutive logical and historical principle of modern statehood. For this central reason, the association of the category of 'sovereignty' with that of 'Empire' – which Michael Hardt and Antonio Negri make in their noteworthy attempt to furnish a theoretical synthesis of the 'new order of globalization' – seems unsustainable. Attentively considered, this association is incongruous within the analytic framework that, developing the ideas of Deleuze and Guattari, correctly identifies the discontinuity with respect to modern logic and politics precisely in the *failure of the critical threshold between the 'inside' and the 'outside'*.

> There is a long tradition of modern critique dedicated to denouncing the dualisms of modernity. The standpoint of that critical tradition, however, is situated in the paradigmatic place of modernity itself, both 'inside' and 'outside', at the threshold or the point of crisis. What has changed in the passage to the imperial world, however, is that this border place no longer exists, and thus the modern critical strategy tends no longer to be effective.[99]

The originality of this framework lies in its ability to side-step the dilemmas of the modern. It does so by fusing the classical idea of Empire and the novel cartography of the global era (which is

---

98   Deleuze and Guattari, *A Thousand Plateaus*, p. 360.
99   Hardt and Negri, *Empire*, p. 183.

characterised by the overlapping planes of the economy, politics and culture), and the post-Fordist pole of immaterial and biopolitical production. In this way, the imperial form is definitively uncoupled from the (still industrial and colonial) paradigm of imperialism and coincides with the hyperspace, with multiple entries of the global pluriverse (which is all-pervasive and yet, in contrast to the modern territorial state, permeable to the omniversality of the multitudes). In the space comprised by this new techno-political and socio-cultural interdependence, the web of power appears to be without a summit and without a centre. The United States figures as only one of the poles of reference. In fact, the open and multicultural character of the space of citizenship contemplated by the American Constitution – 'free of the forms of centralisation and hierarchy typical of Europe'[100] – appears, to them, to correspond fully to an imperial-type logic (and *not* an imperialistic one). The conceptual definition of 'Empire' has three component parts. Empire is: 1) without limits; 2) indefinite in time, that is, it is crystallised in a sort of *epoché*, of suspension *sine die* of order; and, in its paradigmatic configuration, 3) the generalised administration of bio-power (in the Foucauldian sense of molecular control over the totality of the *bíos* and of production-reproduction of life itself).

But it is precisely the rigorous assumption of these premises that leads to the incongruity of asserting the 'old-European' – to use a favourite expression of Luhmann's – cornerstone of the 'paradigm of the Modern' that, incontestably, is found in the concept of 'sovereignty'. If Empire has nothing in common with the old category of imperialism and if the (imperialist) state stands in the same relation to the modern as (diffuse) Empire stands to the postmodern; if the new 'order' has become irrevocably separated from territorial 'localisation' (thus separating the terms of celebrated couple *Ordnung/Ortung*); if global domination, no longer operating according to the centre/periphery schema, ceases to be localisable in one point and so cannot even coincide *sic et simpliciter* with the economic, military and technological power of the United States; if the new decentred and deterritorialised power makes way for hybrid identities, flexible hierarchies, fluid exchanges and modular command networks; if all this is the case, to speak of 'imperial sovereignty' is a *contradictio in adjecto*. Confirmation is given, indirectly, by Hardt and Negri themselves

---

100   Ibid., p. 168.

when, at the very moment they attempt to describe the institutional form of the new order, they turn to the Polybian model of the Mixed Constitution. As is the case with Polybius' account of the Roman Republic, Empire is a synthesis of the three forms of government considered by classical typology. Monarchy is represented by the military-strategic monopoly of the Pentagon and by the control of financial flows exerted by organisations such as the World Bank and the International Monetary Fund. Aristocracy exists in the power of multinationals that organise the production and distribution of goods. And democracy is relegated to the organisms – such as NGOs (non-governmental organisations) and non-profit associations – that organise the tutelage of human rights, acting as new 'people's tribunals'. However, precisely 'mixed government' – re-presented, here, with undoubted efficacy and descriptive pertinence – appeared to Hobbes to be not a solid foundation for Order but as a factor of permanent division and instability, and a menace to the internal peace of the state. Thus, he believed it to be a model incompatible with the logic of sovereignty. A new order founded upon an 'imperial' *civitas*, which is able to bring into its space composed of variable geometries an irreducible plurality of differences, will never be produced in the form of a *reductio ad unum* in accordance with the monopolistic and exclusivist logic of sovereign *potestas*. Instead, it will have to translate into political government and into global political institutions 'the current irregular interdependence between supranational organisms', the different appeals to international law, the *lex mercatoria*, and the 'politics carried out directly by economic power'. All this will have to take place with the lucid appreciation that 'beyond the State, the World State [*Stato mondiale*] does not await us, either in centralised-authoritarian form, or in a federal form'.[101] It is not a new form of sovereignty that emerges from the still chaotic dynamic of globalisation. It is, rather, a new dimension of 'the political', whose likely institutional outlet could be represented not so much by the *civitas maxima* hoped for by Hans Kelsen, as by the multilevel governance system characterised by the paradoxical coexistence (and reciprocal limitation) of a *plurality of sovereign powers*. If what our political future holds for us is a global order, 'it will be neither a statist one, nor a post-statist one (if not chronologically). Nor will it ever be the automatic result of the planetary affirmation of the "laws of the market"'. It

---

101   Massimo Cacciari, 'Ancora sull'idea di Impero', p. 187.

will have to be 'supranational in the precise sense of the term', that is, able to conjugate institutional pluralism with the irreducible plurality of the socio-cultural agents in its space: '*nationes, gentes*, rather than States'. It is only in this way that the new dimension of the political will able to guide 'the process of deconstruction of the artificial state identities, and legitimise itself politically through those subjects, organisms and communities whose power the state had always only ever considered to be "derivative"'.[102]

With regard to structural isomorphism, it is certainly legitimate to interpret the dynamic factors that produce the erosion of sovereignty – from above (supranational organisms, 'ecumenical' agencies and *lex mercatoria*) and from below (regional and localistic-communitarian pushes for independence) – as a 'return' to the *potestas indirecta* that operated in the preceding phase of the modern state's formation and that were neutralised by the centralised power of the Leviathan sanctioned by the 'Westphalian model'. It would, however, be misleading to assume the image of the return literally, because the 'subjects', themes and contents that pull the dynamic factors along are radically new and different. In contrast to the premodern or proto-postmodern past, today the 'indirect powers' assume, on the one hand, the semblances of techno-economic globalism and human rights universalism, on the other, those of the membership of different cultures and public diasporas. Due to the political void produced by the absence of global governance and of a legitimate institutional mediation (at this time suspended between the *no-longer* of the old inter-state order and the *not-yet* of a new supranational order), the sides of universalism and of differences stand in opposition, exacerbating their respective one-sidedness and hardening their position in the glocal pincer. The tension released from the *double bind* takes on the shape of a *conflict of identities* whose logic escapes the procedural *dispositifs* of control of contemporary 'polyarchies'.[103] Therefore, compared with the situation of the modern nation, the current status of world-modernity [*modernità-mondo*] presents a new constellation of relationships between interests and values, one marked by a radical mutation in the form of conflict. This can be observed in the passage from the modern dominance of the conflict of interests to the current dominance of the conflict of values.

---

102   Ibid., p. 188.
103   See Saskia Sassen, *Losing Control? Sovereignty in an Age of Globalization.*

The new constellation projects itself beyond the figure of the Leviathan, the shadow of which was cast even upon its most extreme, 'reformed' and 'expanded' versions: i.e., the Welfare State. In the last phase of his work, the respected neo-contractualist theorist John Rawls forcefully underlined the necessity of reformulating the Hobbesian problem of order starting from the 'fact of pluralism'. But the pluralism in whose presence we find ourselves today, as much in the Western democracies as on the global stage of world-modernity [*modernità-mondo*], is of a different stamp to the 'corporatist' one of aggregate interests that was tested out in the democratic laboratories of the twentieth century, with varied and contrasting fortunes, from Weimar to Roosevelt's New Deal, from Beveridge right up to the models of the social state that took root from the 1950s to the 1970s. We should, however, elucidate a particularly subtle implication of our argument. When we speak of the obsolescence of the paradigm of the 'Leviathan' as a consequence of the passage from a pluralism of interests to a pluralism of values and identities we do not at all intend to affirm that, *first*, there was only a pluralism of interests whereas, *today*, there is a pure and simple pluralism of identities. Construing the thesis in these terms would be a *reductio ad absurdum*. The pluralism of identities, the 'fundamental' conflict between alternative conceptions of the good, with the correlative phenomenon of the intermingling of the political and moral spheres, has played a significant and, at times, decisive role in the modern era as well – and not only before the Leviathan, in the long course of the confessional civil wars, but after the affirmation of the Westphalian model as well. This continued in the preparatory phase of the French Revolution and in the successive revolutionary waves that accompanied the movements for the reform of state power, the Constitution and for the extension of rights. More generally, once the category of 'interest' is no longer comprehensible outside the reference to the cultural and socio-psychological dimension, it follows that the interweaving between the *material* and the *symbolic*, economy and culture, traverses – with different degrees of intensity – all the phases of social change. This is why, as the symbolic dimension permeates even the most materialistic (or, as one used to say, the most 'trade-unionist') of socio-economic conflicts, the logic of class interests or of rank conceals itself even in the most absolutist (or, as one would say today, 'fundamentalist') of identity conflicts. This is the case with the wars of religion between Catholics and Protestants that stained the European earth with blood in the sixteenth and seventeenth centuries, and – why not? – that same strategy of terror and 'global war' led by the most extreme fringes of the Islamic world against Western supremacism.

The question of the relationship between interests and values, strategic logic and logic of identity, should not be set out in terms of presence/absence, but on the basis of the need to identify, bit by bit, the dominant factor that confers on the relationship its peculiar *form*. Today's pluralism is – without a shadow of a doubt – *also* a pluralism of interests, but it has increasingly taken the form of a pluralism of identities. This entails that, today, in contrast to the industrialist (and colonialist) phase of nation-Modernity, interests are no longer the structuring element of the dynamic of social order and social conflict. It is no longer possible to isolate the social dynamic or render its logic autonomous from the constitutive dynamic of identities. The conflicts of interests and class discrimination, which – I repeat – persist as sharply as before, now find themselves inextricably caught within the dynamic of conflicts of identity. Thus, the articulation of interests appears as a *dependant variable of the process of symbolic identification*. Interests come to be interpreted differently according to the context and the form-of-life. That is, they come to be identified on the basis of the *situated existence* of the 'subjects', according to their different cultural-identitarian collocation.

The need to turn to the concept of 'difference', so as to get to the bottom of the dilemmas of the 'post-democratic' era and to open a passageway to a theory and practice of politics beyond the horizon of the state, follows directly from these premises. Such a category should not be understood in terms of an entity with metaphysical (or substantive) connotations. It should be grasped as the standpoint and guiding criterion able to trace the new logics of domination (and of discrimination) that are emerging within the map of the pluriverse that is too hastily being subsumed under the postmodern labels of 'decentring', 'nomadism' and 'dissemination'. The contributions made by the feminist thought of difference,[104] from the perspective of a *post-metaphysical ontology* since the 1970s, have become of vital importance for the identification of new 'fratriarchic' forms of power, as well as of a

---

104   This ranges from the pioneering works of Luce Irigaray and Carla Lonzi to those of Luisa Muraro, Adriana Cavarero, Judith Butler, Françoise Collin, Iris Marion Young, Manuela Fraire, Maria Luisa Boccia, Ida Dominijanni, Chiara Zamboni and of the *Diotima* philosophical community.

liberation of the concept – better still, of the theoretical practice – of the 'political' as much from the mono-logic of the state as from the 'politics of identity' affirmed by neo-communitarian differentialism. A decisive contribution to this endeavour is represented by the radical critique of the *distributive paradigm* that underlies the liberal-democratic theory of justice. This is the paradigm on which, in the final analysis, both the macroscopic eclipse of the concept of power in mainstream political philosophy as well as procedural democracy's inability to 'neutralise' the conflicts of values depend.

The *isometric* logic of the democratic Leviathan is able to govern the conflict of interests but not that of identities. Since there are no parameters for the commensurability of values as there are metrics of interests, political liberalism is forced to take its chances by opting for one of two methods: either the classical method of the *dilatory compromise*, entrusted to the wishful thinking that in the medium to long term envisages identity struggles for 'recognition' turning into redistributive claims; or the method of the *overlapping consensus*, which entrusts the fate of politics to the axiomatic separation between the (irreducibly plural) sphere of 'the good' and the (procedurally uniform one) of 'justice' and, hence, to the technique of *confinement* of questions of principle to the extra-political arena of metaphysics or the meta-political one of the *Weltanschauungen*, 'visions of the world'. Despite Rawls' noble intentions to produce a political philosophy whose aim is to maintain or relaunch the principal achievements of the State-of-Justice of Welfare, the burning question implied by the irreducible plurality of 'comprehensive conceptions of the good', which, in *Political Liberalism* and in other writings, is associated, by analogy, with the wars of religion of the 1500s and 1600s, has ended up being recontextualised in the edifying formula of *multiculturalism*. In practice, under the mask of the 'politics of recognition', this formula has given way to a compartmentalisation of society according to the *logic of contiguous ghettos*.

The fact is, however (and this cannot be separated from the 'fact of pluralism'), that conflicts of identity *overflow* all attempts to confine them within a logic of redistributive quotas. Moreover, in the vain attempt to neutralise them with recourse to the isometric paradigm – this is the method of government conforming to the economic model of 'rational choice' or of 'standard rational conduct' – the 'post-Leviathan' polyarchy ends up crystallising the dynamic of social change in the false

dilemma of techno-political proceduralism or neo-communitarian rhetoric of 'recognition'. Indulging in such a practice of
immobilisation produces a depoliticisation effect on internal
governance, which can then only be symbolically resolved
through the artificial creation of permanent 'states of emer-
gency' and the periodic projection towards the outside of new
images of the Enemy, and means that we lose sight of the real
nature of the *democratic dilemma* that nestles in the 'Babylon-
like heart' of the global era: that 'the political becomes
unpolitical and the unpolitical political'.[105] It is not a merely
mechanical return of the repressed, the eruption of a set of
questions that political modernity had repressed, misrecog-
nised or relegated to the shadow of the inner cavity. Nor is it a
return to the themes of the community or of the social bond
(not even in the shape of the community-without-foundation).
Neither can it be viewed, other than as a pallid analogy, as a
restatement of the Weberian motif of the irreconcilable tension
between *Gesinnungsethik* and *Verantwortungsethik*: the ethics
of non-negotiable principles and ethics of responsibility in
which the consequences of action have to be weighed with care.
Instead, it is a case of a polytheism of *post-nihilistic* and *post-
conventional* values that, from a new perspective, reclassifies
the themes against which the state measured itself in the course
of modernity: from the time of Absolutist politics to the interventions of welfare policy (order and progress, equality and
liberty, the quality of development and the ecological restric-
tions). At the heart of this new perspective is the way that
'Western rationalism' has to this day conceived of and disciplined the forms of our action and our being-in-the-world. One
must locate here, in this polytheistic constellation marked by
the traumatic imbalance between freedom and security, the
very phenomenon of the proliferation of extra-territorial and
ephemeral, hyperindividual consumerist 'explosive communities'. Bauman has focused on this through the hermeneutic lens
of the passage from 'solid' modernity, structured by the principle of stability, to 'liquid' modernity, charged with a diffuse
sensation of precariousness and uncertainty. The dimension of
the conflict of values that institutes an inextricable link between
interests, culture and symbolic identifications puts the utilitarian paradigm and its idea of a univocal, standard model of

---

105   Beck, *Politik der Globalisierung*, p. 29.

rational behaviour in check. Furthermore, in the compression of life-worlds, the epicentre of global conflict assumes the form of a tension between religious faith and modern Western rationality.[106] However, even in this case the cyclical message means little. It is not a case of a simple 'return' to the Sacred that would be adduced to disprove the prognosis (optimistic or pessimistic, depending on the points of view) that secularisation entails its irrevocable disappearance. The resumption of the eternal contest of the ancient gods[107] occurs, today, in terms of the *political function of religion* in the 'global village' – that is, a function that is at once analogous and different from the one operating in medieval, pre-modern and proto-modern times. What emerges is not a new (or nth appeal to a) question *of* meaning. Rather, it is a question *on* the meaning and the destiny of globalisation.

For now we are able only to intuitively grasp the intimate logic of this question, while we await its still chaotic dynamics to become stabilised in a decipherable constellation of signs. However, we can begin to discern what is at stake and its pathogenesis. What is at stake in the 'unpolitically political' question on the meaning of global time – and of the conflict that is propagated by it – is constituted by the relationship between life and technology, existence and the administered world. Conversely, its pathogenesis can be traced back to the shipwreck of an 'impertinent'[108] secularisation, which is indifferent to the contexts of world-modernity [*modernità-mondo*]. In this situation, the religions or the religiously based ethics, by coalescing questions of meaning, become one of the principal factors of symbolic identification. This is so in the Occident, with the exit of religion from the circle of the private (that rendered it invisible) and, in the Islamic world, with the full affirmation of religion as the constitutive dimension of political identity itself. In either case, we are confronted not with a clash of civilisations but of a transcultural conflict that is deterritorialised in nature. Monotheisms, inasmuch as they are religions with a vocation

---

106   Lester R. Kurtz, *Gods in the Global Village: The World's Religions in Sociological Perspective*.

107   The *Vielgötterei* (polytheism) evoked by Weber in an extraordinary passage of his 1917 conference 'Science as a Vocation', in Max Weber, *The Vocation Lectures*.

108   Jürgen Habermas, *The Postnational Constellation*.

to convert and to the acquisition of proselytes, have never kept to their place of origin but have had a universalist and warring vocation from the start.[109]

World Axis and Global Upheaval: 'Orients' and 'Occidents'

The emergence of religions or religious-based ethics as a privileged medium of political-symbolic identification robs the rational choice paradigm of its postulate. In place of the classical ethics-economics nexus or, more precisely, the relationship between moral codes and economic action it poses the need for a comparative, non-ethnocentric approach to the different cultural contexts. This leads inevitably to a reactivation of the comparison between two thinkers whose work, in different ways and with different histories, has never ceased to nourish the decades-old philosophical and historical controversy around the *destiny* of the Occident and its relations with 'other' cultures. I am referring, on the one hand, to Max Weber's extensive, comparative framework of 'world religions' and, on the other, to Karl Jaspers' deconstruction of the Orient/ Occident couple, setting out from the revelation of a subterranean synchrony between the great planetary *Weltanschauungen*. The singular nature of the confrontation is due to the fact that both thinkers adopt a broadly 'Enlightenment' standpoint, one that has learnt the lesson of Nietzschean nihilism but drawn different conclusions from it. Weber does so in the terms of a *theory of irradiation* on a universal scale of the singular event representing 'Western rationalism' (*okzidentaler Rationalismus*) and the 'disenchantment of the world' (*Entzauberung der Welt*); Jaspers in terms of the *theory of convergence* of global cultures towards a rational thought able to constitute, beyond the presumed dualism of *Western knowledge* and *Oriental wisdom*, the common horizon of human being. In order to pinpoint the advantages and the limits of the two theses, I shall first consider Jaspers and then Weber (the reason for this expository strategy will become clear as I proceed).

The comparative study of civilisations is still seduced by the thesis of the 'axial period' (*Achsenzeit*), advanced in 1949 by Jaspers in *Vom Ursprung und Ziel der Geschichte*.[110] This thesis situated the axis of world history in a 'global transformation of human-being' that took place sometime between 800 and 200

---

109 See Marc Augé, *Journal de guerre*, p. 64.
110 Karl Jaspers, *The Origin and Goal of History*, p. 1.

B.C., with the years around 500 B.C. as the critical period. It is possible to observe, at this time, in the 'three worlds' of India, China and the Occident (a term inclusive of Greece but also of ancient Palestine), a synchronic passage from mythical to rational thought, from *mythos* to *logos*. The highpoints of this passage are represented by the Upanishads and Buddha in India; Confucius, Lao-Tse, Mo Ti, Chuang-tzu in China; the prophetic tradition of Elijah, Isaiah, Jeremiah, through to Deutero-Isaiah, in Palestine; and philosophy and tragedy in Greece. The limits of Jaspers' thesis, the importance of which is demonstrated by the fact that till this day it forms the basis of the comparative analysis of cultures carried out, in sociology, by Shmuel Eisenstadt (with a significant shift in the axial epoch from 500 B.C. to A.D. 1) and, in sinology, by Heiner Roetz,[111] are to be found in the extremely schematic nature of its hermeneutic key, which is entrusted to a rather abstract and metahistorical notion of *Aufklärung* or 'rationally clarified experience'. Notwithstanding this, Heiner Roetz believes that one should credit it with producing a liberatory break with respect to the 'Hegelian/Weberian subjugation of the rest of the world to Western supremacy'.[112] In fact, Jaspers – while defending Hegel from those critics who objected that he had included Eastern civilisations which had no 'real contact' with Western events within his dialectical schema – explicitly distances himself from the idea that China, India and the Occident are successive dialectical stages in the evolution of Spirit, which Hegel argues in his *Lessons on the Philosophy of History*. 'It is precisely this succession of stages from China to Greece whose reality we deny; there is no such series, either in time or in meaning'.[113]

In Hegel, the logic of universal historical time follows the course of the Sun with the exactitude of astronomy: 'The dawn of the spirit', says Hegel in the lessons of the winter term of 1822–23, 'is in the Orient. But the spirit is only in its setting [*Die Morgenröte des Geistes ist im Osten, im Aufgang. Der Geist ist (aber) nur ihr Niedergang*]'.[114] Asian civilisation lacks the principle of subjective spirit that, rooted in the 'untouchable sphere of interiority', constitutes 'specifically a determination of European thinking [*eine*

---

111   Heiner Roetz, *Die chinesische Ethik der Achsenzeit.*
112   Ibid., p. 48.
113   Jaspers, *Origin and Goal of History*, p. 10.
114   Georg Wilhelm Friedrich Hegel, *Vorlesungen über die Philosophie der Weltgeschichte*, ed. Karl Heinz Ilting, Karl Brehmer, p. 121.

Bestimmung, die besonders dem europäischen Prinzip eigen ist].[115]
In particular, in the Chinese state, 'the ethical dimension [*das Sittliche*] becomes juridical'.[116] For this reason, what in the Occident belongs to the moral sphere and to internal self-determination becomes, in China, commanded by law and 'regulated by those who govern'.[117] But in this way, the government replaces interiority and the 'principle of subjective freedom is thereby sublated [*aufgehoben*] and goes unrecognised'.[118] We find here one of those passages in which Hegel overcomes the different expressions of oriental culture by incorporating them as dialectical moments of a one-way development. The logic of this passage is in every way isomorphic to that adopted in relation to the problem of truth – as Maurice Merleau-Ponty has noted in some extraordinarily precise pages of his 'Everywhere and Nowhere' in *Signs*. 'So the problem is completely clear: Hegel and those who follow him grant philosophical dignity to Oriental thought only by treating it as a distant approximation to the concept'.[119] Our idea of knowledge and culture is supremacist to such an extent that it poses a drastic alternative to every other form of thought or civilisation: it resigns itself 'to being a first sketch of the concept' or disqualifies 'itself as irrational'. The problem, now, is to verify whether we can truly still lay claim to that absolute knowledge and to that concrete universal which is precluded to the Orient owing to its endogenous limitation, as Hegel does. The inevitable conclusion of Merleau-Ponty's elegantly phrased question is that, if we should answer in the negative, 'our entire evaluation of other cultures would have to be re-examined'.[120]

What appeared to Hegel as a development and an overcoming was, for Jaspers, 'one of contemporaneous, side by side existence without contact'.[121] There were three *independent roots* of one history that, thanks to a mysterious simultaneity, appear to 'lead to the same goal'.[122] The analysis of the nature of the parallelism between the three worlds brought to an end, *ante litteram*, the 'theory of convergence' of civilisations that was destined to play

115 Ibid., p. 145.
116 Ibid., p. 144.
117 Ibid.
118 Ibid., p. 145.
119 Maurice Merleau-Ponty, *Signs*, p. 137.
120 Ibid.
121 Jaspers, *Origin and Goal of History*, p. 10.
122 Ibid., pp. 10–11.

such a significant role in the deconstruction of the universalist paradigm *after the 'American century'*. Decades ahead of Edward Said's unmasking of the stereotypes of *orientalism*, one of the most fecund aspects of Jaspers' philosophical comparativism is his desacralisation of the Orient/Occident dyad by showing it to be based upon a specular reflective mythologem. However, in his labour of disassembling, Jaspers takes the result of Weber's analysis as read. He does not contest the historical circumstances surrounding the 'pre-eminence'[123] of Western rationalism but sets out from this *fact* to critically sift the *meaning* that was ascribed to it by *'us'* Westerners. That only the development of European-Western civilisation has led to the 'Age of Technology, which today gives the whole world a European countenance' and that today 'the rational mode of thought has become omnipresent', would appear to confirm this 'pre-eminence' that 'European self-consciousness'[124] ascribes to itself. But the way in which Europe *justifies* its pre-eminent position, by shifting it from the factual sphere of the 'will to power' to the ethical sphere of value, and thereby transfiguring technical supremacy into moral and civil superiority, can be related back to a *dispositif* of symbolic identification that is radically different from all other civilisations.

What does the European *difference* consist in? Not simply in the border [*confine*] between *us* and *others* that can be traced back to every logic of collective identity: from the tribe to the state, from the clan to the nation. Nor can it be said to consist in the antithesis between Greeks and barbarians, which can also be found in analogous forms elsewhere. 'To be sure, Chinese and Indians have felt themselves to be the truly human peoples and have asserted the self-evidence of this pre-eminence with no less conviction than the Europeans'.[125] More accurately, the European exception lies in the fact that while most other civilisations characterise themselves as 'the centre of the world',[126] Europe constitutes itself through 'an inner polarity of Orient and Occident'.[127] Therefore, the antithesis between Orient and Occident is an exclusive mythical-symbolic property of the Occident. It is a typical Western dualism that is not met with in

---

123   Ibid., p. 67.
124   Ibid.
125   Ibid.
126   It is not by chance that the major Asiatic civilisation, China, intends and defines itself as 'Country of the Centre'.
127   Ibid.

other cultures. The opposition between Asia and Europe, rooted in the self-consciousness of the Greeks since the time of Herodotus, is alien to the civilisations of the Far East – until they became subject to the processes of Western colonisation and modernisation. It is precisely in relation to this process that the elites of those countries coined the formula 'Asian values'. Thus we find ourselves in the presence – as we shall see below – of a macroscopic case of 'imagined community'. That Western reason is inconceivable without this internal polarity and that, therefore, it makes a *necessary* reference to the Other in order to symbolically identify itself confers upon the West's self-attribution of preeminence a significance that is not only of hierarchical supremacy but also of unconscious dependency. It is a dependency inscribed from its inception in the specular nature of the internal relation of the dyad.

The 'Greek miracle' founded the Western world: the *Abendland*, the Twilight Country, the land of sunset. But it did so in such a way that the West 'only continues to exist as long as it keeps its eyes steadily on the East, faces up to it, comprehends it and withdraws from it'.[128] To take up a celebrated adage of Weber's from the Preface to his *Sociology of Religion* of the 1920s,[129] *only the West* feels the need to constitute itself as an identity *per differentiam*, through an originary decision: i.e., as the very etymology of the term suggests, by means of a tearing, a caesura, a cut (to decide [*decidere*] is always to cut off [*recidere*] . . .) from the presumed source in the 'Oriental' *alter ego* – the Asiatic womb. The specular antithesis between *productive* Occident and *seductive* Orient, *free* Occident and *despotic* Orient, Western Frontier and Oriental Permanence is born from this inaugural myth, from this veritable 'primal scene' (to be understood in Freud's sense of *Urszene*) of our *peninsular* European identity. The inevitable consequence of this is that life is projected towards the Outside – in an adventure of novelty and eccentricity – and is permanently accompanied by the anxiety of being sucked back into the great Asiatic womb – the realm of seduction and immobility, of the most abstruse profundity and of unconscious confusion.[130] In the eyes of Jaspers, Asia is

---

128   Ibid.
129   *Translator's note:* This is published as the 'Introduction' to Talcott Parsons's translation of Weber's *The Protestant Ethic and the Spirit of Capitalism.*
130   *Translator's note:* The reference is to the 'confusional states' of Kleinian psychoanalysis. By 'confusion' Klein understands the 'inability, or difficulty, in maintaining a differentiation between the good and bad object . . . In both very

the *symbolic price* paid for the pre-eminent place attained by the West through its productive Project. This project, moving in a linear and punctiform manner towards the technical-scientific expansion of its dominion over the external world, has left the West constitutionally deficient and incomplete when compared to the awareness of another dimension of Reason that is rooted in its most intimate structure and in its very origin.

> Now although objective historical analysis reveals that the West has played a paramount role in shaping the world, it also discloses an *incompleteness* and *deficiency* in the West which render it perennially apposite and fruitful to ask of the Orient: What shall we find there that completes us? What became real there and what became truth, that we have let slip? What is the cost of our paramouncy?[131]

This passage contains the embryo of a thesis that can be found coiled within the anti-Heideggerian component of the *Kulturkritik* of the first half of the twentieth century. The thesis, later developed by Habermas, of the *incompleteness* of the modern project, for which the postmodern rhetoric of the *dérive* and the fragment could not compensate, should instead be offset by the integration of the technical-instrumental side with the dialogical-discursive side of Enlightenment reason. Considering the diversity of the premises and of the theoretical references, the analogy ends here. However, such an analogy appears less arbitrary if one thinks of Habermas' profound agreement with Jaspers' question on the *geistige Situation der Zeit* ('The Spiritual Situation of the Age').[132] Such a question can be resolved by reactivating a dimension of rationality that the West has so far marginalised – despite the fact that, in the last two centuries, it has manifested itself at an inchoative level in some of the crucial transitions [*passaggi*] of society and of the modern public sphere. For Jaspers, it is not a case of enabling the emergence of an alternative source of (presumably 'irrational') knowledge, so much as that of another repressed dimension of the *logos*, one whose genesis is the same as that of the origin of *global history*. This is another dimension of the

---

severe confusional states or its milder forms of indecisiveness, there is a disturbed capacity for clear thought . . . Total immobilization may be the end result' (Otto Weininger, *The Clinical Psychology of Melanie Klein*, pp. 65 and 66).

131   Jaspers, *The Origin and Goal of History*, p. 68.

132   *Translator's note*: The reference is to the volume edited and introduced by Jürgen Habermas, *Observation on 'The Spiritual Situation of the Age'*. See, in particular, the opening pages of Habermas' 'Introduction'.

Aufklärung, of the rational 'enlightening' that – inasmuch as it constitutes a radical interrogation of *Dasein*, of 'situated' existence, of our being-in-the-world – shatters the game of mirrors between Orient and Occident. It breaks through the *Western-Eastern divan* upon which for centuries we have made ourselves comfortable and, thereby, reveals the secret convergence with the questions coming from other worlds.

> The realities of China and India for three thousand years have been just as much attempts to emerge from the indeterminate matrix of Asia. Emergence is a universal historical process, not a peculiarity of Europe's attitude to Asia. It happens within Asia itself. It is the path of mankind and of authentic history.[133]

Thus, at the end of Jaspers' analysis, the faith in the axis of universal history appears to be the only way to avoid being lost in nothingness in an epoch marked – as in Valéry's *Regard* – by a world completely saturated by the planetary expansion of science and technology. 'There is no longer anything outside. The world is closed. The unity of the world has arrived'.[134] In this globalised world there is no problem, action or event that does not affect the whole of the human species, which finds itself at a crossroads between catastrophe or the edification of a new order founded upon right and reciprocal recognition. Despite their radical philosophical differences, Jaspers appears to share with Heidegger a tragic *leitmotiv* that results from the central-European *globale Zeit* debate: in the time of global technology, the main prospect for salvation lies where the danger and the risk of the decision have reached their outermost limit – the *limit-situation* of possible existence. Having said that, for Jaspers the 'widest of all horizons' (*das Umgreifende*)[135] diachronically represented by the axial image of civilisation possesses the structure of a multilateral universalism that is accessible only with that 'method of comparisons', and finds its highest sociological expression in the 'clear and multidimensional conceptuality' of Max Weber's work.[136]

Despite the indisputable grandeur of Weber's analysis, which is to this day unsurpassed, it reveals diametrically opposed limits and advantages to that of Jaspers. The counterpart to Jaspers'

---

133 Jaspers, *Origin and Goal of History*, p. 70.
134 Ibid., p. 127.
135 Ibid., p. 267.
136 Ibid., pp. 266, 267.

thesis of the *mysterious convergence of parallel worlds* (backed
by the faith in the pre-established harmony that supposedly
presides over the development of the three great planetary civilisations), is Weber's tragic post-historical awareness of the
character of *radical contingency of the civilising process* and of
the concomitance of the factors that determine it. As Weber
writes in the splendid *incipit* to the already mentioned Preface to
the *Sociology of Religion*,[137]

> A product of modern European civilization, studying any problem of
> universal history, is bound to ask himself to what combination of
> circumstances the fact should be attributed that in Western civiliza-
> tion, and in Western civilization only, cultural phenomena have
> appeared which (as we like to think) lie in a line of development
> having *universal* significance and value.[138]

Weber's comparative framework describes the process of rationalisation and disenchantment of the world from the perspective of
an 'Occident' understood as a singularity that universalises itself
by radiating out to all other cultures. Jaspers responds to the
Eurocentric limitations of Weber's framework by recognising that
there is a *polycentric dynamic that presides over the development
of civilisation and rational thought*, and that is mediated by the
destructuring of the antithesis of Orient and Occident whose
current crystallisation constitutes the principal cultural obstacle
to the comprehension of the two main epicentres of global conflict:
i.e., the 'anti-global' threat of Islamic fundamentalism and the
'alternative globalisation' represented by the so-called 'Asian
values'. It is impossible to identify these challenges without a
labour of disassembling to elucidate the *plurality within both
terms of the couple.* Were we able to accomplish such a disassembling, we would arrive at the surprising discovery that the
polytheism of values and the multiverse of pictures of the world
that we were inclined to think of as the exclusive prerogative of
the West can be found in equal measure in the 'Orient'. We would
also learn that there exist more 'Orients' and more 'Occidents' –
and that not all the Orients are necessarily in the Orient, and not
all the Occidents are necessarily in the Occident. Once the terms
of the dyad have been disarticulated and pluralised, it will become

---

137 *Translator's note:* see 'Introduction' to Weber, *The Protestant Ethic and the
Spirit of Capitalism.*
138 Max Weber, *The Protestant Ethic and the Spirit of Capitalism*, p. 13.

more difficult to, for example, relate the Europe/Islam relationship to what is presumed to be a symmetrical antithesis of Occident
and Orient. Not only because the reduction of the *dar al-Islam*,
the 'land of faith', to the Orient is as inadmissable as the one-to-
one correspondence between Christianity and Europe once
proposed by Novalis,[139] but also because, thanks to the intercultural interweaving of the globalised world, we have as much Islam
in the West as there is of the West in Islam.

The reassessment of Weber's comparison of universal religions concerns Islam only in a marginal way (it is defined by
Weber as a religion of warriors and of disciplined fighters for
the faith seeking to conquer the world). Prompted by the question of 'Asian values', it is his judgment on Confucianism that
we must now re-examine. Criticism has focused on his definition of Confucianism as an ethics of mere *adaptation to the
world* that is thought to be incapable of producing the practical
and active attitude, and the concern with the transcendent that
is considered to be the property of the religions of redemption.
This definition contrasts with the recently demonstrated ability
of China and the South-East Asian 'macro-region' to put into
effect a form of economic development and social change that is
characterised by a high rate of productivity. For Weber,
Confucian religion was, in the same way as Buddhism, an ethics
of the *tao* (equivalent to the Indian *dharma*). But in contrast to
Buddhism, 'Confucianism exclusively represented an inner-
worldly morality of *laymen*' of 'adjustment to the world, to its
orders and conventions'.[140] What was missing from this 'rational
order'[141] was the 'central force of a salvation religion conducive
to a methodical way of life'.[142] What is at stake in this peremptory and summary judgement is not, simply, the historical and
empirical extension of the analysis provided by this great non-
specialist, so much as whether the categories of 'rationalisation'
and 'Western rationalism' can act as interpretive keys for the
relationship between universal religions and economic ethics in
the global era.

The leading criterion of Weber's comparison of *Weltreligionen*
is constituted, first, by the fundamental antithesis between

---

139   See Franco Cardini, *Europa e Islam*, p. 6.
140   Max Weber, *The Religion of China: Confucianism and Taoism*, p. 152.
141   Ibid., p. 169.
142   Ibid., p. 170.

'adaptation to the world' (*Weltanpassung*) and 'refusal of the world' (*Weltablehung*) and, second, by the fourfold typological partition of the 'degrees and directions of the religious refusal of the world' resulting from the celebrated *Zwischenbetrachtung*.[143] The first aspect allows one to discriminate between *universal religion* and *religion of redemption*. They 'are not, in fact, equivalent terms, because at least a universal religion – specifically Confucianism – exists, which is "a universal religion, but knows nothing of the need for redemption"'.[144] The second aspect provides the four ideal-typical degrees of *Weltablehung*, which can be schematised as follows: 1) mystical, extra-worldly (contemplation as *Weltflucht*, 'flight from the world'); 2) mystical, intra-wordly (contemplation as *Weltindifferenz*, 'indifference to the world', which accepts worldly reality and its secular political order in their naked objectivity, lacking religious value); 3) extra-worldly ascesis (ascetic action as 'withdrawal from the world'); and 4) intra-worldly ascesis (ascetic action as 'domination of the world'). In both cases, Weber adopts the standpoint of the intra-worldly ascesis of puritan Protestantism from which to undertake his comparative analysis of different forms of religious conduct of life (*Lebensführungen*). The tension in relation to the world that is typical of a religion of redemption turns into *action directed to domination of the world*. 'In strong contrast to the naive stand of Confucianism toward things of *this world*, Puritan ethics construed them as a violent tension, full of *pathos*, toward the world'.[145] Moreover, the 'internal' criterion of the synoptic table of the *Weltreligionen* relates back to a more general 'external' criterion: the thesis of the 'disenchantment of the world'[146] and of modern rationalism understood not only as an irrevocable break with magical beliefs but as the linear and irresistible process of *uprooting* of the parental and communitarian ties of the tradition. In this case as well, the 'highest level' from which to draw the elements of comparison *per differentiam* is the ascetic Protestantism of Calvinism.[147] It is this viewpoint that is responsible for the final, inexorable judgement on Confucianism: an

---

143 Max Weber, *Gesamtausgabe*, volume I/19, pp. 479–522.
144 Pietro Rossi, 'Introduction' to Max Weber, *Sociologia della religione*, vol. 1, Torino: Edizioni di Comunità, 2002, p. xxvii.
145 Weber, *The Religion of China*, p. 227.
146 Ibid., p. 226.
147 Ibid.

ethics of 'unconditional adjustment to the world'[148] professed by the intellectual class of the patrimonial bureaucracy which, starting with the emperor, postulates the 'unbroken and continued existence of purely magical religion'[149] and a compliance of the social duties created by a system of parental or group bonds and of purely 'personalist associations',[150] and that has inhibited the birth of modern capitalism in China, notwithstanding its acclaimed vocation for business and commerce. 'In this typical land of profiteering, one may well see that by themselves neither "acquisitiveness", nor high and even exclusive esteem for wealth, nor utilitarian "rationalism" have any connection as yet with *modern* capitalism'.[151] The Chinese merchant, shopkeeper and businessman lacked the 'religiously determined and rational method of life which came from within and which was characteristic of the classical Puritan for whom economic success was not an ultimate goal or end in itself but a means of proving oneself';[152] just as he lacked the 'peculiar confinement and repression of natural impulse which was brought about by strictly volitional and ethical rationalization and ingrained in the Puritan' who was taught to 'suppress the petty *craving for profit*'.[153]

The results of Weber's comparison of Confucianism with the Puritan ethic has led to numerous objections and critical observations at the level of methodology and at the more specifically analytical level. With respect to method, it has been generally noted that the *Religionssoziologie* enquiry proceeds along twin tracks: a positive demonstration that pinpoints the 'spirit of capitalism' in the intra-worldly ascetic of Calvinist Protestantism and a negative demonstration that aims to isolate the pragmatic unity of the 'conduct of life' lying at the basis of modern capitalism by registering and explaining the reasons for its absence in other civilisations. Therefore, we must bear in mind that 'Weber did not study the Orient to know the Orient, but so as to better understand the modern Occident'.[154] Consequently, the criterion that guides the typological assumption of Weber's comparativism

---

148 Ibid., p. 248.
149 Ibid., p. 229.
150 Ibid., p. 236.
151 Ibid., p. 243.
152 Ibid., pp. 243–44.
153 Ibid., p. 244.
154 Laxman Prasad Mishra, 'Le implicazioni antieconomiche della fuga dal mondo', p. 138.

consists in a procedure of subtraction dominated by the figure of
absence. But it is precisely this criterion that renders his evaluation of Confucianism reductive and misleading on the strictly
analytical plane. Chinese civilisation is not characterised so much
by the absence of a 'transcendent conception or tension' as by the
secular definition of such a tension, that is, by the intra-worldly
way of resolving it.[155] Otherwise, it is not possible to explain how
in China, in contrast to other cultural areas dominated by
Hinduism or Buddhism, the encounter with Western Modernity
triggered first a revolutionary transformation and then economic
and industrial development of astonishing proportions. From the
standpoint of certain critics, this is beyond the scope of the possibilities contemplated by Weber in his analysis of China.[156] Setting
aside some of the historical and conceptual errors generated by
the adoption of a number of incongruous categories – above all
the use of the term 'patrimonial' to define the nature of the imperial
and bureaucratic Chinese system – the fundamental weakness of
Weber's analysis of Confucianism (noted particularly in De Bary's
and Tu Wei Ming's criticisms) can be traced to two decisive points:
on the one hand, to the denial of the existence of any tension with
the transcendent and, on the other, to the failure to observe the
dynamic potential that issued not from the break with the past but
from the 'transformation of enduring elements and components of
Chinese tradition'.[157] Such a failure, although it emerges at the
analytic level, reverberates against the very postulate upon which
Weber's entire conception is founded: it puts in question the *terminus comparationis* represented by ascetic Protestantism and the
idea of rationalisation and disenchantment of the world understood
as an unstoppable process dissolving the traditional forms of life. In
other words, Weber is able to understand tradition only as the *ante-
cedent* to Modernity, not as its *counterpoint*. For this decisive
reason, the dialectical figure of a multicentric world-modernity,
marked by the perpetual regeneration of imagined communities
and alternative versions of global history, will continue to be

---

155 Shmuel N. Eisenstadt, 'Innerweltliche Transzendenz und die
Strukturierung der Welt: Max Webers Studie über China und die Gestalt der
chinesischen Zivilisation', pp. 363 ff.

156 See, for example, Arnold Zingerle, *Max Weber und China: Herrschafts-
und religionssoziologische Grundlagen zum Wandel der chinesischen Gesellschaft*,
Berlin: Duncker & Humblot, 1972.

157 Eisenstadt, 'Innerweltliche Transzendenz und die Strukturierung der
Welt', p. 384.

excluded from the theoretical framework centred upon the dominant ideal-type of 'Western rationalism'.

A new transcultural investigation is launched on the basis of
this demand for a decentring and pluralisation of the universalist
paradigm that stems from the global challenge of 'Asian values'.
Such an investigation aims to redefine the criteria of comparison
and amplify the horizons of contrast between the great civilisations of the planet: in a world that is literally dislocated, 'out of
joint', and that appears to increasingly relativise the hegemonic
function of the West.[158] *Religionssoziologie* is without doubt the
most ambitious and far-sighted synoptic framework for global
culture available to us.[159] Nevertheless, as Amartya Sen has noted,
Weber's description is not only in need of updating or enriching
but of revision. Certainly, Weber is the first thinker to relate the
crucial historical event of capitalist Modernity – the emblem and
culmination of Western rationalism – to an ethical dimension of
economic action irreducible to the utilitarian or rationalist paradigm. In doing so, he exposes the fact that if capitalist rationality
had coincided with the pure and simple maximisation of profit, it
would never have been able to give rise to the extraordinary dynamism of social change that is still unfolding before us. On this
basis, Weber establishes a link between modern capitalism, the
activist morality of the intra-worldly ascesis and the domination
of the rationality-of-ends that is able to go beyond the blind 'craving for wealth' and shape a coherent combination of social
relations and institutions founded upon juridical formalism as
well as upon a system of shared rules. But ironically, it is precisely
this 'strong' and univocally characterised definition of capitalist
Modernity that substantially limits the comparison between the
dominant Western *ratio* and the different rationality that, nevertheless, he attributed to other cultures. As we have seen, his
judgement that Confucianism is incompatible with a productive
conduct of life and unsuited to carrying out a role in the genesis of
and development of European capitalism, analogous to that of the
Calvinist ethic of 'renunciation' and the secular ascetic, is particularly erroneous and misleading. Even Weber is occasionally
assailed by doubts or by a presentiment that the future could
disprove his interpretation, to the point that he forecasts (at the

---

158   As Arnold Toynbee had predicted. See Arnold Toynbee, *The World and
the West*, New York: Oxford University Press, 1953.
159   See Carlo Tullio-Altan, *Le grandi religioni a confronto*.

end of his comparative analysis of Confucianism and Protestantism)
that China will be able to appropriate for itself the achievements of
Western economic and technological development and to engender
a full Asiatic Modernity even more effectively than Japan.

> The Chinese in all probability would be quite capable, probably more
> capable than the Japanese, of assimilating capitalism which has tech-
> nically and economically been fully developed in the area of modern
> civilization. It is obviously not a question of deeming the Chinese
> 'naturally ungifted' for the demands of capitalism. But compared to
> the Occident, the varied conditions which externally favoured the
> origin of capitalism in China did not suffice to *create* it. Likewise capi-
> talism did not originate in occidental or oriental Antiquity, or in India,
> or where Islamism held sway. Yet in each of these areas different and
> favourable circumstances seemed to facilitate its rise.[160]

This is clearly not a self-criticism. It is a relativisation of his thesis
that makes it turn on a *so far*, as if Weber – with the critical-scepti-
cal caution typical of a post-deterministic science – had wanted to
limit the scope of the validity of his thesis to the past and, hence,
leave the future course of the world undecided. Let us not forget
that for him the term 'fate' is nothing but 'what came of' human
actions in contrast to 'what he intended' by them.[161] Therefore, it
coincides with the unintentional structure of the historical process.
His prognosis is equally qualified: it only contemplates the possibility of China *appropriating* capitalist technology already developed
in the West; it does not envisage an autonomous creation of an
'other' configuration of Modernity. It is precisely the conditional
form of this stance, which denies to other cultures that original and
independent dynamism, that is vigorously contested by economists
(and moral philosophers) such as Sen.

It is significant that Sen begins by appealing to the anti-individ-
ualist character of the Confucian ethic affirmed by the supporters
of 'Asian values' in order to demonstrate their complete compat-
ibility with the emergence of economically productivist forms of
behaviour typified by a rationality-of-ends, thereby overturning
Weber's equation between capitalism and Puritan ascetic
individualism.

> In sharp contrast with Max Weber's analysis of protestant ethics,
> many writers in present-day Asia emphasize the role of Confucian

---

160   Weber, *The Religion of China*, p. 248.
161   Ibid., p. 238.

ethics in the success of industrial and economic progress in east Asia. Indeed, there have been several different theories seeking explanation of the high performance of east Asian economies in terms of values that are traditional in that region. It is interesting to ask whether values really do play such important roles, and how they influence economic performance in different regions of the world.[162]

Sen concludes that we have learnt from the exceptional economic performance of the Asian continent that other values are able to operate well and can sometimes operate even better.[163] This is the first step of the argument. The second is even more incisive. The communitarian ethic, hierarchically modelled on a collective in contrast to individual rationale, is in no way able to account for the complexity of Asian civilisation. Instead, the Occident projects on its presumed spiritual 'Other' the amorphous and undifferentiated category of 'the Orient'. As Sen observes, it is curious to note how Western culture, which is always so inclined to emphasise the plurality of reasons and multiplicity of versions of Modernity present within it, obstinately continues to be caught within the old commonplace of the Orient as an indistinct reality and homogeneous space.

> The temptation to see Asia as one unit reveals, in fact, a distinctly Eurocentric perspective. Indeed, the term 'the Orient', which was widely used for a long time to mean essentially what Asia means today, referred to the direction of the rising sun. It requires a heroic generalization to see such a large group of people in terms of the positional view from the European side of the Bosporus.[164]

However, the surprising vitality of this stereotype finds an alibi (if not a foundation) in the ideological self-image presented by the intellectual and political elites of China, Japan, Singapore, South Korea, Malaysia, Indonesia and Taiwan through their recourse to the equally generic and indistinct idea of 'Asian values' in opposition to 'Western values'.[165] As Sen warns us, we must not lose sight of the polemical nature of this category that is construed in

---

162   Amartya Sen, 'Values and Economic Success'.
163   Ibid.
164   Amartya Sen, 'Human Rights and Asian Values', p. 13.
165   See William Theodore De Bary, *Asian Values and Human Rights: A Confucian Communitarian Perspective*; Anne Cheng, 'Confucianisme, postmodernisme et valeurs asiatiques'; Flavia Monceri, *Altre globalizzazioni. Universalismo liberal e valori asiatici*, Soveria Mannelli: Rubbettino, 2002, pp. 213 ff.

reaction to the experience of colonial domination. The appeal to
'Asian values' represents, at one and the same time, the conse-
quence and the other side of the coin of the Western ideology of
'Orientalism' – so mercilessly dissected by the Palestinian thinker
Edward Said[166] in what is, in many ways, a valuable work. The
limit of Said's text lies in the way it obscures the break with
Eurocentrism through the reference to oriental civilisations in the
1800s (think of Voltaire and Montesquieu, for example).

Returning to Sen, one should consider carefully the general
statement of his thesis: 'The grand contrast between Western and
Asian values – and other such grand contrasts (including Max
Weber's famous dichotomy) – hide more than they reveal'.[167] The
hidden dimension, which dualistic interpretations promptly leave
out, is that of the *irreducible plurality* of the cultural expressions
and visions of the world present in all the other great planetary
civilisations. True plurality is not the banal one lying *between*
cultures – as the *reductio ad unum* of the logic of identity pretends
– but *within* each one. From this starting point, Sen proceeds to a
systematic dismantling of the current stereotypes concerning the
Orient. He turns the spotlight on how India, which the 'haughty
ignorance' of the West considers the 'home of endless spirituality',
in reality contains 'the largest atheistic and materialist literature
of all the ancient civilizations'.[168] He points out that 'it would be a
mistake to take Confucianism to be the only tradition in Asia –
indeed even in China'.[169] Finally, he shows how fragile the antithesis
between Oriental authoritarianism and Western libertarianism is,
since the '[c]hampioning of order and discipline can be found in
Western classics as well as in Asian ones', and that – in this respect
– Confucius himself does not at all appear 'more authoritarian in
this respect than, say, Plato or St. Augustine'.[170]

His disclosure that not only the West but the Orient too should
be declined in the plural is one of the most illuminating aspects of
Sen's reflections: if there are more 'Occidents' and other variations of Modernity, equally, it is incontestable that there are other
'Orients' and other philosophical and ethical-political expressions
of the generically defined 'Asiatic' mentality.[171] Therefore, the

166 Edward Said, *Orientalism*.
167 Sen, 'Values and Economic Success'.
168 Amartya Sen, 'Indian Traditions and the Western Imagination', p. 168.
169 Sen, 'Human Rights and Asian Values', p. 17.
170 *Ibid*.
171 See Gabriella Sanna and Antonella Capasso (eds), *Orienti e Occidenti*.

epicentre of comparison must shift from the investigation of what is lacking to the explanation of the *autonomous universalising drives* present in the various civilisations. The supposed monolithic character of the Orient, apparently confirmed by the proud claim to 'Asian values', is an effect induced by Western supremacism which, in the space-time compression that typifies the global era, has pushed the dominant classes of the principal Asiatic countries to emphasise – or *reinvent* – those aspects of their tradition that are most radically antithetical to the Occident. For example, setting the rights of the state, the community, the enterprise, the clan, the family, before the rights of the individual; the reasons of tradition ahead of the imperatives of innovation; placing respect for the elderly and the intergenerational bond before freedom and self-affirmation of the individual.

Despite the undoubted significance of the results obtained through the rigorous 'dismantling' of the Orient/Occident dichotomy, it is hard to escape the sensation that, ultimately, Sen's perspective tends to underestimate the function the reactive-conflictual 'Asian values' model can have in the constitution of an 'imagined' mega-community that aims to challenge the Occident, on its own turf: the economy and technology, by presenting an alternative version of global universalism. It is no less effective for the fact that the model was constructed in a specular opposition to the (supposedly) Western values. If, as Sen has indicated, one of the typical connotations of the post-Enlightenment Occident can be found in the 'tendency to extrapolate backwards from the present',[172] the area that characterises South-East Asia, today, seems instead to consist in the tendency to look at the present with the eyes of the past. In this case, we are in the presence of a mechanism of symbolic identification whose motivations are much deeper than those of the ideological slogans that pretend to interpret it – sinking their roots into the 'nostalgic' paradigm which encapsulates the new political forms of conflict on the stage of world-modernity.

---

172   Sen, 'Human Rights and Asian Values', p. 15.

The Nostalgic Paradigm

As we have seen, the conflict of identities in the asymmetrical structure of the global pluriverse marks the simultaneous putting in check of the 'isometric' assumption of the modern state – that was modelled on the dominance of the conflict of interests – and of the utilitarian paradigm of rationality – that was organised around the postulate of a 'standard rational conduct'. With the generalisation of this new form of conflict (the most striking although not necessarily the most important example of which is fundamentalism) the problem of the *representation of identity* becomes the propulsive core of political strategy itself. The clearest interpretive key to the specific dynamic and logic of a world-modernity (in which the reticular all-pervasiveness of techno-economic interdependence is marked by the counterpoint between imagined communities and public-sphere diasporas that constantly regenerate themselves by reinventing their traditions) appears to be the 'nostalgic paradigm'. The 'nostalgia syndrome' becomes the peculiar form assumed by the question of identity in a glocalised world that is no longer anchored to the territorial politics of nation states.

However, nostalgia can be experienced in many ways. Today, in a multidimensional space characterised by the universal experience of uprooting and by the inexorable decline of the classical subjects of modern politics, such an experience takes two forms.

1) The political form of voluntary nostalgia: typified by the strategy of harking back to a past that is supposedly endowed with an identifying symbolical charge. One paradigmatic example would be Bin Laden's evocation of the glorious Ottoman Empire.

2) The impolitical form of nostalgia for the present: its symbolic message, which is in fact destined to indirectly condition the dynamics of individual and collective behaviour with an effectiveness that is, perhaps, even greater than that of explicit political statements, is generally constituted by a nostalgic reference to an image of complete and harmonic community that is considered to be definitively dispelled or irredeemably damaged by the processes of globalisation. As Fredric Jameson and Arjun Appadurai have shown, Filipinos, for example, look back nostalgically to a world – to a set of traditions, behavioural rituals and lifestyles – that in reality they have never actually lost.

The paradox of nostalgia of the present evoked by the poem by Borges placed as epigraph to this chapter can be explained only if the paradigm of Modernity – in which the linear and one-way schema from *Gemeinschaft* to *Gesellschaft*, from (traditional) community to (modern) society – is finally assumed to have dissolved. If one assumes that tradition and community (including so-called organic communities) are not natural or spontaneous facts but are actually artificial products of the modern, then one will have to conclude that the expansion of Modernity is not only reconcilable with the persistence of these forms but that it recreates them constantly, inducing a process of periodic reinvention of their characteristic traits. Once it is clear that Modernity in no way entails the process of dissolution of the traditional communitarian forms postulated by Weber, the 'reaction' to modernisation will appear for what it really is: as the nostalgic claim to a form of life that, insofar as it was never *given* but always recreated and *acted out*, had never been 'lost' – even if today it acquires a newly symbolic, properly identifying significance within the dynamic of the glocal. The thesis stating that modernisation constitutes a menace for 'traditional identities' is nothing but a romantic mythologeme. The spatio-temporal compression of the world does not provoke the decline of identities but their proliferation. It is the present of global time that enables not only the elites, but ever greater strata of the population and ever more diverse cultures to identify themselves through *nostalgic re-presentations* of the moments and salient traits of their imagined community. Only under the push of the global – through the collision and close confrontation rendered possible by the unprecedented contraction of space and time – are the diverse groups led to rediscover (and so to reinvent) their own cultural traditions so as to differentiate themselves from the 'others'.

And yet, the 'heart of darkness' of the global age and of the conflicts generated by it lurks in the intimate bond between world-modernity and the proliferation of new community aggregates. The root of the explosive potentiality for conflict present in the diaspora communities that populate the global stage is found in an *obsession with identity* stemming from the unwitting and stubborn repression of the radical contingency of every civilisation, tradition and form of life, and of the *relational* nature of each (collective and individual) identity. The only response to the real threat of the global age, which is not characterised by a deficit or decline of logics of identity but by their inflation, is a political one. But what is the common location of 'the political' on a global stage characterised by a *passage to the Occident* of all cultures? It

is no longer that of the declining nation state. Nor is it a 'transnational civil society'. Instead, it is a public sphere understood as a
symbolic space that is not a mere container but a dynamic demand
for comparison between diverse 'public diasporic spheres' that are
able to carry out a radical reconversion of the logic of the conflict
of identities. Such a theoretical and practical programme calls for
a capacity to 'think in the plural' (as Simone Weil used to say) and
to redefine the universal from the standpoint of difference:
conceiving the identity of the different 'traditions' not by relating
them through what they have in common but grasping the irreducible specificity of each.

It is clear that the function of a public sphere understood in
these terms cannot be resolved by the search for an 'overlapping
consensus' through rules of procedural justice – as John Rawls
hoped. As we have learnt from Isaiah Berlin and Amartya Sen,
once one begins with values in contrast to tastes, these become a
matter of *est disputandum*. Such a public sphere can only be a
place of open comparison between normative frameworks and
conceptions of the *common good*. The effect of this is to violate
Weber's interdiction that, from the start, denied the discursive
negotiation of assumptions of value that were absolute and incommensurable by definition.[173] Hence, it is necessary to make a clear
philosophical distinction between 'incommensurability' and
'incomparability'. The fact that there is no single parameter of
commensurability of values does not mean that they are incompa-
rable on principle. Nevertheless, it is true that the confrontation
between values and the different perceptions of 'the good' cannot
be resolved through a rational argument modelled on the dialogical principle of a discourse aiming at *Verständigung* (in the double
sense of 'agreement' and 'comprehension'), as Habermas maintains.[174] One must certainly credit Habermas – in a direct polemic
with Rawls – with having indicated the need to redefine the public
political sphere as the medium of a constant exchange between
the set of life-worlds and the practices oriented towards value,
and the negotiation of the formal juridical procedures essential to
any democratic system. The 'third normative model of democracy' he proposes points in this direction: an alternative to
procedural liberalism as well as to substantive communitarianism.

---

173   See Armando Massarenti, 'Introduzione' to Amartya Sen, *Laicismo indiano*, pp. 22 ff.
174   See Jürgen Habermas, *The Inclusion of the Other*.

But in contrast to Habermas, the public sphere that I envisage is not a demand delegated to dialogic interaction and to the rational discussion of values. It is the symbolic space – not merely plural but also dissonant and cacophonic – for an effective (not mitigated) comparison between existentially lived universes of value filtered through experiences of different 'subjects'. A common place of *encounter* that, I would go so far as to say, operates even *in spite of dialogue*. A public political sphere will never be able to call itself truly *political* if it is unable to include within itself the *conflict of values* as a constitutive dimension not only of diverse communitarian cultures but of personal identities themselves. However, recognition of this *fact* in no case authorises one to embrace 'any radical form of relativism or nihilism'.[175]

It is therefore possible that the most suitable strategy for conferring efficacy on a *postnationale Öffentlichkeit*, on a post-national public sphere, is not the dialogic-discursive elaboration of singular and collective experiences so much as *narrative* elaboration. Only through the elaboration of effectively lived singular and collective experiences can values escape the closed, self-referential schema of principles so as to be compared amongst themselves and cross-fertilise. The philosophical implications of such a proposal should now be clear. It is as much a case of overcoming the abstract, 'logocentric' idea that assigns normative primacy to discursive rationality as much as it is a case of overcoming its specular opposite that refers the entire horizon of experiences to diverse and incommunicable islands of the symbolic. In other words, the gamble is to redefine the symbolic dimension – in precisely the opposite way of Habermas' 'philosophical discourse of Modernity' – not as a zone of resistance or as an obstacle but as the medium and privileged vehicle of the rational universal and of *dialégein* itself. Nevertheless, the narration can itself contain a self-justifying mechanism no less powerful than the dialectical-dialogic one. For it to become an effective means of comparison between different or alternative conceptions of the good, the narration must introject the radical *contingency* of each situated existence and abandon all attempts at self-legitimisation by reference to communitarian or relativist axioms of incommensurability of the symbolic universes and their unchallengeable hierarchies of value. The post-national public sphere – no longer inter-national, but not yet global – although allowing rhetoric to exercise its

---

175 Massarenti, 'Introduzione' to Amartya Sen, *Laicismo indiano*, p. 23.

rights – since values are not theoretically *demonstrable*, but only *justifiable* in practice – cannot, consequently, admit rhetorics within its sphere *without* proof, but only rhetorics *with* proof.[176]

Only in this way will the appeal to the 'contingent' be able to open a path to a politics of the *cum-tangere* not only to a simple ethics of the limit. As Michel Serres has noted, contingency is, above all, 'touching a border, and a common border. There is contingency when two varieties touch'.[177] Only by taking this path – in search not of a static *common denominator* but of a dynamic plurality of points of *contact* between different experiences of good and evil, of happiness and pain – will we be able to develop a *universal politics of difference* that is sharply demarcated, on the one hand, from a *universal politics of identity* of Enlightenment stamp and, on the other, from the *anti-universal politics of difference* affirmed in America by the communitarians and in Europe by the strategies of local, regional or ethno-nationalist identities.

In this time of *passage to the Occident*, we will for some time yet have to obey a *double injunction*: writing the word 'universalism' with one hand and the word 'difference' with the other and resisting writing both words with a single hand. Because, in each case, it would be the wrong hand.

---

176   See Carlo Ginzburg, *Rapporti di forza. Storia, retorica, prova.*
177   Michel Serres, *Hermès V. Le Passage du Nord-Ouest*, p. 105.

2

IDENTITY AND CONTINGENCY:
ZONES OF CONFLICT

An Ambiguous 'Present'

Universalism and difference, equality and otherness have, for some time now, formed a strange couple not only within political and moral philosophy but in sociology as well. One of the leading reasons for the revival of ethics in recent years appears to be due to the concomitance between processes of globalisation and the proliferation of intercultural conflicts deriving from the resurgence of logics of identity. But opinions are divided regarding the nature of relations within this apparently opposed couple, opening the way for the most varied and heterogeneous interpretations, and for improvised and incoherent hermeneutics. To be able to tackle this sensitive issue directly, we must begin with a philosophical reflection upon the present – on *our* present.

However, to approach the present as a philosopher does not necessarily mean talking about philosophy, about strictly philosophical subjects. Since the whole set of experiences which can be classed as 'Modern' have gradually developed, the words of the philosopher have exited their orbit and started to invest that dimension we refer to as 'actuality', which is at once involving and fleeing, demanding and transient. From that moment on it is also possible – and, indeed, in a certain sense necessary – to be 'untimely' (in Nietzsche's sense of a discrepancy that is in advance of its time). It is precisely for this reason that we cannot avoid referring – even if only in a polemical or radically negative fashion – to the present.

We will approach the present from the specific point of view delimited by the concept of difference, without losing sight of the longitudinal split that seems to mark our epoch – not to mention the extremely rapid obsolescence and semantic rarefaction of the slogans coined by the academic-advertisement exercises of the

Postmodernists. We define this longitudinal fracture in terms of a *double injunction,* of a conflictive co-existence or co-habitation of two imperatives: the imperative of *atopicality* (the 'non-places' discussed by the anthropologist of everyday life Marc Augé) and that of *belonging* (the compensatory need for community identity manifested in the claiming of stable places and dwellings). As we have seen in the previous chapter, this is not an alternative but an interfacial relation: two sides of the same coin.

This is what we shall shortly attempt to demonstrate. Before doing so, we shall dwell a little longer on the question of places and non-places. In assessing the problems that confront us, it would be as well not to neglect the scale of the morphological-historical differences exhibited by the great geo-cultural areas of the planet. Michel Serres once observed:

> North America has roads but no places. I mean manmade places: it is a space where one passes through. China has places engulfed in loam without even tiny paths, it is a land where one remains, a boundless place. In Europe we have places, roads and paths. At least, as long as paths which create places are not replaced or destroyed by thoroughfares.[1]

But there is still a general aspect which should be borne in mind if we do not wish the debates on the 'decline of ideologies', the 'crisis of foundations', 'drifting' and the 'loss of centre', which have characterised the atmosphere of recent years in Europe and the United States, to degenerate into pseudo-sociological banalities. This aspect affects the constant that traverses all the phases, all the innumerable metamorphoses of the conceptual vocabulary of power in the Occident, and that is represented by its *symbolic space* (and by its code).

The essential lexicon by which power is indicated in the Occident is composed of two elements: violence and perimeter, vitality and geometry, energetics and topology. From this standpoint, the history of power and the history of metaphysics really do coincide, albeit in a much more prosaic sense than that suggested by the path of thought that can be traced from Heidegger to Derrida. The two histories overlap only insofar as they are variants of the same *logic of identity;* only inasmuch as they are complementary ways of denominating the centre, different ways of bringing together two constituent coordinates of self-reference:

---

1 Michel Serres, *Detachment*, p. 22.

identity and borders [*confini*], vitality and spatiality, 'soul' and 'form'. The determination of a turning point, of a fracture within metaphysical substantialism, has suggested that the centre is not a fixed point but a ubiquitous function that cannot be located: an *á-topon*, precisely a non-place, a central meaning which is never present in an absolute way, outside of a *system of differences*.

We must now ask what the consequences are of such a breach in the logic of power and identity. This question throws us immediately into the heart of the problem that we have set out to address.

This problem is formulated from the viewpoint of *difference*. This is a category we intend to uphold not only with respect to the logic of identity, to identity-based *logos* of hegemonic universalism, but above all against the *differences* emphasised by the multiculturalist climate today. I shall reflect upon four areas in quick succession: *borders* [confini], *values*, *language* and *technology*. We shall examine them each in turn, attempting in each case to give an idea of their network of connections and internal concatenations.

Borders

How can the question of borders be viewed today, since the collapse of the mechanisms of threat and protection (mechanisms which are, therefore, symbolically ambivalent) of the bipolar world system?

Let us immediately declare that we are in agreement with those (from Claudio Magris to Hans Magnus Enzensberger) who have characterised the problem in the following terms. With the falling of the visible external walls, the strategic bastions, inner walls have sprung up, the invisible walls from which are produced not only crises of conscience or new friend/enemy aggregates, but from which the tormented ghosts of ancient hostilities also arise – as if they arise from archaic stratifications, from the remote depths of history. Ethnic hatreds which are keen, irreducible and – I fear – have been repressed for too long.

How, then, might we consider the two contrasting diagnoses of our time: the diagnosis which today sees the fulfilment of universal homologation and the 'end of history' under the heading of the *pensée unique* of 'possessive individualism', of an omnivorous and undifferentiated market economy, and that which emphasises diversity, centrifugal forces, and the processes of differentiation?

It is not a case of an either/or of mutually exclusive alternatives. Rather, we find ourselves faced by two half-truths: the two sides of the *present's* coin. The characteristic of our present, or of that-which-we-have-before-us, may be defined in terms of the glocal, that is, of the short-circuit of the global and the local. The phenomena of globalisation, facilitated by modern technology, and the growing interdependence and tendential homogenisation of the various geocultural areas of the planet under the imperatives of competitiveness and innovation imposed by the world market, induce new phenomena of localisation. Therefore, the same vector of *deterritorialisation* gives rise – in a seemingly vicious circle – to the proliferation of phenomena of *reterritorialisation*, which increase exponentially the demands for autonomy and identity-based belonging.

Thus, we experience a return of the community, of the 'little homeland' in all quarters. This 'return' appears differently in the two halves of the West, in the old continent and the new. Since the fall of the Berlin Wall, this return has found its concrete expression in Europe in the upswelling of ethno-politics and in North America it is manifested in the 'politics of difference' (the secular arm of which is that of 'political correctness'). In both cases the notion of the individual – as a value and as hard-won historical achievement – is considered to be a fetish to be overthrown.

In order to grasp the nature of the phenomenon, we must not forget that what we refer to as the 'in-dividual' – that is, an *undivided* subject possessing the sovereign virtues of self-determination – is an event that is not only Western but also specifically Modern. It is the product of the long and bloody religious civil wars which prepared for the advent of the 'great Leviathan' in Europe in the sixteenth and seventeenth centuries: the advent of the secular state based on an apparatus of sovereignty and strictly 'neutral' legal procedures. We must therefore agree upon the meaning to be attributed to the expression 'the return of the community'. Although it is expressed as a nostalgia for origins, this 'return' – precisely insofar as it takes the form of a demand for 'compensation for damages' from Modernity and of a search for a compensatory warmth from the community against the 'Big Chill' of the purely procedural institutions of our democracies – is not really a repeat, a pure and simple rerun of the past, but is a claim which is subsequent to the modern individual, *after the Leviathan*, which follows the neutral styling of political association into a 'large body' composed of atomised individuals, of indivisible monads isolated from one another.

If we wish to adopt more technical formulae, such as those

familiar in the contest between the 'liberal' camp and the 'communitarian' camp which dominated the scene of political philosophy throughout the 1980s (or in the ambiguous debate which followed it around 'multiculturalism', or in the mounting populist revival), then we would have to specify that the essential content of all these challenges signifies, in the current crisis of the Leviathan, the return to the fore of the *conflicts of identity* – and of those irreducible values – that originally paved the way for the advent of the modern state; despite the fact that the latter subsequently managed to neutralise them, declassifying them as mere conflicts of interests.

This brings us to the second part of my argument.

Values

Our present is not a time of ethics in dialogue but a time of *ethics in conflict*. The conflict-breeding – and thus, necessarily, far from edifying – implications that the current centrality of the ethical dimension bears with it, are played out on two levels: on the level (a) of philosophy and on that (b) of the political government of complex societies that are both multimedial and multicultural. It is a good idea to stop, if only for an instant, and examine these two aspects in turn, viewing them in their specificity and autonomy. Then – and *only* then – will we be able to measure the extent of their interdependence.

(a) *At a strictly philosophical level*, we may now see the growth not only of widespread dissatisfaction with utilitarian models of rationality, but also of the idea of an exclusive 'incommensurability' (to take up the expression of Bernard Williams, a well-known critic of utilitarianism) between *value imperatives which are tragically incompatible, however rationally consistent they may be in themselves.*[2] This idea strikes at the heart of the utilitarian paradigm, insofar as the latter necessarily presupposes the axiom according to which there is a single, exclusive model of rational behaviour of 'social agents' – with the consequence that any conflict of value might in the last analysis be reduced to a case of *logical inconsistency*. In short, for utilitarians it is really difficult to imagine that a rational subject might remain rational without following the

---

2   Bernard Williams, *Moral Luck*.

'economic' criterion of rationality based on the calculation of costs and benefits. An agent who does not proceed according to this strictly strategic and instrumental logic is logically inconsistent, or *sic et simplicter* irrational, perhaps insofar as his vision of reality (and of his own interests) is fundamentally flawed by, for example, prejudices, ideologies and false beliefs.

(b) But the consequences of this anti-utilitarian position are no less decisive on the *political level*. Here we have the acknowledgement of the presence, in our Western societies, of mutually conflicting but equally plausible ethical imperatives or normative standpoints which – most important – cannot be lumped together under a single (rationally and universally valid) parameter of procedural fairness or justice. The irreducibility of the conflict of values to some 'metric of interests' or other undermines the model of the contract as understood by modern political philosophy. This has been noted by John Rawls himself, who, twenty years after *A Theory of Justice*,[3] radically revised his neo-contractualist programme in *Political Liberalism*[4] by advocating a theory of 'overlapping consensus'.

In an important discussion with Jürgen Habermas,[5] Rawls openly declares his own renunciation of the claim to derive the model of the 'well-ordered society' from the hypothesis of an 'original position' and attempts to circumscribe the notion of 'justice as fairness' within the realm of the 'Political', understood as an area necessarily removed from the ideological and emotional storm of controversies between different ethical options and *Weltanschauungen* (visions of the world). The strictly political conception of justice, i.e. – crucially – 'non-metaphysical', is therefore specified – in conformity with a maxim which is more classical than even Rawls seems inclined to admit – as a sphere of neutralisation of those 'substantive' questions which are still used as a basis for a pluralism that is finally 'taken seriously'.

---

3 John Rawls, *A Theory of Justice*.
4 John Rawls, *Political Liberalism*.
5 This appeared in the *Journal of Philosophy* 92:3 (March 1995), pp. 109–80. See Jürgen Habermas, 'Reconciliation Through the Public Use of Reason: Remarks on John Rawls's *Political Liberalism*', in *The Journal of Philosophy* 92:2 (February 1995), pp. 109–31; and John Rawls, 'Political Liberalism: A Reply to Habermas'.

The conception of political justice in Rawls' *Political Liberalism* can and must be formulated independently of all 'comprehensive' doctrines (whether religious, philosophical or moral): even if a *Weltanschauung* or a metaphysical version always and in any case constitutes its background.[6] However meaningful it may be, Rawls' new framing of the question nevertheless neglects some crucial questions – as Habermas has also noted, albeit from a different perspective to ours – both at (i) the level of practical proposals and on (ii) the more strictly theoretical plane.

(i)   *At a practical level*: if the pluralistic-conflictive nature of the different perspectives of value and *Weltanschauungen* is such as to render problematic the question of the order of a democratic system (and such – let us add – as to impose a reframing of Rawlsian theory), then on the basis of what miraculous virtues might 'political liberalism' be able to neutralise them in the no-man's-land of a 'reasonable' cooperation?

(ii) *At a theoretical level*: granting, for the sake of argument, that political liberalism can limit itself to the category of the political, leaving philosophy just as it finds it, will it not then be necessary for us to justify this claim in terms of an argument and a 'comprehensive conception', according to which the constitution of the Political can avoid any and all philosophical foundation?

These are questions that cannot be easily avoided if we are to construct a theory of democracy which is effectively equipped to tackle the challenge of our times.

Another influential American political philosopher has recently spoken of two powerful centrifugal forces which are now at work in the United States. One is separating whole groups of the population from a supposedly common centre. The other is affecting single individuals by isolating them. Both these movements of diaspora and distancing from the centre have their critics, who accuse the former of chauvinism or of regressive/reactionary fundamentalism and the latter of pure and simple egoism. The argument between 'liberals' and 'communitarians' plays itself out in a crossfire of accusations. While the liberals regard the separate cultural groups as closed, intolerant tribes, the neo-communitarian critics regard the separate individuals as lonely, rootless

---

6   Ibid.

egoists. Michael Walzer's conclusion (the above observations are his) is that neither of these two criticisms is completely erroneous, nor are they completely exact. The reasons the two tendencies should therefore be made to interact is in order to aid a democratic politics which is open to centrifugal forces and capable of contemplating a plurality of 'spheres of justice'.[7]

This solution is acceptable, but on two conditions. The phantasm of a 'Third Way' must not be allowed back into circulation. This solution had already been tested between the two World Wars and – as we Europeans know only too well – was strewn with dead bodies. And we cannot avoid the politically more arduous problem of the split, which is in my opinion irrevocable, between *citizenship* and *belonging*. The modern democratic idea – of Jacobin origin – of belonging as being fully resolved in citizenship is no longer able to tackle the challenges of contemporary society. We know that there are needs for *symbolic identification* that can never find full realisation in the sphere of citizenship – not even in its broadest imaginable or conceivable form. The possibility of answering social demands with a broadening of the horizon of citizenship (and the corresponding reinforcement of its apparatuses of inclusion) exists as long as one is dealing with political conflicts (over rights of equality) or with economic and social conflicts (over interests or status). But such possibility no longer exists once one enters the field of ethical conflict, the conflict of values.

The idea of a 'moral citizenship' can certainly be affirmed in the abstract or be the subject of academic conjecture. But in reality it leads to the forcible imposition of a mutually exclusive choice between the universalism and relativism of values. Accepting the first horn of the dilemma means assuming one set of morals as universally valid. This is obviously possible only in the presence of a culturally homogeneous population firmly anchored to its own mores. Conversely, accepting the other horn of the dilemma means 'flexibilising' the public sphere in order to render it more hospitable and open to the different groups, once the unsuppressible ethical and cultural heterogeneity of the 'citizens' has crystallised. This is something that inevitably involves a radical revision of claims to universality via a pragmatics of order aimed at resolving conflicts between imperatives and points of view – which are periodically destined to recur – on each occasion that

---

7 Michael Walzer, *Spheres of Justice.*

they arise. And to do so in a manner which is balanced but, for that very reason, unstable as well.

So can we conclude *tertium non datur*? It would seem so. However, the decisive point is another. On neither of the two horns do we really have a broadening of citizenship in a moral direction. On the contrary, we have a limitation and relativisation of its ethical nature, whether implicit or explicit. As a consequence, the presumed or hoped-for broadening of citizenship into moral citizenship leads to the opposite effect in both of the alternatives considered: either due to its anchoring in the 'customs' of the dominant majority group (understood in the double sense of moral styles and standards of behaviour) or through a relativistic readiness to accept the 'rationales' of the different cultural groups present in the population, compensating and neutralising them reciprocally. This situation of theoretical and practical stalemate would seem to be the conclusion of a strictly political and logical consideration of relations between universality and difference. We may, therefore, exclude any examination of the premises (cultural, ethical and, in the last analysis, metaphysical) of politics itself.

Another path might be that of beginning from metaphysical foundations in order to get to the root of the symbolic conflict between *citizenship* and *belonging*. But taking this path would necessarily mean being ready to address the theme of the irreducibility of *difference*, which Western universalism has never managed to conceive of until now – either in philosophy or in politics – outside of the metabolic apparatuses of neutralisation offered by the dialectic or by relativism.

A further problem arises underlying this same set of themes. Is it really possible to elaborate the edifying idea of a *multicultural citizenship* without passing through the great aporia of difference – beginning, of course, with sexual difference understood in the anti-essentialist form of *gender*, i.e., according to the most recent terms of feminist thought, as a 'sociocultural construction' of the differences between the sexes?

In even more general form: is it possible to reframe the question of *being-in-common* (as suggested by one line of anti-metaphysical French thought on the 'inoperative' or 'unavowable' community) without getting to the bottom of those *paradoxes of universalism* that appear to be inextricably linked with that *Western event by autonomasia* that we call 'politics'?

At stake in the conflict that seems to threaten the roots of democratic theory – and that in the United States resonates in an unprecedented crisis of the 'American Dream' – is our capacity to answer this question (and the ways in which we answer it). It is no coincidence that we are now witnessing the return to the limelight of a whole series of decisive ethical questions raised by the Enlightenment in its late phase and emerging in the last part of the eighteenth century through the conflict which places Herder, with his attention to the historical dynamic of languages and cultures, in opposition to Kant's ethical universalism.

Kant's moral idea – Herder objected – is an ideal which is existentially poor. It is a transcendental universal, precisely insofar as it *transcends* the specific forms of life of individuals, who are in reality always immersed in cultural contexts, in linguistic and symbolic networks that no single individual or group can do without. We may, therefore, certainly postulate a universal idea, but the way in which concrete individuals acquire *experience* of those values is always culturally determined and – above all – *mediated by language*.

The different ways of saying, of naming an idea (such as the idea of the good) or a value (like, for example, the values of freedom, of justice, of equality or of 'equal opportunity'), do make a difference with respect to the meaning of ideas and values. But they usually refer to irreducibly different experiences and symbolic nuclei.

This brings us to the third aspect that I proposed to address.

Language

Insofar as it is constituted *by* and *in* language, the self is not in-dividual but is a multiple self. 'The idea that the individual person may be seen as – or actually is – a set of sub-individual, relatively autonomous "selves" has a long history'.[8] We thus find the bold reassertion, by contemporary postanalytic thought, a motif that is dear to the historical adversaries of methodological individualism: the subject is always a social event, and each individual is like a theatrical cavity [*cavità teatrale*] that acts as an echo chamber for the diverse motifs and languages of society. Indeed, the common denominator of diverse contemporary philosophical tendencies such as communitarianism, deconstructionism and hermeneutics is precisely this critique of the metaphysical,

---

8   Jon Elster (ed.), *The Multiple Self*, p. 1.

substantialist premise of the modern subject. For the currents of thought we have just mentioned, this premise is translated politically into a supremacist presumption that lies at the bottom of the emancipatory ideal of universal individualism.

But we cannot do in politics what we deny in philosophy. That is what regularly happens to those communitarian and (albeit to a lesser extent) deconstructionist or hermeneutic critiques of Modernity, which sometimes – with their denunciation of homologation and Anglo-Saxon cultural and linguistic imperialism – appear to pursue the chimera of an *ethics of authenticity* entrusted to the incommensurable autonomy of 'forms-of-life'.

And yet, it is precisely the anti-substantialist idea of an intrinsically multiple constitution of subjectivity through language that should have suggested the useless or pathetic character of the claim to criticise the worldwide imperialism of a language by 'unmasking' the corruptions which it introduces into other languages. It is now many years since the publication of *A Thousand Plateaus*[9] – a work rich in points of interest but much neglected – in which Deleuze and Guattari laid bare the poverty of the critique of the purists against the influence of the English language – the academic or Poujadiste denunciation of *'franglais'*. No language – they stressed – can be 'majoritarian' at a global level, except at the price of being vernacularised or creolised by all the minorities of the world. That is what happened to Latin in late antiquity and it is now happening to English. American itself was not constituted, in its differences from English, without this linguistic work of minorities; for example, the differences that Gaelic and Irish English make to American, or the differences wrought by black English and many other ghetto idioms, to the point that New York is now a city without a language. Anyone familiar with German literature knows that Kafka, as a Jew from Prague, submits German to a treatment that results in the creation of a minor language. In what way? By creating a continuum of variations, negotiating all the variables in order to restrict the constants and extend the variations. By stretching vectors throughout the language so as to achieve heights, durations, timbres, stresses, intensities or even shouts and cries unknown to classical German *Hochdeutsch*. Why should what was true for the German of Prague not be true today of black English or of *Québécois*? And yet . . .

---

9   Gilles Deleuze and Félix Guattari, *A Thousand Plateaus*.

And yet it would be as well to go back to the trajectory of our discussion. The visible results of communitarianism include the emergence of one of the most insidious risks for our democracies: the threat of a *fundamentalism indigenous to the Occident.* Multicultural logic, if abandoned to its own pseudo-natural spontaneity, ends up crystallising into a system of armour-plated differences that, in spite of the celebrated 'politics of difference', act like identities in miniature: monads or insular self-consistencies interested exclusively in tracing sharp borders of non-interference. How is it possible to dissolve this rigid non-interference clause, which apparently extends but in reality confounds the idea of difference by turning it into the mechanical fragmentation and proliferation of a logic of identity?

To attempt to respond to this question, it is necessary to project oneself beyond the present, beyond the complicity of two positions that are only rhetorically contrasting: the position of the technophobes and the position of the technophiles; that of the new apocalyptics and of the new apologists of the thaumaturgical virtues of the new communication technologies.

This brings us to the last phase of our argument.

Technology

The polarisation between those who see in the new technologies of multimedia communications undreamed-of promises of irenic horizontality, of a liberatory interactive diffusion of information, and those who see in them a new dimension of domination, fragmentation and generalised control of subjects, repeats – in its paralysing specularity – the traditional ambivalence of the Western attitude towards technology.

In order to escape from the vicious circle, it is certainly not enough to limit ourselves to repeating the distinction between the level of 'pure' technology and the range of its possible 'impure' uses. This is certainly a long-standing distinction but in some of its aspects it is far from being obsolete. In a democratic regime, as we have noted, nothing is more risky than the transparency of social relations. The telephone itself, a horizontal means of communication *par excellence*, may turn into the most thoroughly permeating instrument of control. Nevertheless, we must make an effort in order to shift the focus of our attention to a further point, which is actually the really decisive one: the way in which technology is *constructed*, even before the way it is used.

Technologies are not just prostheses, but languages, symbolic universes. As such they contain in themselves a metaphorical power: in the literal sense of *meta-phérein*, *trans-ferre*, to carry across, to transport experience from one form to another. At every 'transportation' – from the wheel, the real Big Bang in the evolutionary history of *homo faber*, to sub-atomic particle accelerators, and from the handwritten manuscript to the printed book and the internet – the metaphorical virtualities of a technology sharpen some sides of the human sensorium, marginalise others and reduce them to a state of latency.

If we now examine the new technologies of multimedia communications, we cannot deny that they contain an extraordinary metaphorical power. The universe that they generate is the universe of a 'reticular' technology, the power of control of which becomes effective only if all the given hierarchies are dismantled and deconstructed. It is therefore a power which, by definition, depends on its ability to reproduce itself in a process of incessant self-innovation.

The discussion of the juridical and political consequences of these 'reticular' technologies (in which the so-called human factor is destined to play an ever-growing role: i.e., the ability of the human mind to adapt itself and conform to them) are certainly quite important. But they are secondary (in the sense that they have a secondary-order importance) compared to the crucial, 'primary' problem of the question of codes. Where is the power of 'performativity' to be found? Who establishes the codes? How (and to what extent) is it possible to negotiate them?

With the proliferation of edifying hermeneutics, of apologies for uninhibited translation and irenic theories of communicative action 'free from domination', never has the need been felt more sharply for a *critique of communication*. In the present world, in the Kakanic multiverse in which we happen to live, our salvation cannot be entrusted to a (transcendental or hermeneutic) ideal 'communication community'[10] understood as the 'exchange' of values, projects or models of argument. To think that would be an example of unpardonable 'arrogance of the learned' (Vico). Nor can we be saved by the 'eccentric' self or the 'nomadic' subject, which are currently being debated by Postmodernists and deconstructionists. If it is true – as the most recent products of the same postanalytic thought now suggest – that the individual self is, in

---

10   Karl Otto Apel, *The Transformation of Philosophy*.

spite of its etymology, a 'divided self', and that the conceptual apparatuses developed in the study of *inter*-personal conflicts can – therefore – be applied to the analysis of *intra*-personal conflicts, it follows that in order to be able to interact effectively, we must be willing to *risk the encounter* – the *dépaysement*, the *unheimlich* experience with alterity – *in spite*, even, *of dialogue*. Does not that *peithó* – the persuasive reason at which the Occident has always excelled – emerge as primary already in Sophocles' *Philoctetes*, where he attributes it to Odysseus as the most refined and subtle form of *bía*, of violent stratagem? But in order for this to happen, in order for the encounter, the decentring and disorientating friction with alterity to take place, it is necessary for each to assume – not with regard to others but with regard to oneself – the standpoint of difference. It is always a Stranger who 'makes me feel at home', who gives rise to myself as identity.

It is not enough, however, to say that every identity – whether individual or collective – is made possible by a constitutive difference. It is not enough to take refuge in the formula 'I am a stranger to myself'.[11] It is necessary, on the other hand, to banish all temptation (so widespread in the 'post-philosophical' spiritual exercises of our times) to resolve the critique of the identity-based *logos* in a generic 'heterophilia' or – worse still – in a paradoxical 'xenocentrism', by attributing to the figure of the Other or of the Stranger all the redeeming prerogatives which metaphysical ontotheology once assigned to the all-too-familiar Subject. To classify oneself as *marked by difference* means taking a much more radical step. It means assuming the ideas of 'limit' and 'contingency' as positive – as an existential condition for the opening up of the range of possibilities.

The encounter with radical otherness can produce a comparison of effective experiences only insofar as each identity (from that of the individual to that of a political association or culture) is aware of its own *contingency*. Saying 'contingent identity' is not equivalent to saying 'situated existence'. It is not equivalent to substituting the metaphysics of the One with the post–Metaphysics of the Multiple. The very optical-political power of the present technological apparatus – as highlighted by the postfeminist thought of Donna Haraway – should be enough to show how the passage from the old monological order, structured by ontic isolationism, to the new pluralistic and 'relational' order of semiotically,

---

11   See, for example, Julia Kristeva, *Strangers to Ourselves*.

sexually and culturally situated *differences* is very far from guaranteeing the defeat or weakening of the dominance of the 'neutral'. To start from identity as contingent means, first, assuming *contingency* in the strictly philosophical sense of non-necessary existence; existence not justified by anything but nevertheless not impossible. Existence situated, then, in a kind of *metaxy*, in a precarious ontological interlude between being and nothingness, necessity and impossibility. Second, it means carrying out that change of perspective whereby existence includes the possibility that it could not also not be, or that it could be completely 'otherwise'. In this way, and only in this way, the threshold is opened for that transvaluation of values that consists in connoting as positive the notions of precariousness and limit, transforming them from 'lack' and ontological deficit into conditions of possibility of freedom. Only the contingent has essentially constitutive freedom: the freedom of choice. Even the present identity of each of us is nothing but the result of unrepeatable, or at least highly unlikely, selections and bifurcations. Had we, at certain points in our lives, been faced with other opportunities, or had we, in the face of crucial options, made a different decision from that which we actually made, then we would certainly be different from the people we are today. It is precisely because of this constitutive fragility manifested by each identity (whether of a person or of a collective subject, of a language or of a culture), precisely insofar as it is the result of a *cum-tangere*, of a non-linear series of particular and unrepeatable conjunctions, that it represents a precious asset to be safeguarded and treasured. Indeed, to destroy it or let it die would mean forever extinguishing a light, a viewpoint, a window on the world. Postanalytic thought, therefore, limits itself to dissolving the question of identity in the simultaneous strata of the 'multiple self' (as in Elster) or in the successive series of a 'self' which diversifies itself over time (as in Derek Parfit), thus inadvertently making itself vulnerable to retaliation from the deconstructionist adversary. Instead, we aim to reconstruct the logic of identity as a historical contingency rendered finally accessible from the viewpoint of difference.

Only once we have grasped that freedom is the exclusive prerogative of *contingent identity*, and that the 'otherwise' is the ontological modality proper to our very existence, to our 'being in the world', does an encounter between different experiences become possible under the aegis of difference. This result also ends up decisively affecting the sense of our existential relation with the event and with the universe of technology. Only through the cipher of the 'otherwise' are we made aware of the *paradoxical status of normality* that characterises the hypermodern period, permeated by the metaphorical power of global communication technologies and marked by 'cosmic exile', by the experience of *a-topia* and by universal uprooting.

If it is true, as so many philosophers of Heideggerian descent repeat *ad nauseam*, that technology is a 'destiny' – i.e., that it represents a point of no return and that no problem can be resolved by simply bringing its development to a halt – it follows that the moral position that conforms to the modality of the 'otherwise' certainly cannot be that *ethics of authenticity* advocated by so many once again today. In every ethics of authenticity, whose logical outcome is the extremism of ethnic cleansing, there lurks not only an uncrossable frontier between 'us' and 'them' but also the explanatory key of the identitarian *logos* as symbolic apparatus of appropriation. The logic of the authentic coincides wholly and perfectly with the *proprium*, i.e., the domination of the Identical, which is related to the other only in strictly patrimonial terms.

'If there is, among all words, one that is inauthentic, then surely it is the word "authentic"'.[12] Thus, our task, our responsibility towards the present consists of going back to experience, to the increasingly paradoxical and 'inauthentic' languages with which our experience is interwoven.

In technology as in science, and in politics as in ethics, this means no longer to pursue the woeful illusion of realising the virtual, but to attempt, on the contrary, to *virtualise the real* and, thereby, to open up a new array of possibilities.

---

12   Maurice Blanchot, *The Writing of the Disaster*, p. 60.

3

DÄMMERUNG – *THE TWILIGHT OF SOVEREIGNTY: STATE, SUBJECTS AND FUNDAMENTAL RIGHTS*

The Two Halves of the Occident: *'Continental Model' and 'Oceanic Model'*

Limiting oneself to general questions of identity, of the conflict of values, of language and technology is not sufficient to provide a reliable descriptive framework of the present global era and its problems. It is necessary to descend to a lower level of abstraction to see the more properly philosophical and political aspects influencing the destiny of states, political subjects, institutions and rights in a time marked by the rapid and overwhelming transformation of Western democratic societies.

This problematic will be confronted on the basis of a specific interpretative hypothesis contained in the title to this chapter: *the twilight of sovereignty*. It is important, however, to make an initial clarification so as to dissipate any ambiguity that may arise. The term 'twilight' is not intended in the commonly accepted form of 'declining phase' or 'sunset', which – it is worth noting – took root at the time of the first performance of Wagner's *Götterdämmerung* on 17 August 1876 in Bayreuth. The term is not used so as to flirt with the recurrent literature on the 'End' or on 'Decadence', which is once again widespread. It is adopted, rather, in its original meaning, i.e., the 'diffuse glare' occurring before dawn and after sunset. This semantic ambiguity suggests a structural analogy between the 'before' and 'after', between a genetic-constructive phase and a critical-deconstructive phase of the – characteristically modern – paradigm of 'sovereignty'.

We will attempt to approach this subject in the most rigorous manner, which will not always coincide with the literal interpretations that are commonly in use. In fact, the trinomial provided in the subtitle to this chapter alludes to open questions rather than to available solutions. It alludes to a chain of metamorphoses (some of which have, in part, occurred and others which are, in part, under way) and not to already constituted or actually crystallised entities. With the reference to the plurality of subjects, as well as of rights, it implies a progressive weakening of the classical dichotomy, or, if you prefer, a less prejudicial axiological formulation, a mingling of the traditional borderlines between the countries of the Civil Law and those of the Common Law. Refusing the rigorous demarcation between those systems organised in accordance with Roman law, where the doctrine and praxis of state sovereignty understood in monopolistic terms was formed – first on theological-political bases, then on nature-law foundations and, finally, on rationalistic grounds perfected by legal positivism – and those systems issuing from the common Germanic root, where the production of law is not the exclusive prerogative of a person-state, of a central authority formally invested with power but, rather, the result of the autonomies and dynamic interweavings between diverse 'associations'.

The clouding of the distinction between these great models of order that constitute the *two halves of the Occident* – for brevity's sake we will call one the 'Continental model', characteristic of the European and Latin American states' formalistic–imperative tradition of legal positivism, and the second the 'oceanic model' typifying the Anglophone states' (Great Britain, the United States, Australia) customary-constitutional tradition of common law – poses a series of delicate problems not only for legal theory in the narrow sense but for democratic theory itself.

We shall, therefore, set out from the classical binomial of the 'state' and 'sovereignty' of the Continental model, to questions concerning the present and future problems of democracy, the nature of 'subjects' and the quality of 'fundamental rights'. In this respect, we will need to make a methodological distinction between two tendencies or, rather, two research trajectories (although they are – in fact – interdependent). The first trajectory *(A)*, which privileges the 'internal' aspect of the problem, asserts the definitive *conventionalisation of the concept of sovereignty* understood as the natural point of arrival of a process – at once unitary and two-sided – of *secularisation* and *absolutisation*: moving away from religious authority and towards the foundation of 'intra-worldly' rational-legalistic and technico-juridical procedures for the legitimating of state power.

The   second   trajectory   *(B)*,   essentially   (but   *not* exclusively) privileges the 'external' face of the problem. It proposes to deconstruct this same concept by reversing through its constitutive stages. The implicit wager is that *the current key to the crisis of the state can be traced back to the logic that has historically presided over its edification*, if not to the basic elements, to the 'bricks' with which modern rationalism (in its metaphysical guise even more importantly than in its juridical and political ones) has erected the structure of the 'great Leviathan' over the last four centuries.

For some time, as we have hinted already, we have been convinced that the two trajectories, by traversing or touching upon crucial questions of contemporary politics, end up intersecting or even converging in a number of points. For this reason we struggle to understand the cause of the delay in making them interact on the theoretical plane. This appears much less inscrutable if one thinks of the *prescriptive obsession* that still permeates a large part of political philosophy. This obsession has, to this day, prevented the comprehension or the turning to account, on the specifically philosophical terrain, the revolution in the twin notions of the state and sovereignty produced over the last five decades by historical research – not only juridical, political and constitutional history but also history of religion, anthropological history, social history and the history of ideas.

We shall now examine in turn the problematic core of the two trajectories, so as to then attempt to situate the terms of their possible interaction within the framework of a renewed democratic theory, one that is able to 'temper' prescription and comprehension – beyond any simple antithesis of *analytic* and *hermeneutic*, theoretical approach and historico-critical approach. In other words, we shall attempt to delineate a normative plane anchored to the material and symbolic presuppositions that are woven into the dynamics of 'really existing' polyarchies (and their complex play of exclusions and inclusions, distinctions and mixtures, interweavings and superimpositions between 'interests' and 'values', society and institutions).

Our investigation will make implicit use of the principal foreign contributions on this question (particularly German and Anglophone), without ignoring some important Italian contributions, including those of Paolo Grossi and his school – in particular the work of Maurizio Fioravanti and Pietro Costa on the 'model of juridical sovereignty'; those of Paolo Prodi on the 'sovereign pontiff' and on the 'sacrament of power' – which is to say, on that knot of canon law and public law that lies at the foundation of the attribution of *plenitude potestatis* to the secular state; and Pierangelo Schiera's investigations into the *Verfassung* and the forms of 'discipline' constitutive of the modern state – investigations that were inspired by the methods and results of the 'constitutional and social history' of Hintze, Brunner and Böckenförde. Aside from the significance of these relatively recent studies, we must not lose sight of what is all too often overlooked (at least in the last two decades) by the majority of political philosophers: that the Italian tradition, beginning with Santi Romano, occupies a central place in the landscape of juridical science of the 1900s.

We will seek to identify the nodal points emerging from the two trajectories against this backdrop.

Juridical Experience and the Imaginary of Statehood

The Power of Fiction: the state/sovereignty binomial

A decisive result springs from 'trajectory A', one that sheds light on the *formal value of the state/sovereignty binomial* and on the *fiction of the person-state*. That is to say, the conventionalisation of the *summa potestas* is nothing other than the inevitable upshot of its progressive identification with the law, with the juridical-normative order as a whole. This upshot, as we shall see, reverberates against each of the terms of the binomial.

One of the merits of this tendency is that of having relieved the notion of the state of the misty indeterminacy of many traditional theoretical and historiographic approaches that treated it as a sort of ubiquitous indicator, as universal as it was vague, as indefinite as it was omnipotent and imperious. Such approaches meant that the word 'state' could be applied to the Greek *polis* and the Roman *civitas*, to the *respublica Christiana* and *regna* of the territorial monarchies of the early Middle Ages. This unfounded semantic extension of the term has led us to lose sight of the fact that the state as we understand it, i.e., as a political association founded, in Weberian terms, on the *monopoly* of *legitimate* physical force or violence, which turns on a *dual* and *simultaneous* process of *expropriation-monopolisation* and *legitimation* of 'power', is not only a Western event but a specifically modern one. Its structural identity depends – both in its actual genesis and in its current decline – on historical circumstances that are as determinate as they are specific.

In the modern acceptation the word 'State' is a new word, found in the various European languages only in a period relatively near our own. Its acceptance was linked with certain factual circumstances, with the fact above all that it referred to a new state of affairs, one that differed in many respects from that which was visible to the eyes and imagination of the political writers of antiquity and of the Middle Ages.[1]

The author of the work quoted above Alexander Passerin d'Entrèves, one of the few Italian thinkers able to bring together, in a comparative perspective, the two great political-juridical traditions of the Occident. It was the comparative method that emphasised the diachronic as well as the synchronic peculiarities of the new term. Whereas, historically – beginning with Machiavelli, who is the first to use the term as a noun by means of an abstraction of the *status reipublicae* – it introduces a discontinuity with respect to the past, from the synchronic standpoint it marks the persistence of a break from the 'other side' of Western civilisation represented by the common law. Although the neologism 'the state' had already been introduced into English in the Elizabethan era; although Hobbes, in the introduction to *Leviathan*, had clearly stated the equation between the commonwealth (which was an etymologically precise translation of the latin term '*respublica*') and *civitas* and *state*; although – additionally – even before Hobbes, Pufendorf and his translator Barbeyrac consecrated its use in political theory – nevertheless, the term '*État*' had, for some time already, been adopted in the language of international relations. Despite all this, 'the word "State" does not seem to have fared as well in England and in English-speaking countries as it did on the Continent'.[2] There are complex reasons for this cold reception. They relate back to the division between the two great paths [*indirizzi*] of Western culture, which depend – in the final analysis – on that bifurcation within the development of the juridical concept of 'public person' or 'personality of the state' that had been so admirably delineated by Maitland in *The Crown as Corporation*.

Passerin d'Entrèves' *Notion of the State* was valued more highly in the philosophical sphere outside Italy.[3] This book called itself an introduction to 'political theory' (in the subtitle to the 1967 English edition), or to the 'doctrine of the State' (as in the

---

1   Alexander Passerin d'Entrèves, *The Notion of the State*, p. 29.
2   Ibid., p. 33.
3   For confirmation of its success outside Italy, see Ulrich Matz, 'Staat'.

subtitle to the previous, and less detailed [elaborate] Italian
edition). However, it would not be difficult to find similar statements – i.e., ones marked by an analogous demand to critically
circumscribe the conceptual terms of 'state', 'sovereignty', 'norm',
'legality' and 'legitimacy' to the modern political and juridical
world – in the work of other Italian thinkers (perhaps ones with
a different cultural or ideal orientation). For example, in the
studies of Paolo Grossi, who, over a number of decades, has
advanced the notion of the specificity of 'medieval juridical
experience',[4] rooted in the plurivocal and multiform fabric of a
society without a state. Or in the investigations of his student
Pietro Costa into the question of the *iurisdictio*, that is, into the
semantics of political power in medieval public law. Each of these
enquiries is also decisive for the subject of this chapter, inasmuch
as we extract from them – *e contrario* – the (anything but 'natural') peculiarity of the modern juridical experience, which binds
the production of law to the organs of the state, turning the law
into a purely formal reality.

In an equally precise manner, the results of this line of thought
reverberate against the second term of the binomial, embracing
in a single destiny – that, for some, constitutes a mortal embrace
– 'state' and 'sovereignty'. The modern concept of sovereignty,
beyond the doctrinal antithesis between 'decisionism' and
'normativism', finds its 'natural' presupposition in the *'fiction'*
of the person-state, that is, in that 'nominalism' that – on the
back of traditional study of Roman law and Western canon law
– conceives political association as a *persona ficta*. In this presupposition one can find inscribed, from its very beginnings, the
inexorable destiny of the progressive conventionalisation of the
state. Once the path of the state's metaphysical substantialisa-
tion is rejected, a path taken by the various organicist ideologies
which emerge as counterpoints to the various phases of modernity, the state as 'person' appears as nothing but an artifice and
a legal abstraction. Its 'existence' is, purely and simply, a creation of the law: the personification of a system of norms, imputed
to the 'state'. Therefore, 'taken seriously', the Project of modernity sets out – on the basis of social contract theory – from a
cardinal thesis: the 'life' of the state is an 'artificial' life. One can
only speak *metaphorically* of the 'political body' or the state as
'organism'. And, for Hobbes, it is not only the body that is

---

4   Paolo Grossi, *L'ordine giuridico medievale*.

artificial but also the soul of the Leviathan, which he locates in sovereignty.

It is impossible to underestimate the debt contracted by modern public law with canon law in its elaboration of the 'conceptual fiction' of the person-state (as documented by Paolo Prodi's investigations). The coining of the concept of 'legal person' is drawn from classical canon law. This circumstance alone should suggest just how much modern theorisations are permeated by theological elements. It is thanks to the work of the great Italian canonist Sinibaldo dei Fieschi (the future Pope Innocent IV) that one designates with the expression *persona ficta* an 'artificial subject' that exists only in the construction of law but that, in this construction, has a perfect autonomy and an independent existence (as we have been reminded by Grossi in the wake of Francesco Ruffini's works at the end of the 1800s). At the same time, one must resist the temptation of the continuum, by distinguishing the original meaning of the term from the conventional acceptation that it assumed in its later, secular guise. At the beginning, the adjective '*ficta*' possessed a complex valence, which – in conformity with Latin etymology – indicated both artifice but also the creative dimension of an intellectual design. Subsequently, it became rooted in a rigidly monist conception based upon the iron principle of the hierarchy of sources, that is, on the presumption of a single legitimate source of law and of a single valid order which was identified with the state.[5]

The theoretical regime that presides over this identification has a precise and incontrovertible name: *formalism*. In this respect, the opposition to which we alluded earlier, between 'decision' and 'norm', which since the celebrated controversy between Schmitt and Kelsen has held the attention of at least three generations of European political philosophers (and recently American ones too), loses all meaning. Although it was comprehensible in terms of ideological-polemical polarities in the particular atmosphere in which it arose – that climate of divisions and contrasts that marked the tragic destinies of Weimar Germany and of the first Austrian republic, today the antithesis of decisionism and normativism appears theoretically unjustifiable. The simple but crucial reason for this is that decision and norm, independently of the 'politics of law' that subtend them, are two sides of the

---

5 See Giacomo Marramao, *Dopo il Leviatano. Individuo e comunità*, pp. 326 ff.

same coin: the imperative-formalist coin of legal positivism. No consistent 'decisionist' can today deny that a decision, insofar as it is 'constitutive', is a function of a legal order to which it must *necessarily* give rise. Otherwise, as Schmitt himself underlined in his polemic with 'political romanticism', one would fall back into the arbitrary occasionalism of an *art pour l'art*.[6] Conversely, no consistent 'normativist' can fail to recognise that the system of norms, inasmuch as it is a *valid* legal system, 'exists' only because it has been constituted, that is, *positively* and *formally* instituted, by an act of decision. Otherwise, as Kelsen himself never tired of repeating, one would remain stranded in the metaphysics of natural-right theory.

The current matter of contention is no longer that of the (presumed) dilemma of decision or norm but invests the very stability of the Leviathan model, that is, of a model that is formal and imperative, and founded upon the reduction of all law to state law. However, whereas from the historical-political standpoint one may accept the descriptively anodyne formula of the 'crisis' or 'entropy' of the Leviathan, from the theoretical perspective these general expressions are no longer sufficient. We must acknowledge that – at the level of 'doctrine' – the signs of the crisis, of that entropic tendency, can already be found prefigured in terms of the *dissolution of the concept of the state*. This dissolution is effected through two distinct analytical paths, which we can only outline here: 1) through the definitive conventionalisation of sovereignty into a merely formal axiom of opening/closure of the Order. Kelsen's notion of *Grundnorm* absolves this task. Inasmuch as it is contentless, insofar as it is a pure imperative of observance of all other norms of the system, the 'fundamental norm' indicates – as Georg Henrik von Wright has observed[7] – the decisionistic and 'nihilistic' absence of foundation on which the Leviathan model supports itself. In this respect, Kelsen – and not Schmitt – constitutes the logical end point of the *ius publicum europæum*; 2) through the reduction of sovereignty to cipher for a system of functions or a set of institutions. These functionalist or systemic theorisations, in sociology as in political science, reduce the state to a merely self-referential diagram of functionally differentiated roles or to a hetero-referential parallelogram of social forces.

---

6 Carl Schmitt, *Political Romanticism*.

7 *Translator's note*: See Georg Henrik von Wright, *Practical Reason*; in particular the essay 'Norms, Truth, and Logic'.

In this way, two different theoretical paths converge in the dissolution of the state-sovereignty binomial. And in this respect, it is of little consequence that the 'emptiness' of path A), which culminates in the aporia of the relation validity-effectiveness, is matched by the 'fullness' of path B), which issues in a socio-polit-ical realism that resolves the question of legitimacy in the technicity of the procedure or in the factuality of the relations of power. The crucial aspect is that the result of both paths coincides with the certification of the death of the *magnus homo*, of that mega-machine, or that great artificial organism on which modern rationalism has conferred the name of 'state' through a process of reification that has no counterpart in empirical reality.

But what if the historical and structural reality of the modern Leviathan were something other than its doctrinal, philosophico-political and public law stylisation? What if the notion of sovereignty were only a mask, a symbolic device whose task is to 'sublimate' a whole operational group of concrete interwoven *disciplinary* prac-tices? What consequences should we draw concerning the genesis and destiny of the 'state', were these hypotheses to be on target? Roughly, this was the tenor of the premises of Michel Foucault's investigations. Their aim was to remove the realist foundation of the juridical model of sovereignty, thereby relegating – in a prelimi-nary way – the model to the status of apologetic function of 'self-representation' of the modern state. The shortcomings of Foucault's analysis of power stem directly from his conception of law as a purely negative and repressive *dispositif*. We have already discussed this in *Dopo il Leviatano* and thus will not do so again here. It is important to underline, however, how – despite this limit and this reductive conception – Foucault's investigations converged with demands that, fifty years ago, were made by a number of jurists. We are referring, specifically, to those German jurists (but now no longer only German) who, beginning in the 1930s, inaugu-rated that important course of research called 'constitutional and social history'.

In this way we arrive at the second theoretical trajectory that we wanted to consider: 'trajectory B'.

The Force of Tradition: the return of the 'potestates indirectae' and the multiverse of autonomies

Within 'trajectory B' we discover an indubitably potent and suggestive interpretative key: the destructuring of the Leviathan state would restore the modalities and factors of its birth and constitution, according to a reversed logical and historical order (somewhat like a film played backwards). We have just affirmed that, in terms of logic, in terms of 'pure theory', it is Kelsen and not Schmitt who represents the conclusion of the 'Continental model' structured in accordance with the centralising and hierarchical rationality of public law. Therefore, recent attempts to rediscover or 'overturn' decisionism as a reanimation therapy for a state organism debilitated by procedural, administrative and normative routine are not only anachronistic but sterile, for the simple but fundamental reason that its 'weakness' is nothing but the inexorable result of the imperative (and 'decisionist') principle upon which the entire 'rational-legal' edifice of the modern state is founded. We would be mistaken, however, were we to think we could rid ourselves of the whole of Schmitt's analysis, in particular of that side that – synthesised in *Der Nomos der Erde*[8] – looks well beyond the horizon of 'sovereign decision' and contextualises the very history of the Leviathan in the framework of the various orders that the organisation of power has assumed in the history of the Occident.

At this point we shall advance a thesis that may, at first sight, appear paradoxical or deliberately provocative. Schmitt's thought (the stages of which we shall discuss more fully in the following chapter) is more useful for history than for philosophy. The moment the axis of his thought assumes the perspective of the *longue durée* on European political and constitutional history, his thought becomes more fertile in relation to trajectory B, i.e., to the second axis of investigation into sovereignty. One could sum up his perspective as follows. In the twilight of the modern state the *potestates indirectae*, those autonomous economic, religious, socio-institutional 'powers', the multipolarity of conflict that the absolute sovereignty of the state had 'neutralised', bringing to an end with the Peace of Westphalia (1648) the long and bloody chapter of the civil wars of religion, return to the stage.

We will merely touch upon the problematic implication that this 'long wave' of reflection has on the theoretical intentions of Schmitt's 'decisionism'. In the final reckoning, the *decider* state is revealed to be a *neutralising* state, for the sovereign decision is *de facto* equated with the suspension of internal conflict between

---

8   Carl Schmitt, *Der Nomos der Erde im Völkerrecht des Jus Publicum Europæum*.

'subjects' that, in the previous legal orders, made up the body of political association. The decisive aspect of Schmitt's thesis is given, however, by the fact that the neutralisation, of which the 'mortal god's' birth consists, is exercised over the action of historically specific groupings which aim to model the political order on *ultimate values* that are identified with what they consider to be the only *true* religious principles, i.e., their own. It was not a case of an asymmetrical conflict between absolutists and relativists, between those who considered themselves to be right and those who stopped at the 'penultimate values'. It was a case, rather, of a symmetrical conflict between factions who were united in their belief that they each had a monopoly on the *true religion*. From this perspective, there is absolutely no difference between Catholic and Protestant, between Papists and the variety of 'reformed' sects and tendencies. And so it follows *a fortiori* that the intra-worldly sovereignty of the new form of association that will assume the name of 'state' can be called absolute inasmuch as it introduces a *dissymmetry* that suspends the horizontality of conflict through a form of neutralisation that is itself new. This form, insofar as it revokes the theological element of the conflict, takes the name of *secularisation*. Not for nothing does Schmitt detect the starting point of the process that leads to the construction of the artifice of the state, the 'jewel' of the *ius publicum europæum*, in Alberico Gentili's injunction to the theologians to stay silent: *Silete, theologi, in munere alieno!* Not for nothing does he characterise the current epoch of the decline of the state in terms of the compulsive coexistence of two tendencies: a tendency towards the global technicisation of the political sphere, which turns into a new injunction to stay silent, this time issued by the technocrats to the *iurisconsulti*; the other tendency marked by a return to the world-wide [*mondiale*] sphere of that horizontal conflict that turns on 'absolute enmity' (that is, on value/non-value), which the modern state had managed to 'suspend' at the moment of its constitution.

One crucial circumstance problematises the diagnostic framework. Since history never repeats itself, the 'return' of indirect powers is not tantamount to a pure and simple reproposition of the wars of religion. There are other *subjects*, not only confessional ones. There are other *forms* of symbolic self-identification, not only theological ones. But there is a recurrent *criterion* that presides over their aggregation and disaggregation: the criterion of a hostility that appeals to 'ultimate truths'. Only in this sense can contemporary identity conflicts be made – by analogy – to recall ancient wars of religion. Evoking those wars, the elderly Voltaire declared that Europeans had already experienced 'their own Hell on earth',[9] when they did not hesitate to exterminate 'one another for a parcel of words'.[10]

Beginning with the classic works of Otto Hintze and Otto Brunner,[11] and continuing up to the recent contributions of Gerhard Oestreich and Ernst-Wolfgang Böckenförde, constitutional and social history has deconstructed the public law notion of the state. It has gone on to place the concrete historico-structural dynamics that characterised the course of the *Verfassung* in the European continent at the heart of its enquiry. By visualising the interactive role played by the different socio-institutional components in the transition from the medieval to the modern legal orders, this operation has enabled the decomposition of the phases of the process of selection and combination through which the traits of the new state structure were extracted. It is precisely thanks to this work of decomposition that it is now possible to identify precisely the 'destructuring' factors to which the state's claim to centrality and monopoly is subjected. These factors affect the 'Constitutional State' as much as the 'Social State'.[12] Of these various factors we shall recall those of which we are most acutely aware of today: the regional demands for autonomy, which are structured in an entirely non-state form, put in question the *ius territorii* that formed the starting point for the process of transition from the medieval lordship system to the unitary power of the state; the demand for differential social *and* legal treatment on behalf of interest groups, ethnic and religious communities, and diverse group identities (with the consequent question of the repeal of the legal formula, typical of the modern state, of equality before the law); and the intensification of the conflict of competences (and the multiplication of superimpositions) between the different institutional powers or – according to an expression dear to one of Italy's principal post-war jurists, Massimo Severo Giannini – between the different 'sovereign powers' of the state.[13]

---

9   Voltaire, *Treatise on Tolerance and Other Writings*, p. 48.

10   Ibid., p. 28.

11   Otto Hintze, 'Wesen und Wandlung des modernen Staats'; Otto Brunner, *Land und Herrschaft*.

12   *Translator's note:* This distinction, between the Rights State (*Stato-di-diritto*) and the Social State (*Stato sociale*), roughly translates as the Liberal state and the Keynesian state.

13   See Marramao, *Dopo il Leviatano*, pp. 327–28.

Against this backdrop, the most recent reflections on the relations between sovereignty, subjects and rights have inserted in the
debate a conspicuous dose of descriptive and evaluative elements
of the current phase. For at least two decades, the debate on
divided or – in a celebrated phrase of Norberto Bobbio's – 'dimin-
ished sovereignty' [*sovranità dimidiata*][14] has presented itself with
ever greater insistence. Jurists like Stefano Rodotà have spoken
for some time of the 'fragmentation of the sovereign'[15] in an epoch
marked by new bioethical and biopolitical problems generated by
the exponential growth of technological innovations that increasingly invest the private and corporeal spheres. More generally, in
recent years the conviction has grown that the fall of the Berlin
Wall not only marked the end of the Soviet empire and of the
bipolar system but has also brought to an end the epoch of the
nation state that began with the French Revolution.

The emphasis is placed on what appears to be a paradoxical
phenomenon: the simultaneity and belonging together of global
and local, the process of globalisation [*mondializzazione*] and
drives for autonomy and for decentring. On the one hand, the
homologation of the planet under the 'unitary model' of the world
market is said to multiply, in a geometric progression, the phenomena of migration. For this reason, it is said that the mobility of
human beings, capital, commodities and information is irrevocably eroding the territorial logic on which our societies are founded.
On the other hand, the end of the system of nation states is
thought to trigger the compensatory phenomenon of the search
for security and anchoring in an identity within homogeneous
regional legal orders. For the new theorists of the 'end of democracy' (we are thinking specifically of a homonymous work by
Jean-Marie Guéhenno),[16] the current crisis can be linked with the
decline of the great institutional constructions of modernity. We
are told that the contemporary world is heading towards the
diffusion and pulverisation of the powers that – disaggregating all
coagulations of sovereignty, and with that the very idea of Western
democracy – is leading us towards an 'imperial' world, that is, a
multiverse of tendentially centrifugal communities, cemented by

---

14 Norberto Bobbio, *Which Socialism?*, p. 82.

15 Stefano Rodotà, *Tecnopolitica*.

16 *Translator's note:* In English this has been translated as *The End of the
Nation-State* rather than as, more literally, *The End of Democracy* (*La fin de la
démocratie*).

'technopolitics'. From here stem the crucial questions concerning this end-of-century transition. In such a scenario, where the 'manager' takes the place of the 'sovereign', where 'rules' supplant 'values' and 'principles', what future is being prepared for human communities? In what way will individuals be able to construct their identities and affirm their rights? What rules of the game and what spaces of freedom will emerge in a world suspended between the alternatives of technocracy, populism and Bonapartism?

In comparison to these extremely disenchanted and (anything but baselessly) pessimistic scenarios, the line of investigation indicated by 'trajectory B' has the advantage of offering an Ariadne's thread enabling us to orientate ourselves in the intricate labyrinth of corridors and bifurcations, twists and turns, that characterise the current political multiverse. As we have indicated, this thread is constituted by deploying the perspective of the *longue durée* that alone enables us to track those constitutive conditions of sovereignty and of modern law whose disarticulation lies at the bottom of the confusion and the discomfort in which we find ourselves today.

But how can we reformulate the crucial political questions of our time, making them converge – in accordance with the demand we posed at the start of this chapter – with the nodal points that emerged from the two trajectories? With this question we have at last arrived at the final section of this chapter.

Common Law and Civil Law: Diaspora and Contamination

The question of rights

In order to radically redefine the problems confronted so far, the convergence of the perspectives must essentially concern two levels: *a*) the methodological level and *b*) the theoretical-comparative level.

a) On the *methodological* level: it is a case of grasping the effective *depth of field* of the crisis of the state by making the two trajectories outlined above, that is to say, the results internal to the doctrine (i.e., to strictly legal and political philosophy) and the results acquired by historical investigation, interact.

b) On the *theoretical-comparative* level: it is a case of visualising the latitude and complexity of the problems that assail the contemporary 'polyarchies' as a whole, comparing the 'Continental model' and the 'oceanic model', the experience of countries with a codified legal regime (civil law) and that of the anglophone countries with common law.

Both these operations are now unavoidable, if we are to effect a qualitative leap in our discussion and institute a not-subaltern confrontation with the great theoretical elaborations from abroad, which appears to us to be entirely obvious. It is certainly no accident that in international investigations (not only German, but also Anglo-American), in recent years, the prevalent concern has been with the process of transition and formation of sovereignty rather than with strictly doctrinal questions. It is enough to mention the renewed attention to the pioneering enquiries by William Maitland and John Neville Figgis, to the return to the great themes of 'twin-born majesty' or the 'two bodies of the king' tackled by Ernst Kantorowicz in a work that has since become a classic, or even to the revival of the institutionalism of Santi Romano and of Gierke's *Genossenschaftsrecht*. All these are motifs that, by accentuating the aspect of originality and independence of the law from the state, solicit supplementary investigations of some of the 'self-evident truths' of the Continental doctrine and a closer comparison between legal and political traditions in which the Occident has 'bifurcated' in the thorny transitional phase from the Middle Ages to modernity. In view of current concerns, such a comparison appears unavoidable. This is all the more the case because – beginning in the 1920s and increasingly since the end of the Second World War – the boundaries between the two models have begun to fade and intermingle. We will limit ourselves to a schematic confrontation of the two models, considering, first, the question of fundamental rights, and second, that of subjects.

The dual movement of diaspora and contamination between the two great legal and political frameworks of the Occident is particularly instructive in relation to the question of the nature of fundamental rights. The crucial question is: what is the nature of fundamental rights? Is it a case of natural human rights, of customary rights or of positive rights? For example, if we take the *Habeas Corpus* Bill of 1679 or the Bill of Rights of 1689, which consecrates the Glorious Revolution of 1688, we must reply that the rights are *not* natural rights but, rather, traditional rights based upon common law. In fact, in neither bill do we find universal or abstract proclamations. To see these customary rights transformed into 'natural' rights, we must wait for the Bill of Rights of the American colonies, which rise up against English domination.

In this respect – we must add – there is no substantial difference between the *Déclaration* (the Declaration of the rights of man and the citizen) voted by the French National Assembly in 1789 and the American Declaration of Independence. Both speak of natural rights that pre-date the *pactum societatis* that the state must recognise as 'inalienable' (in the American formulation) or 'imprescriptible' (in the French formulation). These differences of definition, which are important for the qualification of rights, are entirely indifferent with respect to the relationships between right and power. In fact, in both cases, rights (founded upon custom, as in the English bills, or on nature, as in the American Revolution) form/configure a *pre-existing limit* to political sovereignty.

The distance of the Anglo-Saxon from the Continental conception of law can be measured here in its entirety. In the tradition of legal positivism, fundamental rights are subjective rights conceded to individuals (or groups or communities) by the state. Thus, it is not an external limit of power, rather – to take up an expression adopted by Georg Jellinek in the *System der subjektiven öffentlichen Rechte* – of a 'self-limitation' of sovereignty. Furthermore, it is significant, even if only as a counterpoint, that the *Grundgesetz*, the Fundamental Law of the Federal Republic of Germany, does not provide for any constitutional revision for citizens' rights. In this way, it overturns the entire German public law tradition founded on the theory of the 'self-obligation' of the state.

However, an essential difference between the two traditions also remains in relation to the institutional mechanisms for the protection of rights. In the countries in which civil law is present, such protection is assured by the division of powers and the 'inclusive' extension of the institutions of participation. In the countries of common law it is guaranteed by the constitutional limits approved by the legislature, thus, centrally, on the formula of 'government of law' or 'rule of law'. In contrast, in the Continental model the formula of *Rechtstaat*, coined by German jurists in the nineteenth century, has ended up, under the influence of positivism, emptying the law from all evaluative content, flattening the crucial question of legitimacy in the determination of 'effectiveness', that is, on the factual existence of the law itself. Therefore, any really existing positive legal order is, by definition, a state-of-law.

The question of subjects

We thus come to the final theme: subjects. We shall not be concerned with the merits of the *debates* on the rights of nations, that is to say, of the 'subjective' insurgencies on the international stage. The question, which for some time has been the object of important investigations, has been taken up – in Italian philosophy of law – by Luigi Ferrajoli with regard to the relations between 'internal' sovereignty and 'external' sovereignty.[17] In strong agreement with some of the studies we have examined above, Ferrajoli makes the concept of 'sovereignty' coincide with the 'course of that specific juridical-political formation that goes by the name of the state, which was born in Europe a little over four centuries ago and that has been exported across the whole of the planet in this century and that is today in decline'.[18] From this premise, Ferrajoli develops three working hypotheses concerning the 'aporias of the doctrine of sovereignty'. 1) An aporia internal to the *theoretical* constitution of sovereignty: the 'construction of a natural law framework that served as the basis for the legal positivist conception of the state and of the paradigm of modern international law'.[19] Therefore, at the origin of juridical modernity and in conflict with it, there lies a 'premodern relic'. 2) An aporia concerning the *history* of sovereignty, that bifurcates in 'two parallel and divergent paths': whereas the course of internal sovereignty coincides with its 'progressive limitation and dissolution' through the constitutional and democratic state of law, the course of external sovereignty results, in its 'progressive absolutisation', in a system of international relations structured by the politics of power and by the 'permanent threat of war and destruction for the future of humanity'. 3) An aporia inherent to the *conceptual* legitimacy of sovereignty, conditioned at root by the 'irreducible antinomy between sovereignty and law'.[20]

Some problematic knots emerge from this dazzling reframing of the historico-theoretical problem of sovereignty, which we shall indicate in summary terms. First, to what extent is it possible to distinguish the legal positivist construction of the state and the consequent conventionalisation of sovereignty from the

---

17   Luigi Ferrajoli, *La sovranità nel mondo moderno*.
18   Ibid., p. 8.
19   Ibid.
20   Ibid., pp. 8–9.

theological-juridical one? Second, to what point is it legitimate to interpret the history of sovereignty as an opposition between progressive internal limitation (on the plane of state law) and progressive external absolutisation (on the plane of international law) without rehabilitating natural law theory? Ferrajoli appears to be aware of these difficulties, since he affirms that the two processes constitutive of the modern state – secularisation and absolutisation – 'invest both dimensions of sovereignty, the external and the internal, and are at one with the formation of the modern idea of the state as artificial person, as the exclusive source of law and, at the same time, as free from law'.[21] Recourse to the tradition of natural right thus appears inescapable once it is a case of delineating an alternative to this model and to its aporetic implications. At the time of the 'twilight' of the *statu nascenti*, the alternative can be found in the idea of a world order hinging on the 'natural rights of peoples' developed, 'well before the notions of internal sovereignty of Bodin and Hobbes',[22] by Francisco de Vitoria in the *Relectiones* at the University of Salamanca in the 1520s and 1530s.

Ferrajoli's approach to the themes of sovereignty, subjects and rights involves very significant theoretical consequences for the present; consequences which it is not possible to investigate further here. To conclude, we will limit ourselves to a marginal gloss on a terminological question. We have the impression that the course of Ferrajoli's argument has the paradoxical effect of rehabilitating – from a radically democratic angle – the German term *Völkerrecht* in contrast to that of 'international law'. Indeed, taken literally, the expression 'inter-national law' signals a law *between* legitimate state-based and sovereign nations. That is, it implicitly presupposes the state system as given. In contrast, the German term *Völkerrecht*, which is a literal translation of the locution *ius gentium*, poses a problem – both ancient and new – that emerged in the (still pre-state-based) phase of transition to modernity: the problem of a law that was not only *between* states but also *of* peoples. We propose to reinterpret the judgement on the 'extraordinary modernity' of Francisco de Vitoria from the standpoint of the *longue durée*, which we have already tried to delineate by isolating the *crepuscular* elements of the 'before' and 'after', of the dawns and sunsets of the Leviathan. Ironically, this

---

21   Ibid., p. 20.
22   Ibid., p. 11.

thinker's proto-modern framework is fertile for us today, precisely because we are situated in a hypermodern (and post-Hobbesian) climate.

We are now at the crucial point. The question of subjects is, today, strictly interrelated with a new phenomenon in which the course of the two Western juridical and political traditions tend to converge: the *pluralisation of sovereignty*. This motif, familiar to the anglophone world since the nineteenth century has, since the 1920s, been at the heart of extremely important reflections on the European continent as well. We have already gestured towards the importance of institutional theory in Italy and France. We are convinced, however, that the very theme of 'corporatist pluralism' – which was in vogue in the United States around the 1970s[23] – is largely anticipated (as was observed by a historian of the standing of Charles S. Maier) in the interwar debate in Germany and Austria.[24] In our judgement, one of the high points of this debate is to be found in the concept of 'collective democracy' (*Kollektive Demokratie*) developed by Ernst Fraenkel,[25] where the attention to the associative dynamic erupts into the 'Continental model' which possessed analogous exigencies to those that, in those very years, were being advanced by American social sciences.

Today, however, we are faced with phenomena of pluralisation that are far more intricate and complex. Whereas corporate pluralism – in the half century between the 1920s and the 1970s – referred to interest groups, the present-day phenomena of differentiation and pluralisation are produced by aggregates not only of interests but above all of values. For this reason the scene of pluralism – as its principal twentieth-century theorist, Isaiah Berlin, has indicated – appears to have substantially mutated due to the surging up of the *culturally differentiated* subjects, for whom culture is the identifying value *par excellence*. Thus, we are living in an epoch whose guiding star is Herder rather than Kant or Hegel. The demands advanced by these subjects – which in Europe manifest themselves in the form of ethno-politics and in America in the communitarian and populist critiques of liberal democracy – are not easily confronted by a political theory and praxis that is not prepared to put in question the 'monist'

---

23 Schmitter, Lehmbruch and Berger, to mention just some of the most important thinkers in this respect.

24 Charles S. Maier, *Recasting Bourgeois Europe*.

25 *Translator's note:* See Ernst Frankel, 'Kollective Demokratie'.

assumptions of its operations. For Berlin, such monist presuppositions do not only belong to the Continental European
tradition but equally to the Anglo-Saxon tradition, which is so
accustomed to 'dealing with' and governing conflicts of *interests*
but not conflicts of *identity*. Not for nothing the battle cry of the
various neo-communitarian positions is, in the United States,
heard in the critiques of the universalising and homologating
pretences of procedural liberalism (whose unmentioned metaphysical basis is said to be that of atomistic individualism). To
the 'rational kernel', which this critique doubtless contains,
answers the 'mystical shell' of the 'ethics of authenticity',[26] for
which cultural difference is something that – by definition –
excludes any form of normativity. Berlin is an intellectual who is
much more aware than the American communitarians. But for
him cultural differences tend – following Herder – to present
themselves as natural as well. That is to say, human nature has
the faculty to differentiate itself culturally. Human nature
supposedly involves a sort of 'generative grammar' of cultures,
with the consequence that the distinction between *ius naturae*
and *ius gentium* is suppressed.

Setting out from an objection, which in many respects is legitimate, to the philosophical presuppositions of the atomising
individualism and of the political instruments of 'procedural
universalism', the communitarian and 'multicultural' challenges
issue in the affirmation of the community as 'factual *a priori*'[27]
and as the only authentic, trans-individual subject of rights. The
logical political translation of these premises can be nothing other
than the constitution of 'armour-plated' differences, operating
within the instrumental schema of *iustitia commutativa* that is
resolved in a simple redistribution of 'quotas'. Despite the
proclaimed politics of difference, communitarianism ends up
reproducing – as the American feminist Jean Cohen has correctly
noted – all the risks of the politics of identity.

With these final comments we have reached the threshold of a
yet more delicate and crucial question: that of the *reconstruction
of a democratic theory* fit to confront the challenges of the present.
The objective should be that of the reconstruction of a concept of
'deliberative democracy' that is distinct from the communitarian
and from the procedural one; a concept, therefore, which is able

---

26   Charles Taylor, *The Ethics of Authenticity*.
27   Karl Otto Apel, *The Transformation of Philosophy*.

to produce an effective interaction between *universalism* and *difference*, not merely a rhetorical one.

The work to be done is vast. As we have attempted to show, it requires not only a rethinking of the metamorphoses of the 'political' from the standpoint of a 'historical sociology'. More important, it demands a drawing together of different theoretical traditions and styles of analysis. Above all, it demands an innovative effort that is capable of projecting juridical and political reflection beyond the theoretical and practical confines of the modern state. That is to say, beyond the horizon of the Leviathan.

But we must question whether the problem before us is so far away from the needs expressed by Michel de l'Hôpital in 1562 on the eve of the Huguenot wars: 'How it is possible to live together is what matters, not what the true religion is.'

4

THE EXILE OF THE *NOMOS*: CARL SCHMITT AND THE *GLOBALE ZEIT*

A Jurist on the Fringes of the Law

One of the most extraordinary anticipations of the themes of the global epoch is to be found, as we have already seen, in the work of Carl Schmitt. He represents one of the most significant and controversial figures in European political and legal philosophy in the twentieth century. His name and work have long been associated, from the standpoint of political ideology, with his compromise with the Nazi regime and, from a strictly doctrinal aspect, with the alternating fortunes of 'decisionism' – a theoretical position in which the foundation of the state's sovereignty would not rest on the impersonality of the law or on a norm, but rather on a primal decision. Schmitt's assumption expressed, principally, in his controversy with the 'normativism' of Hans Kelsen – but more generally with all the 'proceduralistic' and 'pluralistic' ways of viewing the state, whether liberal-conflictive or associative-corporative – has caused some interpreters to consider Schmitt's thought equivalent to a realistic political science outside legal science. Or, according to the polemical judgement of Massimo Severo Giannini,[1] it is a 'degeneration' of the great thread of German legal positivism that begins with von Gerber and Laband through to Jellinek and Kelsen.

However, such a judgement clashed with the understanding of his own work that Schmitt offered on several occasions. Until the end, he identified himself as a jurist. In spite of his documented 'ignorance' of private law and his 'particularly polemical attitude toward any pandectistic[2] and neopandectistic view of

---

1 See Massimo Severo Giannini, 'La concezione giuridica di Carl Schmitt: un politologo datato?'.

2 The Pandectic School was the offshoot of the Historical School of Law of

public law from Laband to Kelsen',[3] Schmitt – according to his autobiographical testimony in *Ex Captivitate Salus*,[4] which he wrote while in prison from 1945 to 1947 – was familiar with 'two areas of legal science, constitutional law and international law'.[5] These two disciplines, both of which include a grasp of public law, are exposed to 'danger from "the political"'.[6] From this danger, Schmitt noted, obviously arguing against any form of legal 'purism':

> [N]o jurist in these disciplines can escape, not even by disappearing into the nirvana of pure positivism. The most he can do is mitigate the danger either by settling into remote neighbouring areas, disguising himself as a historian or a philosopher, or by carrying to extreme perfection the art of caution and camouflage.[7]

The trail of Schmitt's theoretical reflection should begin, ideally, in 1919 with *Politische Romantik*,[8] his first important work, then continue with his celebrated *Die Diktatur*.[9] *Die Diktatur* had considerable effect on the so-called 'conservative revolution' but also on Marxists. The volume's subtitle – 'From the Origins of the Modern Idea of Sovereignty to the Struggle of the Proletarian Class' – is a sign of Schmitt's broad and complex approach to the problem, which aimed at an unbiased confrontation between historical-ideological components that are different, or even opposed (this was recognised at the time by intellectuals coming from different camps, from Walter Benjamin

---

Friedrich Carl von Savigny. Indeed, it was founded by a student of Savigny's, Georg Friedrich Puchta (a line of thought later developed by Immanuel Bekker and Bernhard Windscheid). The school takes its name from the study of Justinian's *Corpus iuris civilis* (in particular from the section entitled the 'Pandects'). Using the logico-systematic method of Roman law, the 'Pandectic paradigm' brought changes to a number of different areas of German law in the nineteenth century, from civil to public law. In particular, it led to a deepening of the divide between the dogmatic legal framework of civil law countries and the case-based law of common law countries (which rested on the concrete rather than abstract formalism).

3   Ibid., p. 447.
4   Carl Schmitt, *Ex Captivitate Salus: Erfahrungen der Zeit 1945/47*.
5   Ibid., p. 55.
6   Ibid.
7   Ibid.
8   See Carl Schmitt, *Politische Romantik* and *Political Romanticism*.
9   Carl Schmitt, *Die Diktatur: Von den Anfängen des modernen Souveränitätsgedankens bis zum proletarischen Klassenkampf*.

to Ernst Robert Curtius). It is, in fact, in this text that he first introduced the distinction between 'commissioned' or transitional dictatorship (contemplated in the Roman legal system) and an 'institutional' or 'sovereign' dictatorship, which Schmitt would take up again later in the framework of his pitiless diagnosis of the constitutional dispositions of the Weimar Republic, a work he had begun in his *Die geistesgeschichtliche Lage des heutigen Parlamentarismus*.[10] Other key texts of Schmitt's in the 1920s include *Politische Theologie*,[11] *Der Begriff des Politischen* – which appeared for the first time in 1927 in the *Archiv für Sozialwissenschaft und Sozialpolitik*[12] – and *Verfassungslehre*,[13] in which he proposes the themes of the antiformalist polemics of the preceding years. His works from the early thirties, *Der Hüter der Verfassung*, *Legalität und Legitimität*,[14] and *Staat, Bewegung, Volk*, continue along the same course as those of the preceding decade. A further systematisation of his thinking is attested to by *Über die drei Arten des Rechtswissenschaftlichen Denkens*[15] and by his 1940 collection of essays *Positionen und Begriffe*. It should not be forgotten, however, that Schmitt, again during the thirties, assiduously confronted the work of Thomas Hobbes, most notably in his 1937 essay 'Der Staat als Mechanismus bei Hobbes und Descartes', and with the volume he published the following year, *Der Leviathan in der Staatslehre des Thomas Hobbes*.[16]

Beginning with the years of World War II, Schmitt's approach to the problem undergoes a significant shift. The themes related to the genesis-structure and to the parabolic path of the modern state are increasingly absorbed within a cosmic-historical circumstance, hinged on the earth/sea binomial, whose alternating circumstance would mark the destinies of the *Nomos*, understood as the countersign of a universal law of 'appropriation' and, for that reason, the point of origin of every law. This phase of his thought, which began in 1942 with the slim book *Land und Meer*, culminated in 1950 with what represents Schmitt's *magnum opus* and one of the

---

10   See also Carl Schmitt, *The Crisis of Parliamentary Democracy*.
11   See also Carl Schmitt, *Political Theology*.
12   See also Carl Schmitt, *The Concept of the Political*.
13   See also Carl Schmitt, *Constitutional Theory*.
14   See also Carl Schmitt, *Legality and Legitimacy*.
15   See also Carl Schmitt, *On the Three Types of Juristic Thought*.
16   See also Carl Schmitt, *The Leviathan in the State Theory of Thomas Hobbes*.

great books of the century, *Der Nomos der Erde im Völkerrecht des Jus Publicum Europæum.*[17]

In the subsequent thirty-five years of his life, Schmitt dedicated himself to a deeper understanding and a precise definition of the important categories of his thinking, rather than to a true development – not, therefore, with the aim of systematisation (since his thought is characterised by a conspicuously anti-systematic attitude), but as if wanting to fix its cardinal points. Of this final phase, it is enough to mention some of the salient passages: the 1953 essay 'Nehmen/Teilen/Weiden',[18] conceived as a corollary to a theory of the *Nomos*; the 1960 article 'Die Tyrannei der Werte'; the slim 1963 volume *Theorie des Partisanen,*[19] which presented a kind of intertextual integration of *The Concept of the Political*; and, finally, *Politische Theologie II* of 1970,[20] which constituted a significant defence of the category of 'secularisation', engaging in a controversy with the thesis of the 'legitimacy' or 'self-affirmation' of the modern advanced by Hans Blumenberg. To put this controversy in context, I take the liberty of referring to my works *Die Säkularisierung der westlichen Welt* and *Potere e secolarizzazione.*

To provide a methodological compass suited to orientating oneself in the vast and tight weave of these works – today the subject of a significant, though ambiguous, revival in various countries – it is necessary to use as reference points the three fundamental nuclei that articulate Schmitt's thought: 1) political theology; 2) the concept of the 'political'; and 3) the theory of the *Nomos* as concrete order. These three items are simultaneously gathered, both in their specificity and distinctiveness, and in their interactive coexistence [*compresenza*], into an 'epochal' vision of the modern state and its parabolic path. They will be addressed, albeit separately, to bring about their confluence into a large diagnostic framework that assumes the 'crisis of the state' within the more general development of what Schmitt defines – following Max Weber – as 'Western rationalism' (*okzidentaler Rationalismus*).

---

17   See also Carl Schmitt, *The Nomos of the Earth.*

18   Carl Schmitt, 'Nehmen/Teilen/Weiden: ein Versuch der Grundfrage jeder Sozial- und Wirtschaftsordnung vom Nomos her richtig zu stellen', *Gemeinschaft und Politik* 3 (1953).

19   See also Carl Schmitt, *Theory of the Partisan.*

20   See also Carl Schmitt, *Political Theology II.*

Political Theology

'The Sovereign is he who decides on the state of exception'.[21]
Political Theology of 1922 begins with this peremptory statement. The text has as its central theme the concept of sovereignty.
For this reason, many jurists have wondered why the title was
chosen. The reason for their surprise is to be found, evidently, in
their failure to note the category to which Schmitt gave the task of
interconnecting the problem of sovereignty as a 'decision'
(*Entscheidung*) about the 'state of exception' (*Ausnahmezustand*)
with the context of political theology: the 'secularisation' category. This connecting function is made explicit only in the *incipit*
of the third chapter of the book, with the statement that all 'significant concepts of the modern theory of the state are secularised
theological concepts'.[22] Thus, the secularisation category provides
the key to accessing not only the historical development of those
concepts, passing from theology into public law – '[F]or example,
the omnipotent God became the omnipotent legislator'[23] – but
also their 'systematic structure'. The 'constructive' analogy
running between theology and jurisprudence allows Schmitt to
read the entire development of the doctrine of the state over the
last four centuries from the point of view of the antithesis between
'deism' and 'theism'. Here, Schmitt neatly outlined his opposition
– which will remain, from this point on, a constant in his thought
– to the 'deistic' theological-metaphysical presupposition of the
'modern constitutional state', which 'rejected not only the trans-
gression of the laws of nature through an exception by direct
intervention, as is found in the idea of a miracle, but also the
sovereign's direct intervention in a valid legal order'.[24] The case
of an exception, repudiated by the 'rationalism of the
Enlightenment'[25] in any form whatsoever, 'in jurisprudence is
analogous to that of the miracle in theology'.[26]
   The bridge between *political theology* and the *theory of sovereignty* has thus been cast. Schmitt did not, in fact, limit himself to
declaring *sovereignty* a limit-concept to be applied in a limit-case.

---

21 Schmitt, *Political Theology*, p. 5.
22 Ibid., p. 36.
23 Ibid.
24 Ibid., pp. 36–37.
25 Ibid., p. 37.
26 Ibid., p. 36.

He above all underlined its 'systematic, legal logic foundation',[27] which makes the state of exception 'truly appropriate for the juristic definition of sovereignty'.[28] The non-rhetorical and non-occasional attitude of this insistence on the properly legal character of the definition of sovereignty is newly and exactly verified by Schmitt's refusal to adopt the sociological equivalents of the concept:[29] 'It would be a distortion of the schematic disjunction between sociology and jurisprudence if one were to say that the exception has no juristic significance and is, therefore, "sociology"'.[30] Sovereignty is, for Schmitt, a *conceptus terminator*. It is precisely the *terminus* of every normative system, in the double sense of the 'border' and 'line' that defines it. But precisely as the line that defines it, that delimits it, sovereignty cannot be expressed in normative language, but must instead be correlated to what the *decision* requires: sovereignty, therefore, as the power to decide *about* the state of exception.

However, it is necessary to pay attention to an essential detail of this defining formula if one does not want to run the risk of misunderstanding the meaning of the entire discourse. The dimension of *Entscheidung* is certainly 'extra-normative' but *not* extra-legal. Thus, the function of the case of exception is precisely that of making manifest the 'specifically juristic element – the decision in absolute purity'.[31] For Schmitt, it is precisely Enlightenment rationalism that does not take into account the crucial nature of the distinction between 'legal' and 'normative': it 'assumes that a decision in the legal sense must be derived entirely from the content of a norm'.[32] If, on the one hand, only the limit-case 'makes relevant the subject of sovereignty, that is, the whole question of sovereignty',[33] on the other hand, such a subject is qualified by its limit-position, which places it, paradoxically, both outside and within the legal system that is in force. It is *outside* it, because otherwise it would not be the subject of a decision. But *within*, because it has the 'competence' of deciding to suspend the constitution *in toto*.

---

27   Ibid., pp. 5–6.
28   Ibid., p. 6.
29   I am thinking, for example, of Weber's *Herrschaft*, or dominion in the sense of 'legitimate power', countered by *Macht*, or 'de facto power'.
30   Schmitt, *Political Theology*, p. 13.
31   Ibid.
32   Ibid., p. 6.
33   Ibid.

Access to the paradoxical ambivalence of sovereignty would be inexorably precluded for the 'deistic' mechanicism, which is a presupposition of the doctrine of the state of law: from Locke through Kant up to its 'normativistic' dissolution accomplished in the theories of Krabbe and Kelsen. Schmitt countered this 'degenerative' process with his own decisionistic definition of sovereignty, tracing it back to an alternative line which, beginning with Jean Bodin (whose merit consists precisely in having 'incorporated the decision into the concept of sovereignty'[34]), would reach the 'theistic conviction' of Catholic philosophy in the Counter-Revolution, represented by the classic names of de Maistre, de Bonald, and Donoso Cortés.

It is hardly necessary to point out the enormous interpretive forcing undertaken by Schmitt in his attempt to fabricate a genealogical tree for 'decisionism'. First, with respect to Bodin: if it is true that, in fact, we are in debt to the *Les six livres de la République* (1576) for the first legally accomplished definition of the *summa legibusque soluta potestas* as an 'irreducible unit' of the prerogatives of absoluteness, perpetuity and indivisibility, and as a *puissance de donner et casser la loi* (the power to make and to abrogate the law), it is at least as true that such a *puissance absolue* is anything but 'unlimited', as Schmitt maintains,[35] since it must be exercised both in keeping with the natural laws imprinted on the world by the supreme authority of God, and in observance of the fundamental (today we would say constitutional) laws of the state – for example, the law of the crown – which exist to safeguard the continuity of the bureaucratic and administrative apparatus upon which sovereignty stands. Second, with regard to the thought of the Counter-Revolution: if it is in fact true that it supports the 'personal sovereignty of the monarch'[36] theologically, it is at least as true that such support cannot be arbitrarily expunged, setting aside the controversial legitimist call for tradition, the ethical-religious appeal to providence and to ecclesiastical authority, which for these theoreticians always represents – as Schmitt himself is forced to admit – 'the last decision that could not be appealed'.[37] For these aspects, and

---

34 Ibid., p. 8.
35 See Giacomo Marramao, *La passione del presente. Breve lessico della modernità-mondo*, pp. 300–310.
36 Schmitt, *Political Theology*, p. 37.
37 Ibid., p. 55.

more generally for Schmitt's 'Catholic' positions, one could see his reflections on 'representation' and on the *complexio oppositorum* contained in a work that appears marginal and stands alone in his production during these years.[38]

Beyond this historico-philological forcing of the interpretation (which incidentally also affects an early attempt by Schmitt to give a decisionistic interpretation of Hobbes), what matters in this context is his isolation of the fundamental theoretical nucleus of 'political theology'. It lies in defining sovereignty *legally*, not as a monopoly to 'coerce' or merely to 'rule' but as 'a monopoly over [the] last decision'.[39] The decision is freed 'from all normative ties and becomes in the true sense absolute'.[40] Therefore, Schmitt's wager rests on the chance that the case of exception, too, will remain 'accessible to jurisprudence because *both elements, the norm as well as the decision, remain within the framework of the juristic'*.[41]

As we have said, the character of the decision is paradoxical: it transcends the norm while it is, at the same time, the presupposition of every norm. Through decision 'authority proves that to produce law it need not be based on law'.[42] The paradox now seems to reverberate on the very category of exception, conferring on it an ambivalent status. The exception stands in relation to 'normality' exactly as the decision stood in relation to the norm. Its status would seem, therefore, eminently methodological. Only by carrying problems to their extreme, to a limit-concept, is it possible to manifest the truth or essence of the 'normal situation',[43] made routine by procedure, and neutralised by the automatic order of norms. This would seem to be the tone in which Schmitt's proposition must be understood, where the exception is 'more interesting' than the 'normal case'. While the latter 'proves nothing', the former 'proves everything'.[44] This is why the exception proves the rule, and not vice versa. However, Schmitt does not limit himself to that. Instead, he tends to hook the 'primality' of the *Ausnahmezustand* (or of the *Ernstfall*, or of the *Grenzfall*) to a metaphysical *lebensphilosophisch* assumption – derived, that is

---

38 See Carl Schmitt, *Roman Catholicism and Political Form*.
39 Schmitt, *Political Theology*, p. 13.
40 Ibid., p. 12.
41 Ibid., pp. 12–13. Emphasis added.
42 Ibid., p. 13.
43 Ibid., p. 12.
44 Ibid., p. 15.

from a 'philosophy of . . . life': 'Precisely a philosophy of concrete life must not withdraw from the exception and the extreme case, but must be interested in it to the highest degree'.[45] And again: 'In the exception the power of real life breaks through the crust of the mechanism that has become torpid by repetition'.[46]

The ambivalence of status mentioned above now seems to be translated into an indelible ambiguity of Schmitt's entire theoretical construction. The existential and anti-normative dimension assigned to the decision – with Nietzsche and, perhaps, even Stirner as guides – tends, on the one hand, to assume a 'negativity' and 'groundlessness' that breaks with all the traditional substantialist views of order. On the other hand, Schmitt's 'positive' radicalness aimed at reaffirming the supremacy of the state's existence and of its 'right to self-preservation'.

From the first perspective – in contrast to those interpretations that aim to reduce him to the stereotype of reactionary statism that emphasise the problem of order and institutional stability – Schmitt seemed to emphasise the innovative aspect, the beneficially 'catastrophic' break of the decision with respect to the constitutional equilibrium in force; and, from a general theoretical standpoint, to share with Max Weber (the author who is closer to Nietzsche in this than is commonly believed) an element of substantive discontinuity with the European political tradition: namely, the crisis of foundations which supported the classical subject of sovereignty. Moreover, the German term *Entscheidung* indicates the same act of cutting, of breaking-away, expressed by the Latin *de-caedere* and, of distinguishing, in order to make a choice, expressed by the Greek term *krísis*, from *krínein*, 'to separate', 'to discern', the meaning which underlies its derivatives 'criticism' and 'criterion'. This is the root of the 'caesura' that separates Schmitt from the reactionary German statism of the nineteenth and twentieth centuries, in which he perceives a return to the regressive utopia where conflicts are resolved, reposing on the pretext of refounding the state's identity in an organicist-corporative mode. Here also lies the reason for his constant polemic with the different variants of corporativism, from the Romantic-reactionary version of an Othmar Spann to the very differently formulated one of Otto von Gierke, and up to the 'pluralism' of G. D. H. Cole and H. J. Laski. But at the same time,

---

45 Ibid.
46 Ibid.

the decision's character as break, founded on nothing (*auf Nichts gestellt*), tends to sharply distinguish itself from aestheticising and Romantic 'occasionalism', with which Schmitt – in any event – had settled his accounts almost as a preliminary to his political-theological treatment of sovereignty in *Political Romanticism*. The decision is not a *coup de théâtre* – a mere arbitrary gesture for its own ends, a sort of *art pour l'art* – but the cut, the innovative schism, which is the origin of every concrete, actually existing legal system. But the *Entscheidung* cannot be deduced from the form of the legal system, since it never is the effect or the result of a process of formation or constitution. It is, however, *constitutive* of it. Conversely, the fact that the decision always gives way to a new constitution (*Verfassung*) in no way means that it depends on it. In fact, it is precisely the point at which the constitution itself takes place. Upon this scheme rests the formulation Schmitt gives to a classic problem of constitutional law, that of the relationship between *legality* and *legitimacy* – which is confronted in an important text from 1932.[47] From this viewpoint, there is no radical difference between Schmitt's and Weber's positions. Schmitt's criticism of Weber – that Weber reduced legitimacy to legality, as does normativism – is largely imputable to Kelsen's forced assimilation of Weber's theses in 1922, in *Der soziologische und der juristische Staatsbegriff*.[48] If it is true that, for Weber, the legitimisation of power cannot descend mechanically – as in Kelsen's 'pure theory of law',[49] which in this respect falls prey to the 'naturalistic fallacy' that reduces law to fact – from the simple empirical encounter with *effectiveness* (with the continuity of the coercive legal system that obtains obedience), it is equally true that, for Weber as for Schmitt, legality and the legal system are not the *cause* of legitimacy but only its *necessary form*.

However, beyond the threshold of this statement of the non-self-sufficiency of the criterion of legality, Schmitt's thought seemed to run into an aporia even greater than Weber's. Indeed, from the 'positive' perspective mentioned above, the decision seems to be constituted in its 'absolute' – and, therefore, *unrelated* – autonomy as the symmetrical reverse side of the general and intermediate nature of the liberal scheme.

---

47   See Schmitt, *Legality and Legitimacy*.
48   Hans Kelsen, *General Theory of Law and State*.
49   Hans Kelsen, *Pure Theory of Law*.

The decision frees itself from all normative ties and becomes in the true sense absolute. The state suspends the law in the exception on the basis of its right of self-preservation, as one would say. The two elements of the concept *legal order* are then dissolved into independent notions and thereby testify to their conceptual independence. Unlike the normal situation, when the autonomous moment of the decision recedes to a minimum, the norm is destroyed in the exception. The exception remains, nevertheless, accessible to jurisprudence because both elements, the norm as well as the decision, remain within the framework of the juristic.[50]

So where does the reason lie for the theoretical *preference* for the *decision* instead of the *norm*? Schmitt answered that it is to be sought in the existential priority of the state: 'The existence of the state is undoubted proof of its superiority over the validity of the legal norm'.[51] Therefore, it is the appearance of the *existential* dimension that interrupts the vicious circle of norm and decision, in which one of the most representative figures of the 'public philosophy' of Weimar had felt it necessary to see a sterile game of mirrors ensnared in formalism. In *Die Souveränität*, Herman Heller wrote, 'Schmitt's will without norm [*normloser Wille*] resolves the problem as little as Kelsen's norm without will [*willenlose Norm*]'.[52]

But through the folds of the existential dimension, we now glimpse the emergence of the other conceptual pole of Schmitt's thought: the 'political'.

The Concept of the 'Political'

For Schmitt, the concept of the 'political' constitutes the *presupposition* for the concept of the state, understood – according to the tradition of civil law, rooted in Roman law – as the *status* 'of a people organised on a closed territory'.[53] All the possible characterisations of the definition of the state (machine or organism, person or institution, society or community) take on meaning only in light of the 'political' and, conversely, are incomprehensible if the essence of this term is misunderstood. For Schmitt, this essence is to be found in its irreducible autonomy by breaking the *circulus vitiosus* of 'political' and 'of-the-state'. The fact that the

50   Schmitt, *Political Theology*, pp. 12–13.
51   Ibid., p. 12.
52   Herman Heller, *Die Souveränität*, p. 62.
53   Ibid.

'political' is the inescapable presupposition for what is 'of-the-state' does not mean in any way that it is to be identified with it (as the modern mythology and jurisprudence of the state would have it). The 'political' cannot be circumscribed, confined or topologically delimited, even if the spatial dimension constitutes, as we will see, one of its chief correlates. It can only be temporarily 'located' in those set of dimensions or forms in which, from time to time, it manifests itself historically. It is, in fact, a 'criterion' *stricto sensu*, an attitude that is explained – like the decision that, inasmuch as it forms the far limit of the 'legal', bears its counter-mark – not by refounding or recomposing but by *settling*, by *dividing*. This criterion is to be taken in its peculiar specificity and 'distinction', with respect to other 'various relatively independent endeavours of human thought and action, particularly the moral, aesthetic and economic'.[54] This is an extremely important point, in which some have found – not without the complicity of Schmitt himself – analogies to Benedetto Croce's 'philosophy of the distincts'.[55] Once it is assumed that the distinctive criterion of the moral is provided by the opposites good/bad, that of the aesthetic by the pair beautiful/ugly and that of the economic by the pair useful/harmful, or profitable/non-profitable, the problem of the *essential definition* of the 'political' coincides with the identification of a set pair that is irreducible to the preceding couples.

The 'specific political distinction' consists, for Schmitt, of the 'distinction of friend [*Freund*] and enemy [*Feind*]'. It represents the autonomous, irreducible 'criterion' to which 'all actions with a specifically political meaning can be traced'.[56] The two indispensable correlatives of this specific distinction are its *existentiality* and its *public nature*. Two unavoidable consequences follow. First, the concepts of friend and enemy must be assumed, not as metaphors or symbols but in their concrete, 'existential' meaning. Second, not only must they not be confused with other criteria (according to which, for example, the enemy would be morally bad, aesthetically ugly or economically disadvantageous), but neither must they be understood 'in a private-individualistic sense as a psychological expression of private emotions and

---

54   Schmitt, *The Concept of the Political*, pp. 25–26.

55   See Schmitt's lecture 'Das Zeitalter der Neutralisierungen und Entpolitisierungen' from 1929, where he cites Croce, in *Der Begriff des Politischen: Text von 1932 mit einem Vorwort und drei Corollarien.*

56   Schmitt, *The Concept of the Political*, p. 26.

tendencies'.[57] Friendship and enmity, therefore, must be conceived exclusively *in a public sense*: 'The enemy is solely the public enemy . . . The enemy is *hostis*, not *inimicus* in the broad sense'.[58]

For the aspect of the 'political' as well, as was already the case with that of the decision, Schmitt employs the methodical criterion of the 'extreme' as the truth for normal cases: the closer a grouping comes to the extremity and purity of the friend/enemy antithesis, the more political it is. This produces the definitive detachment of political acting from any topological referent, which has led some to see in Schmitt a definition of politics that mirrors and is the opposite of, the relational, functionalist, or systematic models of *power-influence*. 'The political . . . does not describe its own substance, but only the intensity of an association or dissociation of human beings'.[59] Since 'purity' and 'autonomy' are part of the criterion, not the realm in which it is made explicit, it follows that any aggregation of intensity near the friend/enemy antithesis itself assumes a perfectly political character whether it is manifested in religious (confessional civil wars), national (interethnic conflicts) or economic (class) conflicts.

Given this state of affairs, how is the concept of the 'political' related to the 'political-theological' dimension of state sovereignty? Due to the two sets of consequences that it brings to the development of Schmitt's thought, this is a crucially important question. The question a) *directly* affects Schmitt's polemic with regard to the constitutional arrangements of the Weimar Republic,[60] and also b) *indirectly* affects the way in which his diagnosis of the parabolic path of the modern state is inserted into the framework of a general vision of the alternating succession of law and power, order and conflict, earth and sea, which spans the development of 'Western rationalism' from its beginnings in classical Greece up to its current expansion on a planetary scale. Let us proceed to an examination of these aspects, treating them in the order we have just stated them.

---

57 Ibid., p. 28.
58 Ibid.
59 Ibid., p. 38.
60 For a historical and conceptual appraisal of the Weimar political and constitutional debate, see Giacomo Marramao, *Il politico e le trasformazioni*.

Against Weimar: Depoliticisation and the Ascendency of Technique

If one looks closely, Schmitt's definition of the criterion for the 'political' is characterised by an unmistakeable trait: it institutes a drastic caesura between *the essence of the 'political'* and *the form of the exchange-contract*. However, a caesura of this type involves – for the years in which it was formulated (between 1927 and 1932) – an implied violent polemic towards the Weimar Constitution. It was a 'Constitution without decision'[61] (*Verfassung ohne Entscheidung*, as Otto Kirchheimer, a militant pupil of Schmitt in the ranks of the Social Democrats, would define it), since it had passively accepted the euthanasia of the 'political' in the contracting and translating of the enemy into the competitor. For Schmitt, the effects of such passiveness were deadly in their inexorable automatism. The 'pluralistic' dynamics of conflicts and transactions between various pressure groups and institutional 'bodies' appeared, to his eyes, as the re-emergence from a long state of dormancy of those *potestas indirectae* which had once been 'neutralised' by the affirmation of the modern state and that now threatened to take their revenge by undermining the sovereign unit at its root. The legal and constitutional literature generally has dwelt on the 'therapeutic' aspects of Schmitt's contributions in the years bridging the 1920s and 1930s, beginning with his tendentious exegesis of Article 48[62] where – in explicit disagreement with Kelsen – Schmitt identified the guardian of the 'true' Constitution with the President of the *Reich*, 'legislator in the case of extreme necessity',[63] and not with a jurisdictional collegial body such as the Constitutional Court, which, in his opinion, remained an eminent expression of the pluralist fracturing. Beyond these technical-juridical aspects, the background for the Schmitt-Kelsen polemic consisted of a genuine axiological and political-ideal antithesis – which emerges clearly from the confrontation between these two figures assembled in Hans Mayer's memoirs[64] – between a position that considered political parties a

---

61   Otto Kirchheimer, 'Weimar – and What Then? An Analysis of a Constitution', p. 71.

62   See Schmitt, *Legality and Legitimacy*.

63   Carl Schmitt, 'Der Hüter der Verfassung'.

64   See specifically Hans Mayer, *Ein Deutscher auf Widerruf: Erinnerungen*, pp. 140–51.

disintegrative element of the political system and one that aimed, instead, at fully legitimising them as constitutive factors in modern democracy. The theoretical indicator of the stakes was, in the final analysis, represented by the diametrically opposed assessments that the two authors supplied for the concept of 'the people'. For Kelsen, this was nothing more than a totemic mask, a metapolitical illusion concealing or dissimulating a pluriverse of interests, ethnic groups and cultures. For Schmitt, on the other hand, the self-identification of the *Volk* constituted the existential presupposition for every political unit.[65] Hence, the singular pastiche represented by Schmitt's *Verfassungslehre* was his attempt – paradoxical, to say the least – to bring Rousseau's democracy of identity together with the doctrine of *pouvoir neutre* from Benjamin Constant, Rousseau's philosophical adversary.

Beyond these technical-juridical and constitutionalist aspects, it is important to underscore the philosophical outlines of Schmitt's reflection. They concern, at this point, the relation that is instituted between the concept of the 'political' and 'political theology', which hinges on the concept of sovereignty. The text in which the interconnection between these two fundamental coordinates is most coherently and suggestively expressed is his 1929 lecture 'Das Zeitalter der Neutralisierungen und Entpolitisierungen'.[66] Here, the historical-ideal succession in modern Western civilisation is described as a sequence of stages in which the political essence of the will to power becomes secularised. The stations along this path – that Schmitt cautions us not to confuse with the traditional schemes of an ascending philosophy of history – go from the 'theological' to the 'metaphysical', from the 'moral' to the 'economic', up to the current 'era of technology'. Therefore, the process of secularisation unfolds by means of a gradual shift in the centre of gravity, in which, from time to time, the 'political' settles and is 'normalised'. Modern secularisation is thus characterised by an alteration between contrasts that are determined by the actualisation of the friend/enemy antithesis and its successive 'neutralising' arrangements. The *eruption* that renews the 'political' and *neutralisation* represent a non-modular polarity of the process of secularisation. 'European humanity is constantly migrating from a field of

---

65 On this point see Giacomo Marramao, *Dopo il Leviatano. Individuo e comunità.*

66 Schmitt, *Begriff des Politischen*, pp. 78–95.

conflict to neutral ground and the neutral ground, as soon as it is conquered, is immediately transformed, once again, into a battle-field. It then becomes necessary to seek new neutral spheres'.[67] The contemporary epoch, marked by the ascendency of technology, is nothing more than the landing place of 'a series of progressive neutralisations'[68] of areas where, in the course of modern history, the centre has successively shifted from the 'theological' (the theatre of the wars of religion in the sixteenth and seventeenth centuries), to the 'metaphysical' (the space of scientific-political conflicts in the fifteenth century), to the 'moral' (the ground for cultivating the rationalism of the Age of Enlightenment and its revolutionary outlet), to the 'economic' (the pedestal for the doctrine of the 'neutral and agnostic state' of the nineteenth century and its overturning in the Marxist theory of classes). But, technique, as the final derivative of the process of neutralisation, does not permit further depoliticising shifts. In fact, it is 'culturally blind'. It does not, in itself, possess the criterion for its possible uses: 'it can be revolutionary and reactionary. It can serve freedom and oppression, centralisation and decentralisation'.[69]

Technique always awaits a legitimate subject to use it. Yet this cannot be an impersonal, abstract subject, such as the 'state of law' that, since it reduces politics to a bureaucratic-administrative machine, is itself technical, a neutralising and depoliticising form. It must be a subject capable of reviving the specifically political criterion for identification. In this way, Schmitt links the concept of the 'political' to the theme of the decision, which – even if, as we have seen, it leads to the attribution of every innovative dynamic to the extra-normative sphere of existence and concrete life[70] – in no way should be confused with a romantic refusal of technology. Technology is accepted not only because it represents, at this point, an irrevocable destiny, but also because it is precisely to the process of disintegrative secularisation of the metaphysical, culminating in the ascendency of a technical-conventional order, that the decision owes its character of *groundlessness*. The 'bottomless abyss' of a freedom capable of producing the state of exception suspends the norm

---

67   Ibid., p. 89.
68   Ibid., p. 88.
69   Ibid., p. 91.
70   Schmitt, *Political Theology*.

and is able to determine a new friend/enemy grouping in complete autonomy.

Setting aside the burning controversies raised by Schmitt's category of 'decision' – which would later be related, in the framework of a comparative conceptual analysis, to the concepts of Jünger and Heidegger[71] – here it must be underscored once more that the thesis of successive secularising neutralisations is detached from the framework of traditional philosophies of history because of two decisive aspects. First, it reduces progress, as does Weber's thesis of the continuum of Western rationalism, to the progressive rationalisation of means that gives rise to formalism *without foundations*, to a purely conventional order. Second, the succession of *Zentralgebeite* in no way fits into a new doctrine of 'stages' (if anything, later Schmitt appears to lean towards Arnold Toynbee's 'rhythmic' theory of cultures based on the *challenge/ answer* scheme), since, far from denoting a rising motion, it is limited to underlining the points of crystallisation for the 'pluralist' dynamics of Western *Kultur*, whose presuppositions are 'existential and not normative'. In other words, the 'centres of reference' never subsume the multiplicity of phenomena in each epoch, but only polarise the dynamic contexts with which the neutralisation and control of conflictive tensions is determined. Therefore, the passages do not occur in the dialectical form of *Aufhebung* (in which the final step sublates and includes within itself all those that preceded it), rather in terms of a lateral shift from one context to another. It should not be surprising, therefore, that this paradoxical status of the 'political' as an *atopical* criterion – but one mysteriously capable, at the same time, of giving way each time to very concrete topographies of order – could appear to some as a veritable philosophical aporia. In a celebrated essay from 1935, Karl Löwith noted that Schmitt cannot in reality say where the 'political' is located, if not in a totality that goes beyond every determinate area of reality, *neutralising them all in the same way, even if in a direction inverse to that of depoliticisation.*[72]

However, the philosophical kernel of Löwith's severe judgement – in which the concept of the 'political' would only specularly restore the empty formalism of neutralisation, leading

---

71 Christian von Krockow, *Die Entscheidung: Eine Untersuchung über Ernst Jünger, Carl Schmitt, Martin Heidegger.*

72 Karl Löwith, 'The Occasional Decisionism of Carl Schmitt'.

to an indeterminateness that is fungible on occasion in every content and purpose – would hit the target only on one condition: that of ignoring the overall design in which Schmitt inscribes all these moments, including the concepts of politics and the state.

The theoretical scheme presupposed in this picture is represented by his conception of the *Nomos* as a concrete order.

The Theory of the Nomos as 'Concrete Order'

The parabolic path of the modern state, born out of the civil wars of religion in the sixteenth and seventeenth centuries, takes place, for Schmitt, in perfect parallelism with that of its doctrinal framework: the *ius publicum europæum*. As a 'specifically European phenomenon,' jurisprudence is 'deeply involved in the adventure of Western rationalism'.[73] The authority that it assigned to the sovereign functions of the new secular state retraced at the beginning, with a near obsessive faithfulness, the entire range of theocratic attributes. The absolute nature of the appropriation of those attributes on the part of the secular sovereign was thus guaranteed precisely by this perfect formal correspondence with the source. As a translation – as rigorous as Hobbes could want – of theological prerogatives into 'mortal' and 'worldly' prerogatives, the secularisation originally performed by public law still was not a profanation. Instead, it neutralised religious conflict by installing a new order, no longer based on creed but wholly civil and political. Here lies the key to Alberico Gentili's warning, taken by Schmitt as the inaugural formula of the modern state: '*Silete, theologi, in munere alieno!*' Except that, in the course of secularisation, the structure of the state has become ever greater, transforming itself into an inanimate machine and neutral apparatus from which the 'representative-sovereign person' was first relegated to the background and then definitively removed. With the age of technology, this profanation has reached its natural conclusion and, in the presence of the 'new objectivity of pure technicality', it now is the jurists' turn 'to receive the injunction to be silent'. Thus, *Silete, theologi!* is replaced by *Silete, iuriconsulti!*

---

73 For these questions, see Schmitt, *Ex Captivitate Salus* and *Der Nomos der Erde im Völkerrecht des Jus Publicum Europæum*.

Behold two singular orders to be silent, at the beginning and at the end
of an epoch. At the beginning there is an injunction to be silent that
comes from the jurists and is addressed to the Just War theologians. At
the end there is the injunction, aimed at the jurists, to follow a pure,
that is totally profane, technicalness.[74]

The pessimistic tone of *Ex Captivitate Salus* echoes in many of
the motifs of Schmitt's thought after the Second World War. 'The
epoch of the great philosophical systems has now been left behind',
we read in the preface to the 1963 reissue of *Der Begriff des
Politischen*.[75] Today only two styles of thought are possible: a retro-
spective historical glance (which reflects the great epoch of
Continental public law) and the aphoristic style. Since it is impossible for a jurist to make the 'leap into the aphorism', the first 'way
out' becomes obligatory.[76] This is what Schmitt attempts in *The
Nomos of the Earth*, which can be considered his greatest work.

The fundamental concepts of Western jurisprudence – the
'political' and the state – are framed and related to the development of the *Nomos*. With his theory of the *Nomos*, Schmitt offers
to delineate the primary prerequisites of all law. It is no longer,
however, a matter of the positive law of modern jurisprudence but
of a kind of primitive law, which is accessible from a metalegal
and tendentially anthropological viewpoint. The essential coordinates of this primordial are those of the pair *Ordnung/Ortung*
(order/location). In other words, there is no law without land (the
iustissima tellus), since all law rests on the cardinal presuppositions of territorial acquisition and spatial order. Based on a radical
etymological hypothesis stated in his 1959 essay 'Nomos Nahme
Name', Schmitt has the Greek noun *nómos* derive from the verb
némein, in its triple meaning: to take/conquer, to partition/divide
and to cultivate/produce. These three meanings are said to correspond to as many primary modes of acting and social existence as
can be encountered in all the phases and all the orders of history.
In this way the existential motif of the concrete ordering presents
itself once more. In the course of the development of Schmitt's
thought, this problematic takes a form that is yet more primary
and profound than the 'polemological' one (centred on the concept
of the 'political') and the nihilistic one (turning on the category of
'decision'). In his 1934 essay on the three kinds of legal thought,

---

74   Schmitt, *Ex Captivitate Salus*, p. 75.
75   Schmitt, *Theorie des Partisanen*, p. 11.
76   Schmitt, *Ex Captivitate Salus*, p. 81.

Schmitt had already forcefully relativised the 'decisionist' kind, seeing it as an interface of the 'normative' kind and tracing it back to the seabed of an institutional and 'orderly' vision. It is interesting to note how, anticipating a *leitmotiv* of anti-decisionist criticism, he lucidly stated in this text that 'pure decisionism presupposes *disorder* that is transmuted into *order* due simply to the fact *that* a decision is made (it does not reveal *how* the decision is formed)'.[77]

Looking at the results of Schmitt's complex – and not always consistent – itinerary, the theme that must be emphasised here, is that concerning the conceptual pair that supports the diagnosis of the *globale Zeit*, or 'planetary era', in *The Nomos of the Earth*; namely, 'earth' and 'sea'. In the light of the eternal affair of earth and sea, we can find an explanation not only for the point of arrival of the *ius publicum* but, also, for the course of the modern itself and for its most unequivocal manifestation, the industrial revolution. The *ius publicum* runs aground on the ascertainment of the technical-neutral euthanasia of the 'mortal God', the Leviathan state, and with the underlining of its specific consequences, such as the dissemination of the friend/enemy polarity and the emergence of new figures of 'the political', such as the 'partisan'. The global framework produced by this revolution – the unification of the world under the domination of a planetary technology – is, for Schmitt, understandable only through the opposition between land and sea. The true cosmic-historical turn to Modernity took place when, at the end of the sixteenth century, Britain detached itself not only strategically but culturally from the destinies of the continent to undertake its own adventure on the seas. The effect of this detachment is that the 'ancient, purely terrestrial *nomos*'[78] was replaced by a 'new *nomos* that included the oceans in its own order'.[79] From then onward, all 'further pushes towards the cosmos by an unstoppable technique' – wrote Schmitt in an important dispute with Ernst Jünger in 1955 – have only 'meant turning the star where we live, the Earth, into a spaceship'.[80]

It is certainly true that, despite its ostentatious and, at times, self-satisfied radicalness, this diagnosis is anything but resigned

---

77   Carl Schmitt, *Über die drei Arten des rechtswissenschaftlichen Denkens*, §2.

78   Carl Schmitt, 'Die geschichtliche Struktur des heutigen Welt-Gegensatzes von Ost und West'.

79   Ibid., pp. 165–67.

80   Schmitt, *Ex Captivatate Salus*, p. 75.

about the possibilities of relaunching the classical themes of the
'political' and of Order in the heart of the *globale Zeit*, perhaps in
the form of a new historical-dialectical synthesis of earth and sea.
Such a possibility becomes real by the fact that technology has
definitively saturated space. For that reason, today's 'appeal from
history' is no longer 'identical to that of the epoch in which the
oceans were opened'.[81] All this is true.

Yet, in the final analysis, the underlying tone of Schmitt's
thought remains pessimistic. It is basically no different from the
psychological attitude that had taken shape thanks to the wisdom
from his years in prison. This attitude, lying between pride and
nostalgia, was dictated by his acute recognition that he was the
'last' in a great tradition; the final witness and spokesman for a
greatness that was inexorably nailed to the past:

> Every situation has its secret and every science bears in itself its own
> *Arcanum*. I am the last conscious representative of the *ius publicum*
> *Europæum*. The last to have taught and investigated in an existential
> sense and be living out the end just as Benito Cereno lived out his
> voyage on the pirate ship. Here it is well and it is time to be silent. We
> must not be frightened of it. By being silent, we remember ourselves
> and our divine origin.[82]

---

81 Schmitt, 'Die geschichtliche Struktur des heutigen Welt-Gegensatzes von
Ost und West', pp. 165–67.
82 Schmitt, *Ex Captivatate Salus*, p. 75.

5

GIFT, EXCHANGE, OBLIGATION: KARL POLANYI AND SOCIAL PHILOSOPHY

Beyond the State and the Market

To get to the bottom of the problems of the 'political' and of the gap between technology and values that characterise it today, we will need to adopt a perspective beyond the state-market coupling.

For the most part, this theoretical and methodological assumption is drawn from the work of Karl Polanyi. In this chapter, we shall attempt to approach his work from the perspective of 'social philosophy'. We will take our cue from the themes for which Polanyi has become famous: the comparative analysis of the diverse ancient and archaic economic systems. Polanyi is an intrepid thinker. His inquiry winds along the borderline between different areas of influence and distinct disciplinary territories: history and 'science of culture', social theory and economic anthropology. We will initially draw these themes together on the basis of the results provided by the reception of his celebrated work *The Great Transformation*, which was dedicated to the passage of the Western economy from the system of the 'self-regulated market' in the 1800s to the 'organised capitalism' of the 1930s. We will then demonstrate that the two lines of investigation are interdependent and interact with one another.

The aim of this chapter is to gauge the possibility of taking up again the fundamental categories of Polanyi's investigation – 'gift' and 'exchange', 'political obligation' and 'social bond' – from the perspective of a social and political philosophy capable of transcending the classic modern hendiadys of market and state. Even if the dichotomies that turn on this couple are – on following Polanyi's work – thought to be secondary forms of sociality, the modern philosophical and political debate, and the theoretical-economic one as well, appears largely polarised by the opposition between state and market, and by the false alternatives or pendulum swings to which it gives rise. A good example of this is the ongoing discussion on privatisation as a response to the crisis of the welfare state. The therapies proposed seem to make way for an ideological division between the champions of the state and those of the market. The problematic of a difficult choice and decision appears to result in a drastic either/or between a social configuration of the economy regulated by state authority and one where privatisations are said to establish a free-market society that is emancipated from bureaucratic-administrative tutelage, as well as from the fiscal bonds of the 'great Leviathan'. What escapes the 'current' debate is that the important element – i.e., the properly political dimension – is situated between the state and the market. Hannah Arendt diagnosed a 'public sphere' caught in the pincer composed by the poles of the Leviathan state, with its centralised institutions, and civil society, reduced to the sphere of production and labour, to a system of needs and mercantile competition. Still today (and perhaps more so than yesterday) this appears as a literal and faithful account of our political present. Therefore, to posit the need to overcome the dichotomy of state and market is to question the real factors that make up the social bond. It involves one going in search of that *primary institution* of society that is the presupposition of any form of conventional institution – be it 'artificial' or 'contracted' – and thus of the Leviathan itself. That is, of the state understood in terms of its modernity, constructed in accordance with the formal criteria of the *ius publicum*. The logic of institutionalisation must be understood as a process whose roots are buried in a social bond whose *normativity* operates on a much deeper level than that of the practices that institute the social contract, or of the codes and formal rules that guide action and its *rationality*. Polanyi's perspective aims to pierce the screen of rationality in order to grasp the dynamic that operates behind it, silently supporting and nourishing it.

Overcoming the antithesis or the complementary duality of market and state goes hand in hand with the theoretical need – felt in many areas today – to rethink the question of community in relation to the status of the modern individual. In so doing, the classical contraposition of individualism and holism is overcome as well. A preliminary clarification is necessary at this stage. The thesis that I am about to state does not merely gloss and integrate Polanyi's argument but – rather – *puts it in question*. As Alfredo Salsano has correctly observed, the relation between the state and market society is never theorised adequately by Polanyi. One could – to be provocative – assert that the specifically modern market (characterised by the 'invisible hand') is literally unthinkable without the legal regulative and administrative *dispositifs* established by the sovereignty of the state and by the system of relations that has emerged between sovereign states. Absolutism and mercantilism are coeval. Colbert would not have been conceivable without a Sun King. An all-too-familiar ideology of our time – widespread not only in economics but also in mainstream political science – exalts the thaumaturgy of an undifferentiated market, reduced to an amorphous notion, forgetting (and leading us to forget) that the market has always been a 'determinate market' and that the modern capitalist market is nothing but one of the diverse forms of market that have successively arisen in the course of the history of human societies.

Pressing our provocation further, we could add that the current global age, far from sanctioning the triumph of liberal-competitive rationality, appears to be marked by a *crisis of the market* provoked – to be precise – by the crisis of that sovereign nation state which had made possible, through its *dispositifs* of internal and international rules, the birth and development of a historically 'determinate' market, *rationalised* in the form of the contract, i.e., of the exchange between abstract, legally 'free' and 'equal' subjects. In short, in the current process of globalisation we discover a mercantile arena over which the uncertainty of law and the precariousness of rules reign supreme. So neither the 'heaven on Earth' of the market that brings history to an end nor the spectre of World Government is able to provide us with the cipher of the new phase. It is marked, rather, by a competitive game between financial capital unchained from productive processes and allocated in 'real time' from one point to the other of the planet. New, frequently anonymous powers operate incalculable concentrations of 'nomadic' money over which the single states, including the United States of America, are – literally – powerless. Neo-liberal apologetics, which even appears to have taken root in some sectors of political philosophy, should take lessons in disenchantment from the most lucid operators of international finance. Were it do so, it would quickly learn – from the words of Joseph Stiglitz or, even, of George Soros – that the pervasive reigning rhetoric of the 'global' is based upon a false premise: that the activity of private capital, once this has been liberated from the institutional ties and bindings, spontaneously adjusts the dynamic of the system towards a stable point of equilibrium. In reality, as was demonstrated only a few years ago by the South-East Asian stock market crisis, the exact opposite is true. The system tends towards instability. Moreover, this instability comes not from the outside but from the inside. It is not the product of some 'exogenous' trauma. It depends, instead, on factors that are in each and every way 'endogenous', innate to the physiology of the system of international markets and exchanges in the current *interregnum* between the old inter-state framework and a new framework that has yet to be defined. The idea that the 'free market' tends naturally towards equilibrium comes from classical political economy. As the experts in the field know all too well, experience demonstrates that this may be true as far as ordinary goods are concerned but not for financial markets. The instability of this type of market depends upon the importance assumed by the psychological element of expectations. The most sophisticated economic theories, those that have been accustomed to draw on the results of anthropology and other social sciences, have for some time indicated the decisive function of symbolic factors in the dynamic of the market – I am thinking above all, but not exclusively, of the works of Albert O. Hirschman. A reflexive feedback effect that modifies the course of things interferes in all human behaviour. The 'reflexivity' inherent to the symbolic dimension of expectation assumes a particular degree of intensity precisely in financial markets. Our expectations concerning the future influence the current value of money, of stocks and shares at the very time they are exchanged. But precisely because expectations escape quantification, it follows that financial markets can oscillate far beyond equilibrium and never rebalance.

The philosophy of a major market operator such as George Soros thus appears more disenchanted and penetrating than that of many 'professional philosophers'.

> There is much talk about imposing market discipline, but if imposing market discipline means imposing instability, how much instability can society take? Market discipline needs to be supplemented by another discipline: maintaining stability in financial markets ought to be the objective of public policy. This is the general principle that I should like to propose.
> Despite the prevailing belief in free markets this principle has already been accepted and implemented on a national scale. . . . But we are sadly lacking in the appropriate financial authorities in the

international arena. We have the Bretton Woods institutions – the IMF and the World Bank – which have tried valiantly to adapt themselves to rapidly changing circumstances. Admittedly, the IMF programs have not been successful in the current global financial crisis; its mission and its methods of operation need to be reconsidered. I believe additional institutions may be necessary.[1]

Despite the technocratic illusion that can be detected in this final proposal, Soros' diagnosis posits three demands that are difficult to escape:[2] 1) a differential analysis of the market form; 2) the observance of the 'non-mercantilist' presuppositions of the regulation and functioning of the market; 3) the critique of the paradigm of equilibrium understood as the natural vocation of the free market. This last motif – the disenchantment concerning the 'self-regulated market' – brings us back to the theme that lay at the heart of Polanyi's analysis of the 'great transformation'.

The Great Transformation was composed in 1944 but, as Michele Cangiani has correctly noted, it was assimilated only much later. It is little consolation that the thirty-year delay in the appearance of an Italian edition is less than the forty-year delay in the French translation. Nonetheless, in this case the date of publication is not unimportant to the fate of the work. Given the time it was published in Italy, 1974, it is entirely natural that it became – for the most part – incorporated into the debate on 'neo-corporativism' and 'corporatist pluralism' that, at that time, was particularly intense. This created enormous problems of an interpretive and historiographical order. The motifs that were emphasised to bring the analysis up to date meant that the overall design of the work was overlooked. Conceived as an interpretation of the origins of our time within the mitteleuropean milieu of the great Viennese culture, the Vienna of the exchange between diverse cultural and disciplinary languages, the author linked those origins (following a periodisation that was not at all obvious or, as we shall see, painless) to the period between the wars. Cangiani has observed that the book is characterised by the will to contest the neo-liberal tendencies of Hayek and Schumpeter's theorisation of neo-classical democracy of the time, in a sort of transatlantic continuation of the celebrated Viennese disputes. George Dalton underlined how Polanyi was, fundamentally,

---

1   George Soros, *The Crisis of Global Capitalism*, p. xvi.

2   Incidentally, at the start of *The Crisis of Global Capitalism*, Soros announces that he has reread Polanyi's *The Great Transformation*.

captivated by two great problems throughout his investigations. The first was that of the origin, growth and transformation of capitalism in the nineteenth century. The second problem was, more generally, that of the relation between economy and society. The centrality of this latter theme shows Polanyi's connection with another great social scientist of the 1900s, Max Weber, although they are distinguished by their distinct interpretations of the link between economy and society in primitive and ancient cultures. A first set of difficulties arises here. To speak of primitive *and* ancient systems brings us to a peculiarity of Polanyi's path of investigation. He argued that the ancient phases of Western culture are able to furnish important interpretive results when compared to so-called primitive cultures, which form the object of anthropology. The core of the thesis consists in the equal treatment given to 'ancient' and 'primitive', historical distance and cultural distance, that is, by defining the distant peoples studied by ethnologists in the same way as ancient peoples 'contemporaneous with us'. The theoretical weight given to this analogy gives us the measure of the divergence between Polanyi's and Weber's 'comparativism'. Although Weber robustly underlines the exceptionalism of Occidental culture in comparison to other cultures, he also maintains that its 'singularity' – as we saw in the first chapter – does not begin with the modern. Rather, it has its origins in those typical features of *okzidentaler Rationalismus*, the early signs of which he glimpsed in the ancient world (Greek *logos*, Jewish prophecy, Roman legal rationalism). We will come back to this aspect, which is crucial in so many ways. Returning to Polanyi, it is important to note that the two thematic axes that we identified as central to his work – the enquiry into the origin, growth and transformation of nineteenth-century capitalism, and the examination of the relationship between economy and society in primitive and ancient systems – are strictly interdependent. Indeed, when we observe Polanyi's intellectual development, we see how the comparative analysis of ancient and archaic systems has the function of clarifying the present, i.e., what was happening in the contemporary world with the crisis of industrialisation. In his eyes, this crisis constituted an epochal threshold that was able to elucidate the sense of the decline of the ideology of the self-regulated market itself, that is, of that doctrine of *laissez-faire* which represented the compendium and cipher of nineteenth-century, Victorian-Mancunian, capitalism. In one of his most important articles, 'Our Obsolete Market Mentality' (1947), Polanyi underlined that the fundamental problem is that of understanding how the exit from industrialisation can result in a new technological framework that is not destructive of the environment but that is able to merge with and adapt to the needs of human existence. It is not easy to discover such a precocious sign of the ecological thematic, even for someone who is used to interdisciplinary raids. Returning to our problem: can these two poles of Polanyi's work be defined in terms of a 'short wave' and a 'long wave'? The short wave – relatively short anyway, since we are talking of one hundred and fifty years of history, that is, of the period that begins with the start of industrialisation until the end of the hundred years' peace that is marked by the outbreak of the First World War – coincides with the parabola of 'liberal-competitive' capitalism and what Polanyi considered to be a veritable utopia more than an ideology: the idea of a self-regulated market that was able to stabilise itself with autonomous and independent rational *dispositifs*. This market, according to Polanyi, goes definitively into crisis in 1929. The Wall Street Crash drags down with it the 'great illusion' of maintaining the stability of productive growth without some form of regulation. By examining the Great Crash, Polanyi raises – with a display of radicalism unknown to the 'enlightening' debates of our day – a problem that Keynes had already posed when analysing the first years of Soviet Russia. He asked himself if the drive for acquisition and earning can truly be considered a natural disposition of humanity. A crucial aspect comes into view here, one that tends to be casually overlooked or to become ideologically rigid in the work of today's economic theorists. The question raised by Keynes was worthy of a classic of political economy. By posing it, the Bloomsbury Group economist was touching the confines [*i confini*] of economics and ethics – political economy and moral philosophy – raising the question, as Adam Smith did, of the deep anthropological roots of political economy. Does something exist that, by its persistence and homogeneity, is able to support the definition of 'human nature'? If it exists, to what extent can we legitimately affirm that it is univocally characterised by egotism, by the acquisitive drive, the propensity to earn and the pure maximisation of profit? These are – practically letter for letter – Polanyi's questions. They are the crucial questions underpinning the 'long wave' of his analysis.

Economy and Society: Karl Marx and Max Weber

The attention paid to the long wave – to the thousand-year-old relationship between economy and society, within which the liberal market economy represents nothing but a segment or episode – leads Polanyi to an enquiry into the meaning of 'modern capitalism' in accordance with the developments of the social science of his day. It is the same question asked by Marx and Weber, Sombart and Schumpeter, and all the great social scientists of the 1800s-1900s. *What is 'modern capitalism'?* In the same way as his illustrious predecessors, Polanyi looks for an answer *per differentiam* – in his case through a comparison with ancient and primitive societies. We will see this more clearly below. But before we do so, let us pause to consider this short wave for a little longer.

We have already hinted at the controversial aspects of the peri-odisation proposed by the Hungarian theorist. Situating the 'great transformation' in the 1930s has raised a number of lively reac-tions amongst historiographers. The sharpness of the disagreements can be explained by the size of the stakes of Polanyi's thesis. Does the rupture consist in the First World War or in the 1929 Crash? If the 'hundred years' peace' concludes with the First World War – as Polanyi maintains – should the rupture not be situated there? The dilemma affects the interpretation of a decisive moment of recent history [*storia contemporanea*] that still concerns us today: the shift from the framework of the 1920s to that of the 1930s. Depending on the different periodisations, we can – to this day – still hear the echo of two distinct and contrasting interpretive choices echo in the 'conflict of interpretations' concerning the traits of the twentieth century. Consider, for example, the recent dispute around the notion of 'short century' or 'long century' that followed the publication of Eric J. Hobsbawm's book. In brief, those who privilege the 1930s – like Polanyi and many other thinkers, amongst whom we can mention Georges Bataille or, on other grounds, Hannah Arendt – identified the hermeneutic key for the interpretation of the twentieth century in the concept of 'totalitarianism'. Those, on the other hand, who privilege the 1920s focus their attention on the notion of 'mass society'. If the break lies in the constitution of mass society, the 1920s, with the emergence of the middle classes and the 'corporatist pluralist' articulation of the interests that typify them, constitute a decisive exit from the dichotomous 'classist' structure of nineteenth-century capitalism. A good example of this second approach is provided by a work that was published in Italy at much the same time as *The Great Transformation*, namely the American historian Charles S. Maier's *Recasting Bourgeois Europe*. The comparative analysis it rested upon – concentrating on three cases, Germany, France and Italy – focused upon the decade that followed the end of the First World War, namely 1918 to the crisis in 1929.

What are the advantages and what are the risks of situating the break in the 1930s? Without a shadow of a doubt the advantage consists in signalling the strategic significance of the New Deal and of the so-called Keynesian State (although, as is well known, Keynes had no time for Roosevelt's policy). Then again, making the break absolute involves a somewhat risky consequence: the assimilation – under the rubric of 'politics of the masses' – of diverse regimes, such as fascism, Nazism, Stalinism and the New Deal. The new phase, characterised by the intervention of the state and by the inclusion of the masses within the political-institutional dynamic, would thereby end up exhibiting two divergent results: on the one hand, the theme of Keynesianism and the New Deal, typically thought of as the apex of the twentieth century; on the other, its perverse double, totalitarianism (a category as comprehensive as it is generic, such that it is able to include national-socialist and fascist dictatorships, as well as the Soviet or Stalinist one). There is no doubt that this line of interpretation is still prevalent. Today we witness a revival of what Franz Neumann, in strongly critical terms, called *Totalitarismustheorie*, the theory of totalitarianism. Although this is the dominant line of interpretation, already in the 1970s some historians questioned whether this obsessive concentration on the category of totalitarianism did not result in one losing sight of certain essential differences and distinctions – for example, between the fascist regime and the Nazi one, and between both of these dictatorships and Stalinism – and by so doing, hiding one decisive element: the 'great transformation' that invests the state in the thirties does not annul but, rather, introjects the pluralistic-conflictual framework that the thirties had inherited from mass society of the twenties. The adoption of *Pluralismustheorie* as hermeneutic key was mediated by the return of the idea, which in part can be traced back to Franz Neumann's *Behemoth*, according to which the very dynamic of the dictatorships is conditioned – in its very foundation – by a precarious equilibrium between different 'bodies' and power blocs in reciprocal conflict. On this interpretation, the resulting war turns out to be nothing other than the inevitable projection outwards of contradictions that appear irresolvable within each single regime. Were we to continue with this 'deconstruction' of the concept of totalitarianism – which turns on Hobbes' dichotomy of Leviathan and Behemoth – we would have to conclude that the return today of *Totalitarismustheorie* finds itself subject to the serious risk of becoming ideological. Many contemporary readings of the work of Hannah Arendt appear to move in this direction. These develop an interpretation of twentieth-century mass society that is dangerously generic when compared to the terms in which the problem was posed in the great work of Neumann on the structure of National Socialism, which has influenced the work of some historians and social scientists in the 1970s and 1980s.

We come now to the crucial question underpinning the 'long wave' in Polanyi's work: the definition of modernity and of modern capitalism. His thesis appears as the exact opposite – although not necessarily the antithesis – of Max Weber's. To conclude, I shall try to explain why this reversal of Weber's position can be summed up – in terms different from Polanyi's own – as the privileging of the optics of normativity in contrast to that of rationality. Whereas the social sciences have, to this day, shaped their standards of rationality on the model of action-towards-an-end which was essentially economic (based upon the utilitarian cost/benefit analysis), Polanyi understands the social import of the economic normatively.

We shall set aside, for now, the distinction between rationality and normativity, and turn to an analysis of the way that Polanyi confronts one of the *topos* of twentieth-century philosophy and social science: the parallel between Karl Marx and Max Weber. In his view, Marx's limit consists in his ignoring that the economic is dominant only in capitalist society. In a section, significantly entitled 'Economy and Society', of the collection of Polanyi's essays edited by George Dalton,[3] he writes: 'The discovery of the importance of the "economic" under a market economy induced him to overstress the influence of the economic factor generally, at all times and places. This proved a grave mistake'.[4] If this was Karl Marx's error, what was Weber's? The answer is equally significant. Weber's limit consists in his considering the economic through a lens provided for him by Marx. This identification of a limitation involves no desire to denigrate. Indeed, Weber shares

---

3   Karl Polanyi, *Primitive, Archaic and Modern Economies*.
4   Ibid., p. 134.

the Marxian influence with the main non-Marxist social scientists of his time: from Ferdinand Tönnies to Werner Sombart, and Franz Oppenheimer to Karl Lamprecht. But in Weber this conditioning has a paradoxical outcome. Weber accepts, at least heuristically, the primacy of the economic. However, being convinced of the supremacy of the market system, his attitude is not Marxist but 'marketist'. Paradoxically, therefore, Weber's 'marketism' is said to stem directly from Marx's description of capitalism. According to Polanyi, the inescapable ambiguity of Weber's notion of the 'economic', which is characterised by an unresolved oscillation between a substantive and a formal meaning of the term, follows from this.

To grasp the sense of this last distinction it is necessary to turn to the important article 'Economy as Instituted Process', in which Polanyi distinguishes the two senses of 'economic'. He relates the substantive sense to the natural bond, that is, to the procurement of the means for the satisfaction of natural needs. The formal sense he relates to rules. In the strict sense, only action is 'rational' for Weber. In the case in point, only *zweckrational* economic behaviour, i.e., rational in relation to an end or strategic-instrumental behaviour is rational. Between the two senses of the 'economic' there is the same distance that separates the realm of 'subsistence' from that of 'rules'. The indicator of the ambivalence is given in the core of Weber's thesis, which presupposes the two-way relation between the economic and the rational: rationality is always economic; there is no possibility of a project outside of *oikonomía*, of a calculating *ratio*. We touch upon a very delicate matter here. Weber does not criticise Marx's historical materialism for having put the economy at the centre of things, but for the 'monist' pretence of having deduced from it general laws, cancelling from the concept of 'the economy' its fertile tension with the ethical moment from which the dimension of rationality springs. According to Polanyi, the bond between the economic and the rational does little else but reflect the situation of capitalist economics. It is unable to operate as general principle. Thus, it is precisely Weber's presumption of 'universality' that makes his schema inadequate to economic history.

Having said this, we must ask, did Weber really take the stand that Polanyi ascribes to him? This is a crucial question, one whose implications enable us, amongst other things, to begin an examination of Polanyi's interpretation of the gift and exchange. In our view, the answer can be answered only negatively. The impression is that this reading of Weber is not far away from the sociological vulgate that has traditionally privileged his *Wirtschaft und Gesellschaft* over his other works. However, the structure of this work – which is the result, as is well known, of an assiduous but questionable operation of 'montage' by his student Johannes Winckelmann – is certain to be completely taken apart in the labours around the *Max Weber Gesamtausgabe*. Aside from the historical and philological significance of this event, it must be recalled that, already by the late 1950s, and then more intensely in the 1970s and 1980s, a new course of research emerged in Germany and the United States that contributed to shifting the centre of gravity of the interpretations of Weber from the *Wirtschaft und Gesellschaft* to the *Religionssoziologie*. The principal figures of this new line of enquiry range from Wolfgang Mommsen to Friedrich Tenbruck, from Reinhard Bendix to Wolfgang Schluchter and to Habermas himself. In this context, a decisive turn in the theoretical reconstruction of Weber's work as a whole (and of the whole comparative framework that supports it) is without question constituted by Schluchter's *Die Entwicklung des okzidentalen Rationalismus*. What is the common denominator, the hermeneutic quality that characterises this new line of enquiry and, particularly, this last work? The salient fact, above and beyond their different trajectories, for both Weber and Polanyi, is the exceptionalism of modern Western culture. It is worth repeating that such a thesis follows from an eminently comparative conception, which can be derived more clearly from *Religionssoziologie* than from *Wirtschaft und Gesellschaft*. But there is a crucial difference. For Weber, modern capitalism, characterised by the universalisation of the *Zweckrationalität* (of a rationality-of-ends), does not so much represent an episode, as Polanyi maintains, so much as the high point and the point of arrival of Western rationalism. In other words, Western rationalism forms a continuous arc whose parabola constitutes, in its entirety, an exception, a *unicum* when compared to all other cultures. Both in the *Vorbemerkung*[5] and in the celebrated *Zwischenbetrachtung* of the *Religionssoziologie*,[6] Weber never uses the phrase 'only in modernity'. Instead, he repeatedly adopts the much more telling expression 'only in the West'. Consequently,

---

5 *Translator's note*: translated in English as the 'Preface' to Max Weber, *The Protestant Ethic and the Spirit of Capitalism*.
6 Max Weber, *Gesammelte Aufsätze zur Religionssoziologie*, vol. 1.

for Weber, the 'singularity' is not constituted only by 'modern civilisation' but by Western culture itself, whose genetic make-up is constituted by three fundamental elements: the Greek *logos*, the *ratio* of Roman law and Jewish prophecy. It is these traits that constitute, in their interweaving and reciprocal combination, the 'differential' that turns the Occident into a *unicum* amongst human cultures. To sum up, whereas for Polanyi the exceptional character of the modern is formed by the peculiar dominance assigned to the 'economic' (which separates it not only from other cultures but also from its own ancient and archaic past), in Weber the exception affects, from its very origin, the entire orbit of *okzidentaler Rationalismus* insofar as it forms a general process of secularisation and 'disenchantment of the world'. From the Weberian perspective, rationality is not an autonomous value relating to some form of self-sufficiency of the economic, but is, rather, a variable dependent upon an excess. We will see more clearly later in what way this *topos* of symbolic excess is important for Polanyi as well. For the present, it is enough to bear in mind that, whereas the Polanyian 'excess' is led back to the dimension of the sacred and to the persistence of the rites of exchange modelled on the gift, the Weberian 'excess' – the genetic site of the 'singularity' of the production of the Occident's 'deviation' – consists in the paradox inherent to the *Entzauberung*, that is, the paradox of a disenchantment that, in its advance, represses its origin, letting the irrational presuppositions of rationality fall into oblivion.

For Weber, the disenchantment of the world is – in contrast to Polanyi – a phenomenon of desacralisation and deritualisation. The practical conduct of life and the fundamental ethical and religious attitudes which this disenchantment induces upset ritual organisation and perpetually uproot social bonds. In this sense, Jewish prophecy lies at the origin of the process of disenchantment manifested in modern science's '*Entseelung der Natur*'.[7] Furthermore, this process finds in the Calvinist ethic and the puritan ethic of sects the fundamental energetic transformer enabling Western rationalism to turn its singularity into a generalised dominion, thereby producing the paradoxical dynamic of a unity that generalises itself.

---

7   Ernst Cassirer, 'Zur Logik der Kulturwissenschaften'.

'Aristotle was right': the Critique of Modern Individualism

In diametric opposition to Weber, Polanyi tries – as in a chemical experiment – to isolate the elements of the modern market economy from the great riverbed of the general economy of human societies 'normally' regulated by excess. The horizon in which his conception is situated is the one delimited by the themes of that great ethno-anthropology that starts with Marcel Mauss' *Essai sur le don* (1923–1924) and is then developed theoretically by the Collège de Sociologie in the course of the 1930s. It is no coincidence that, in recent years, the French anti-utilitarian school has had a leading role in the Polanyi revival. However, I wish to distance myself from the theses avowed by MAUSS (*Mouvement anti-utilitariste dans les sciences sociales*) for two sets of reasons. First, because I am not convinced that Polanyi's work provides a final resolution to the relationship of the market and other forms of social bond, such as obligation. Second, because I most certainly do not believe that the alternatives within contemporary social and political theory can be derived from the antithesis between utilitarian and non-utilitarian. While generally sharing with Alain Caillé and others behind the *Revue du Mauss* the need for a critique of the utilitarian paradigm of rationality, I believe that their 'anti-utilitarianism' does not so much constitute an alternative, as the other side of the coin of utilitarianism. One will never resolve the problem by opposing to the republic of exchange the realm of the gift. As I hinted at the beginning, it is necessary instead to confront the difficult choice between rationalism and normativity. I will come back to this aspect – which is decisive for the reconstruction of the concept of 'social philosophy' – in the final comments of this chapter. Before doing so, let us try to reconstruct the later passages of Polanyi's enquiry.

The fecundity of Polanyi's perspective consists in underlining, in the face of the international debate's drift towards veritable religions of the market, that the exchange relation is nothing but one of the factors that compete in the determination of the complexity of the social dynamic. Today, 'our obsolescent market mentality' in its desperate attempt to reduce to unity a multiverse of ungovernable relationships appears to issue the worst of fundamentalisms. The ethnocentric prejudice that lies at the foundation of this mentality reproduces itself by assigning to the market an exclusive on universality. If one tries to indicate, today, where the universal resides, one falls back on the banal observation that we all drink Coca-Cola, that we all dress in more or less the same manner, etc. One can find more or less everywhere the paradoxical utopia that we can call – with Marc Augé – the universalism of non-places. It is as if rules, technologies, artifices, airports, golf courses, supermarkets, fast food and Coca-Cola could make different individuals, from different continents and cultures, equal and homologous. In the presence of this 'bad' universality, Polanyi shows us that in reality every market is a determinate one and that no form of market can, by itself, reduce to unity an entire pluriverse of socio-cultural differences. In reality, there has never been, in the history of the market, a market that was not a 'determinate market' (to use an expression that appears more than once in Gramsci's *Prison Notebooks* and that represents an important starting point for the critique of utilitarianism and of *homo œconomicus*). Every market is structured by different and heterogeneous dynamic factors within which the same functions play different roles. The fact that each system includes money – except for those based on barter – does not mean that money always plays the same role. The fact that in all systems there is exchange does not mean that it always plays the same role. Therefore, these categories, these containers, these forms should not be taken in the peremptory form of their definition. They must be understood in accordance with the specific variations that they assume in each system. The very function of the economy is not taken as invariable. It is defined in each instance within the dynamic of social relations, to the extent that each of the forms we are speaking of – money, exchange, market – far from constituting singular and unitary facts, represents instead a constellation, a complex of factors stemming from the same source.

Another characteristic motif of Polanyi's conception stems from this: his critique of modern individualism. Just as the indeterminate market, the individual 'without qualities' of the moderns is not only ideological but, above all, utopian. So Robinson Crusoe's world – the heart of bourgeois ideology – is pure utopia. That world is nothing other than the utopia of possessive individualism, that is, of that *homo œconomicus* that represents the anthropological referent of the modern market. Polanyi contrasts the idea of the social individual to the Crusoesque character of modern political economy, as does Marx. For Polanyi, individuals are not social only because they join together (although one must not forget Polanyi's significant assertion that 'Aristotle was right', Man is *zoon politikón*, is a social animal); individuals are social for a much deeper reason: because within each individual one finds a community. Each of us is like a theatrical cavity in which the voices of communitarian traditions that have moulded and constituted us echo. Therefore, all communities – including the individuals who are constituted only in community – are nothing but institutionalisations of the exchange-gift. I will say little more about Polanyi's critique of modern individualism, of the modern idea of individual sovereignty. Anticipating some of the arguments advanced by contemporary communitarianism and neo-Aristotelianism, Polanyi maintains that the modern affirmation of the absolute freedom and autonomy of the individual rests upon the presumption that the individual is independent of the communitarian dynamic that is alone responsible for constituting him or her. The liberal conception that presupposes the individual, which considers him or her to be already constituted instead of produced by an 'exogenic' (and not 'endogenic') process of constitution, ends up emptying the individual of meaning. By reducing the individual to an *á-tomon* – i.e., *individuum* – such a conception extrapolates from those links, those ties, those constitutive processes that alone are able to constitute him or her as an individual. It is important not to (mis)understand this critique as a devaluation of the individual in favour of the social or the collective. Polanyi is extremely interested in the fate of the individual, to the point of not wanting him impoverished to the extent of becoming pure abstraction or acquisitive marionette. In short, the valorisation of the individual is no different – as far as Polanyi is concerned – from the richness of social determinations that he or she is able to express. Naturally, when we assert that all the communities within which the individual constitutes herself – and that, at the same time, inhere in the individual – are institutionalisations of the exchange-gift, some extremely delicate problems of a theoretical, as well as semantic, nature arise.

One I will be able to mention only in passing: the problem of the convergence between the anti-utilitarian movement in the social sciences and the rehabilitation of practical philosophy. This convergence is evident, above all, in the emphasis with which the theme of social integration is underlined. It must not be forgotten that, for Polanyi, exchange, reciprocity and redistribution are fundamental forms of social integration. In other words, from his perspective the social bond assumes an absolute theoretical and conceptual priority. The signal of this priority is constituted by the theme of the exchange-gift, which forms the ground of the debate between Polanyi, Mauss and Bataille. It must not be forgotten that it is from Marcel Mauss himself that George Dalton drew the phrase placed as exergue to his introduction to *Primitive, Archaic and Modern Economies*, almost constituting a seal of approval of Polanyi's thought: 'It is only our Western societies that quite *recently* turned man into an economic animal'.[8] I have italicised the adverb precisely because it marks the distance between an approach such as that of Marcel Mauss (or Karl Polanyi) and that of Max Weber. The *incipit* of the phrase – with the expression 'only our Western societies' – appears to suggest an analogy with the celebrated adage of Weber's (which we considered above), '[o]nly in the West'.[9] With the addition of the adverb 'recently', Mauss provides the occasion for Polanyi's theme of the exceptionality represented by *homo œconomicus*: this exceptionality is a recent fact, a singularly modern event. Bataille understands this exceptionality in the same way, through the distinction between 'general economy' (characterised by phenomena of 'excess', like the gift and sacrifice) and 'restricted economy' (characterised by typically modern phenomena of production and exchange). Indeed, his text from 1933, *The Notion of Expenditure*, constitutes a suggestive return to a philosophico-social reconversion of Mauss' ideas.

Bataille poses the problem of the normality of unproductive expenditure and the exceptionalism of the productive project. In other words, the productive project is an exception in the course of human society while unproductive expenditure is its resplendent norm. For Bataille, 'normality' is positive precisely insofar as it is the normality of excess. It is modernity which renders that excess *extravagant* through a disciplining (that Caillois and, following him, Foucault would turn into the focus of their investigations) which relegates to/casts into the realm of perversion what previously was a resplendent norm: the unproductive expenditure, the continuous investigation of the most intense expressions of life and personality. The notion of unproductive 'expenditure' is understood by Bataille as the passage from the Hegelian restricted economy to what he calls 'general economy'. This is not the place to confront in detail the philosophical background of this operation. We shall merely signal the fundamental passages of the reading of Hegel that Bataille develops on the

8   Polanyi, *Primitive, Archaic and Modern Economies*, p. ix.
9   Max Weber, *The Protestant Ethic and the Spirit of Capitalism*.

basis of Kojève's analysis. This reading can be grasped in terms of the attempt to tear the negative away from the subordinate role it played within the logic of Hegelian supersession (*Aufhebung*).

In the modern project, as expressed by Hegelian philosophy, the negative has a 'servile' function. All power, all excess is somehow given a productive function. In the Hegelian dialectic, the servile nature of the negative resides in its being submitted to a logic of production and progress. But, argues Bataille, once it has been emancipated from this servile function, once it is torn away from the project, the negative magically returns to its sovereign dimension. Sovereignty consists in a type of constellation-like structure, which is not project-driven but is defined by the terms 'excess', 'sacrifice', 'death', 'gift'. For Bataille, the existence of a negative finally become absolute is what properly constitutes sovereignty; in literal terms, *ab-solutus*, unchained from all servile bonds, in-dependent from all types of projective function or end. Sovereignty is that which presents itself as excess without useful employment. Therefore, *dépense*, expenditure, is the marginal quantity of energy deployed but not employed by subjects. Sovereign energy is that which is deployed in existence, but which never allows itself to be employed for something, such as for the constitution of a product or an oeuvre. Thus, sovereignty is the absence of an oeuvre. Consider the influence of this Bataillian motif of 'inoperativity' on recent French thought's engagement with the notion of community (from Jean-Luc Nancy to Blanchot and Derrida). However, Bataille's thought has a singular double-edged force. It operates not only on the plane of philosophy but also on that of socio-anthropology. Or, rather, on the borderline that, paradoxically, is also conjuncture or shared border between the two approaches. By pushing the philosophical concepts to the limit one is led to the logical and symbolic presuppositions of social order. The same occurs when one touches upon the outer margin of sociological concepts. The spirit of the Collège de Sociologie was nothing if not this practice of the border.

Bataille himself draws attention to the 'sociological' implications of his thesis. Since the useless and unproductive deployment of energy is the 'normal' way societies are cemented, the folly of modern capitalist society consists in the idea of a project directed towards the suppression – that is, the 'overcoming' (*Aufhebung*) in dialectical sense – of unproductive expenditure by the productive project. But this utopia will do nothing but lead the project itself to its death. Thus, according to Bataille, at the heart of each of our existential experiences there operates that same unproductive energy that holds society together. The 'cement' is not the architecture projected by rational actors coming to an agreement through a contract, by means of a convention. On the contrary, society is held together by precisely those 'sovereign' expressions of existence that rationalist modernity despises or relegates to the ghetto: art, laughter, eroticism and so on.

The Paradoxes of the Gift: Polanyi, Mauss and 'diagonal sciences'

The connections with *Essai sur le don* are self-evident. This text, considered by many to be the greatest work of twentieth-century anthropology, is a book of Mauss' maturity. However, already with *Essai sur le sacrifice* – which he published with Hubert in 1899 at the age of twenty-seven – Mauss had lain the bases for his theory of the gift, positing the question of sacrifice as the exchange between sacred and profane mediated by the sacrificial victim. This theme would then return with that of '*mana*'. In *Essai sur le don*, Mauss investigates the forms taken by the exchange of gifts in different tribes. He recognised that these forms did not merely have a mercantile function, i.e., a function directed to an immediately economic end. Instead, the exchanges were symbolically dependent on the act of giving and counter-giving. The gift, because it bears with it an obligation, appears to Mauss as a foundational and autonomous element of the social bond. In other words, the significance of the gift consists in its creation of a constant circulation of objects without commercial value in accordance with precise procedures – the rules of rituals – whose only aim is that of establishing a bond between different groups. The theme of circulation is very important because it reveals how, depending on the gift, the structure of exchange is not an axial, rectilinear structure but, as Jacques Derrida has opportunely noted, a circle that describes the curved flight of the boomerang. As we have mentioned, this circuit is foundational of the social bond. What, however, guarantees the bond, the necessitating structure of the exchange which obligates one to the gift, that is, to the acceptance and restitution of the same gift? What is the energy that animates the circuit, the force that makes it move the hand that releases the boomerang? According to Mauss it is the power of *mana*, that same force that sustains the movement [*transito*] (once again, the exchange . . .) between sacred and profane. In the forms of exchange of archaic societies and in the so-called primitive societies that form the object of ethnology – for example, in the system of *potlàc* of certain indigenous populations of North America or in the exchange of goods of the Polynesian region, such as the *kula* described by Malinowski – it is a case of establishing what force is enclosed within the gift that makes the gift a force of obligation. Anticipating a theme that Polanyi would take up in almost identical form, Mauss argues that this force is not reducible to 'value'. That is, it goes beyond the exchanged objects, for it is itself the true (symbolic) motive of the exchange.

The distance separating archaic civilisations from modern society is to be measured entirely in these terms. Modern language is the language of value. It is a language that permeates even the realm of ethics and interpersonal relations. To us moderns, it appears entirely natural to identify morality with the 'sphere of values'. But 'value' is a term from economics. Therefore, modernity lives – to take up one of Carl Schmitt's favourite expressions – under the *Tyrannei der Werte*, the 'tyranny of values',[10] that is, where the economic and the market spheres infringe on the ethical sphere. Mauss anticipates another motif which Polanyi will discuss in a number of works: the obligating force is not reducible to value. It is precisely for this reason that the economy is not self-referential and that the self-sufficiency of the economic is mere utopia. People do not live together because they are hungry (as in the common prejudice of liberals and Marxists), they stay together for other reasons. Indeed, they live together despite the fact of being hungry. The force encapsulated in the gift and in the circuit of the gift is not reducible to material and economic value, because it is a symbolic force, it is a symbolic power. It is an energy, a *mana* that goes beyond the objects exchanged, because it is the true reason for the exchange.

Going beyond Mauss and, perhaps, Polanyi, we can ask ourselves if the fact that this force goes beyond the objects exchanged is true only of 'normal' societies or whether it is true of modern capitalist society as well; if it is not possible, in other words, that the energy continues to operate in the sense of a transcending of the value of goods as such as well, in the form of a

---

10   Carl Schmitt, 'Die Tyrannei der Werte'.

symbolic investment – as in the case of status symbols, for example. Such goods appear as a form of a social glue, i.e., as a paradoxical function of belonging and so as a type of stabilisation. But this is a difficult subject that it is not possible to discuss in depth here. Let us not forget, however, that for Mauss the first and fundamental 'unproductive' and 'obligating' exchange is, in all cultures without distinction, that with the gods and dead spirits. Thus, the anti-utilitarian dimension of the 'excess' remains the explicatory key of that event which we call 'society'.

This theme has been developed in an original manner within the Collège de Sociologie in the programme for a 'sacred sociology'. With this expression, Bataille and Caillois do not mean a religious sociology. The 'sacred' is understood, rather, in the rigorous sense of the term introduced by Bataille in an illuminating intervention at the seminars of the Collège and then by Caillois in *L'homme et le sacré*.[11] The '*sacred* character' is specific to 'everything in human existence that is *communifying*'.[12] Furthermore, the 'sociological' perspective which is able to detect in society something more and other than the sum of the individuals that constitute it can be termed 'sacred'. If we maintain that society cannot be reduced to the summation or mere assembling of the presumed individual atoms that compose it, then we are in the area of the sacred. The problem of the nature of the energy constitutive of the social bond has already been posed. Let us, however, read Bataille's definition in its entirety:

> [T]he question of the nature of society is inherent to any social science and particularly to the domain that we have designated by the name of sacred sociology. It would be impossible, therefore, and futile at the same time, to try to evade this question. Indeed, for us sacred sociology is not just a part of sociology as is, for example, religious sociology, with which it risks confusion. Sacred sociology may be considered the study not only of religious institutions but of the entire communifying movement of society. Hence, it regards power and the army, among other things, as its rightful object, and it contemplates all human activities – sciences, arts, and technology – insofar as they have a communifying value, in the active sense of the word, that is to say, insofar as they are the *creators* of unity.[13]

---

11 Roger Caillois, *Man and the Sacred.*

12 Georges Bataille and Roger Caillois, 'Sacred Sociology and the Relationships between "Society", "Organism", and "Being"', p. 74.

13 Ibid.

Whereas 'the whole present-day culture' goes no further than to 'add contracts to individuals', the perspective envisioned by sacred sociology identifies, instead, '*in addition* to the individuals who make up society . . . an overall movement that transforms nature'. Hence, we can understand the interest of thinkers such as Bataille and Caillois for those 'diagonal sciences' characterised by the ability to cross from one discipline to another, which would later be privileged by Polanyi. These sciences provide us with the key to the phenomenon of 'society'. The constitutive dynamic of the social is supported by an elementary yet latent structure that is not detectable empirically; by a symbolic energy whose excess of meaning is never entirely translatable in a system of meanings. To conclude: the symbolic dynamic that holds society together is never entirely translatable by a 'structure', although it fertilises and nourishes all the systems of rules and signs.

According to the socio-anthropological line of thought of Mauss-Polanyi-Sahlins, one need not start from rationality (and the different models of rationality of the agents) to explain society, as do Weber and methodological individualists who, thereby, submit to the hegemony of the economic that characterises the major schools in the social sciences of the 1800s and 1900s. The idea of society as the product of rational projects and actions does not explain the total social fact, but pretends to resolve it in a knotted web [*rete di intrecci*] of diverse intentionalities (whether strategic or cooperative, communicative or conflictual). Rather, to explain society one must set out from normativity, a latent, pre-reflexive normativity that regulates not only the processes of collective symbolic identification but also those of individual self-identification. In this regard one should recall that Mauss introduces into his work the question of the relationship between personal unconscious and collective unconscious. In this way he anticipates the theme of the instability of the borders between normality and madness, and in this manner, turns the latter into a dependent variable of the forms of institutionalisation of the 'normal'.

Before we conclude, I should like to take up again – in the light of what we have spoken of so far – the comparison between Weber and Polanyi. Whereas Weber privileges the perspective of rationality and Polanyi that of normativity, I do not believe that their conceptions are necessarily alternatives or exclusive of one another. Instead, they represent two sides of the same problem: that of how we understand the phenomenon of 'society'. The social dynamic is not only founded upon normativity but on projects as well. Therefore, normative and rational represent the two sides of the same coin of social integration. Those who emphasise the normative tend to privilege the element of binding and underestimate the element of conflict. Conversely, those who emphasise the rational tend instead to privilege the moment of conflict in terms of the competition between individuals, not realising that the same conflict – precisely insofar as it involves the recognition of the contending parties – presupposes a 'communifying movement'[14] anteceding all covenants (i.e., all conventions and contracts). In short, we could say that while Weber speaks of us, Polanyi speaks of the world, of reality or of the contexts in which we live and reproduce our symbolic – even more important than material – conditions of existence. Weber speaks of the way that the forms assumed by our projects and our everyday behaviours have been constituted in the course of centuries, through the phases of the evolution of Western rationalism. Polanyi refers to the great anthropological roots that nourish the different socio-economic systems, showing how the constitution of modern subjects and their behaviours stem not from a 'universal' standard but from an exception.

Weber would have shared this concept of the exception, insofar as he considered the paradox of Western universalism as a singularity that stretches over the world in a single form: the technical rationalisation of the forms of domination. The Occident is universal because it dominates by unifying; because it realises the universal in its very etymology. It casts everything into a single place, *universum*, as into a basket or bin. The Occident knows only one modality of the universal: that of domination. This domination has its root in a particular declension of rationality, which is even more central than the logic of power. Certainly, 'ships and cannons' also play their part, but the most effective armament that the Occident has been able to rely upon over the centuries has been without question its particular form of 'rationalism'. This depends – aside from technology and the economy – on the emergence of specific forms of 'practical-rational behaviours' that have no adequate parallels in other cultures. Even Weber would have had no difficulty in admitting that the behavioural attitudes of individuals from the modern Occident are not really universal but are, rather, the product of an exception that tends to project itself outside its place of birth, expanding across

---

14 Ibid.

the entire world. But, in contrast to Polanyi, he would never have relegated that exceptionalism to industrialism, which he defined as 'a precariously grafted scion upon man's age-long existence'.[15]

The phrase just quoted is drawn from the already mentioned article 'Our Obsolete Market Mentality', in which we had already discovered a significant anticipation of the environmentalist thematic. The problem, for Polanyi, is that of adapting the artifices of technology to the needs of human existence. Studying what precedes industrialism is the only means for anticipating and comprehending the framework destined to follow it, although Polanyi's prognosis is not at all optimistic:

> Our condition can be described in these terms: Industrial civilization may yet undo man. But since the venture of a progressively artificial environment cannot, will not, and indeed, should not, be voluntarily discarded, the task of adapting life *in such a surrounding* to the requirements of human existence must be resolved if man is to continue on earth. No one can foretell whether such an adjustment is possible, or whether man must perish in the attempt. Hence the dark undertone of concern.[16]

If we want to glimpse the future that awaits us, we will have to study what has already happened, retracing the stages and the constitutive moments. Polanyi's observation, formulated while keeping in view what precedes and what – presumably – will follow industrialism/isation, appears fruitful even with respect to the development of the modern state and its current dissolution. In my book *Dopo il Leviatano*, I attempted an analogous operation on the basis of the hypothesis that, in order to outline the possible contours of what awaits us after the state, one must reconstruct phase by phase, piece by piece, the history of its formation. The wager consists in conceiving the process of destructuring of the Leviathan like a film played backwards. As if the crisis of the Leviathan state could return in inverse order the bricks from which it was built: indirect powers, the corporations that have determined and structured it, the various ingredients of which its legal form and constitutional framework is made.

It is this that I believe constitutes the relevance of Polanyi today. Studying the before is useful to understand the afterwards, to understand the outlines of the global world that is being formed

---

15 Polanyi, *Primitive, Archaic and Modern Economies*, p. 60.
16 Ibid.

before our eyes. It is a world that we cannot view with the eyes of Robinson Crusoe or with those of Descartes. It is a world that, beyond the appearances and the ideological illusions *à la* Fukuyama, appears increasingly resistant to our 'obsolete market mentality'. It is a world that appears to escape the equations of modern universalism precisely because it is characterised by the paradox of the *glocal*: of a globalisation destined to increasingly flip into a new process of localisation (or – as often described in the unconsciously ethnocentric quality of our everyday language – of 'retribalisation'). To grasp the discontinuity of this world in relation to the 'first modernity', we will need to found a new comparativism – as Amartya Sen has, to some extent, already begun to do. This comparativism will need to take up Weber's great plan of a comparison between ethico-religious codes and economic behaviour. But it will also have to integrate it and correct it by accounting for a dynamic that is progressively uprooting the Occident from its hegemonic pedestal, shifting the centre of gravity of the world economy towards geocultural areas – such as China, India and South-East Asia – that traditionally shape cultural alterities that are irreducible to the table of values of modern individualism.

The centre of gravitation of theoretical interest shifts from the hendiadys or, rather, from the dichotomous tautology of state and market, to the nexus – and field of forces – of technology and values, economy and ethics. This is the simple but decisive reason for the current relevance of Polanyi's work of reconstruction of the concept of 'social philosophy', following the important efforts of the interwar period (that of the Parisian Collège de Sociologie and of the Frankfurt School). This contemporary relevance of his work asserts itself despite, or perhaps precisely in virtue of, the aporiae and limits that we have indicated.

After all, are we really so sure that the global era in which we happen to live does not represent a new, dramatic but fascinating chapter of the 'great transformation'?

6

UNIVERSALISM AND POLITICS OF DIFFERENCE: DEMOCRACY AS A PARADOXICAL COMMUNITY

Western Difference

Let us return to the core themes of our argument – technology and value in the 'global era' – from a standpoint that complements the one expounded in the first chapter: the paradoxes of universalism. As I shall argue particularly in the final section of this chapter, this is a demanding choice that involves the adoption of an unusual perspective compared with what commonly (or from the 'disciplinary' standpoint) is understood by 'political philosophy'. The theme of the paradoxes of universalism draws directly upon that *symbolic* and *cultural* dimension of the conflict of values that is generally repressed or considered secondary by the prescriptive models, namely neo-Utilitarianism and neo-Contractualism, which have dominated the 'doctrinal' field over recent years. Therefore, it is necessary to immediately specify that the expression the 'paradoxes of universalism' is adopted here in its most rigorous sense. It is not our intention to speak, generally, of contradictions, limits, perverse effects, counter-finalities, etc., but – literally – to speak of *paradoxes*. That is, of something that is in contrast with the *dóxa*, with current opinion and the commonsense view of 'universalism'. We will attempt to underline the tacit implications or the 'un-thought' (as one used to say) of universalism. This is a difficult operation to be carried out through a series of incisive and radical critical steps. However, we will not aim to denounce or eliminate the foundation of the universalist platform. We shall advance the *reasons* (plural) of universalism and its (this time in the singular) originary cultural *premise*, no less than its initial promise of emancipation. That its verification is not only essential, but even a necessary preliminary step on the way to the correct framing of the question (of which Steven

Lukes is so fond) 'What is left?' – in the dual sense – is so obvious that it is not worth dwelling on.[1]

On the rare occasions when political discourses transcend
concern with single issues by considering what causes them or what
they have in common, one encounters a curious phenomenon. The
paradoxes of universalism gravitate obsessively around a single
point. They tend to gravitate around the same slogan, which also
aims to serve as a *passe-partout*: the ethnocentric character of the
Western 'universalist' horizon. This is something entirely different
from the 'glaring disparity' – of which Tzvetan Todorov speaks at
the start of his *Nous et les autres* – 'between what people in power
said and the lives they led and allowed us to lead'.[2] It is a much
more profound phenomenon even than the way official doctrines
'robbed the noblest terms of their meaning: "liberty", "equality",
and "justice" became words that served to mask repression and
favouritism, the flagrant disparities in the way individuals were
treated'.[3] The paradox, as explained above, indicates instead that
the emancipatory universals of the Occident (from the idea of
communicative reason to that of the freedom of the will) underlie
ab originibus a closing monocultural axiom. In other words, they
constitute a set of values and guiding principles valid for all people
and for all climates. But they also find themselves wrapped in a one-
dimensional envelope that is entirely typical of the specific cultural
source that generated them, i.e., that literally 'conceived' them and
brought them into the world. In turn, that source bears the precise
and unmistakeable markings of the *logic of identity* and of *identification*. This is the *dispositif* of the Western *logos*, furrowed since
birth by a profound and invisible wound: the abstraction from
corporeity, from naturalness, from the originary bifurcation of the
species. It is unnecessary to insist on the decisive importance of this
theme. We shall merely note, in passing, that it would not only be a
pointless delusion but also a woeful error to hope to exorcise it on
the grounds of the indisputable (and sometimes frankly unbeara-
ble) mannerism with which the critique of so-called logocentrism
– or better still, 'logo-phono-centrism' – is to this day presented by
some of the 'super-contemporary' representatives of the French and
Italian thought of *différence*. While bearing in mind the breadth of
the problem, we will focus on the triptych that for the last two

---

1   Steven Lukes, 'What Is Left?'.
2   Tzvetan Todorov, *On Human Diversity*, p. vii.
3   Ibid.

centuries has represented modern Western rationalism: liberty, equality and fraternity. To this day, and even more so since the 'second '89', these three great themes perform the role of legitimating resource of the political organisations and institutions of the Occident.

A first and crucial problem arises concerning the *viability* of these principles in the face of the challenge of a 'global era' that is characterised by the irruption of *irreducible ethical and cultural differences*. The question directly concerns the destiny of the democratic form as well as the historical and emancipatory content it encapsulates, because those principles, which describe the horizon of *politically incisive* universalism, are also – as Edgar Morin has correctly noted – the *guiding terms* of the left.[4] These are *gigantic words*, the importance of which stretches across the entire political arena and which divide up the world not despite but because of the collapse of the old ideological walls. They are *hyperdense words* that appear to concentrate within themselves a maximum of meaning and truth. They are *nuclei words* forming centres around which our ideas gravitate as do our conflicts. They are *cardinal words* that indicate the zenith and the nadir, the old and the new, the north and south, the low and high, the left and right. They are, finally, *strategic words* forming fortresses for our beliefs.

It is my firm conviction that these words have now become *proprietors* of reality. They are *hyperreal*. For this reason I believe that behind their apparent self-evidence there hide the ramifications and enigmas that must be extracted through rigorous conceptual analysis as well as through an unbiased interpretation of real phenomena. If we want to be fully prepared to face the challenges of our time, we must have the courage to analytically adopt/assume and politically master two distinct but interrelated phenomena: a) the 'Promethean disproportion'[5] – as Günther Anders used to call it – between Man and the world produced by Man (that is, the instrumental and linguistic universe of technology); and b) the *cultural gap* produced by the conflict between values and their existential translation, between the principles of politically incisive universalism and their practical realisation in the framework of the 'material constitution'.

Holding together these two aspects in a productive tension

---

4   Edgar Morin, *Pour sortir du XXe siècle*.
5   Günther Anders, *Die Antiquiertheit des Menschen*.

represents our only credible chance of relaunching contemporary democracy. We are tempted to close these opening comments by returning to the ancient but still valid exhortation *Hic Rhodus, hic salta!*

But we should not be so precipitous. What we have said so far is merely the tip of the iceberg.

The 'Big Chill'

In order to approach the problem adequately and to not remain ensnared by the scenarios we have just outlined, we will have to carefully avoid two sterile and risky attitudes. On the one hand, we must ban from our discourse 'Nobel Prize–style statements'. That is to say, we must avoid all generic formulas that the language of politics has perniciously transmitted even to 'intellectuals', who have been called to comment upon anything and everything. Such language has not moved on since the nineteenth century, notwithstanding the impact that the twentieth-century revolutions had upon expressive forms, from the arts to the sciences, and to the very way we look at experience. The archetype of such sententious phrases is best represented, naturally, by the extraordinary 'discovery' that the current situation of humanity is characterised by the alternative between great dangers and great possibilities. In other words, and more specifically, we must steer clear of the 'dual' perversity of the postmodern, the oscillation between the hermeneutics of euphoria (weak thought, theory of the simulacra *et similia*) and a heuristics of fear (the common attitude to the 'dark' aspect: from Arnold Gehlen's *posthistoire* to Hans Jonas' 'principle of responsibility'). On the other hand, we must also avoid setting up our own 'Western-Eastern Divan' (the allusion is to Goethe's *West-östlicher Diwan*) by rambling on about yet another (in truth antediluvian) 'discovery' concerning the relationship between the Orient and the Occident.

Let us try to grasp the bull by the horns while doing our best not to be gored. Today, the Occident is an *exploded cultural sphere*. The explosion, whose fragments we find ourselves trying to administer, occurred not despite but as a consequence of the apparent global victory of its model. So what characterises the 'spiritual situation' of our age? The imposition of homologating Western parameters under every sky and over all cultures? I do not think so; or, rather, I do so only in part. We must signal that we are faced with a crucial point. To do so we will go against the current of the *discordia concors* of all those 'apocalyptic' or 'integrated' intellectuals who, *from within the Occident*, either jubilantly salute the triumph of the Western model or babble in defeatist manner against the universal homologation supposedly introduced by such a model, without recognising that *for some time now the stick has been bent in a diametrically opposed direction to that of universalism*. The climate threatening to mark the passage to the new century is that of the *politics of difference* championed by different groups in their increasingly widespread and intense rebellion against the universalist Western model. I refer – for those who have not already understood – to the battle of the American Communitarians against the democratic pact. This is a far more subtle and insidious phenomenon than even the nationalistic and sub-nationalistic 'tribalism' that has rent the European continent since the fall of the Berlin Wall and the break-up of the Soviet Empire. The battle of the neo-Communitarians is more socio-cultural than political. For this reason, it risks taking root in ethnic groups and strata of the population that are traditionally indifferent to the course of the *politique politicienne*. For these veritable *'indigenous' fundamentalisms* of the Occident, the institutions of universalism represent the realm of the 'Big Chill' because they are irredeemably typified by a physiological *indifference* towards the *different* 'politics of recognition' engaged in by the multiple 'communities', that is, towards the links of solidarity that can exist not between atomistically divided individuals (according to the schema of the 'social contract' from Hobbes onwards) but between concrete, *culturally alike* subjects. We begin to glimpse the outline of the unsettling neo-Communitarian challenge. From its perspective, not only is the instrumental and strategic *dispositif* of universalism ethnocentric (i.e., the technologies, the conventions, the formal rules of democracy), but so is its 'communicative reason', that is, the very idea of rational dialogue. *Persuasion*, in other words, is viewed as a more civilised model of the *conversion* of the 'barbarian' and the 'infidel'. It is seen, therefore, as essentially a means to neutralise cultural 'alterity'. Moreover, the emphasis on the concretion of the forms of life tends to draw the themes of solidarity and sharing of values back to the riverbed of cultural specificity.

In the face of the most extreme forms of communitarianism and 'multiculturalism' (the other key phrase of these years), there is a strong temptation to see in them 'nothing new', as if they were merely an anachronistic reaction to the victories of

Western democracy and rationalism; but to do so would be merely to shut one's eyes, entrenching oneself in a sterile and pathetic defence of our certainties. It would mean failing to 'understand' the reasons for a challenge that is drawing into its orbit not only substantial social groups but also combative and well-prepared intellectuals: from Robert Bellah to Alasdair MacIntyre, from Charles Taylor to Martha Nussbaum, from Michael Sandel to the late, lamented Christopher Lasch, right through to the brilliant 'liberal-communitarian' hybridisations of Walzer and Rorty. Moreover, are we so sure that the themes of solidarity and the bond of the community are adequately accounted for by the great equations of universalism? To answer this question it is necessary to rapidly analyse the components of the revolutionary-emancipatory 'triptych'.

The Forgotten Dimension

As we have already suggested, behind their apparent self-evidence, the three principles of modern universalism conceal some enigmatic and paradoxical ramifications that still need unpacking. The paradoxes of universalism taken in the sense of politically incisive universalism (i.e., which is constitutive of the politics and freedom of modernity) are essentially of two types: A) the *paradoxes inherent to the ideal/conceptual structure* and B) the *paradoxes inherent to the historical dynamic and experience*. We shall examine each of these aspects.

As is well established, the age-old dispute among liberalism, socialism and democracy has almost exclusively concentrated on the two poles of liberty and equality. It has either posed itself the problem of distinguishing between the two dimensions or it has attempted to conjugate them in a superior, or simply more acceptable, synthesis. All of the political, economic and social doctrines that allied themselves to each of these great idealities (and attempted, more or less successfully, to bring them together in the forms of liberal democracy, social democracy or 'liberal social-ism') engaged with this bipolar tension. *Fraternité* was the *forgotten dimension* – at least from the theoretical standpoint. It is rare to find a specific entry in political dictionaries for this term. For example, there is no sign of an entry for this term even in the revised *Dizionario di politica* (1983) edited by Norberto Bobbio, Nicola Matteucci and Gianfranco Pasquino. This is not an unimportant omission, given that it is one of the key principles of the triptych. There is, however, a profound reason for this absence. The problem of 'fraternity' represents a veritable thorn in the side for the triad of modern universalism, precisely because it poses the question of the link, the bond of solidarity and community that no logic of pure freedom or mere equality is able to grasp or resolve. The logic to which the values of freedom and equality answer is the – strictly modern – logic that underlies the historically and anthropologically cultural model of individual choice. In the final analysis this model rests on a foundation of *individualism*. Therefore, in the very conceptual and symbolic structure of universalism there is a latent conflict between the (general) logic of *citizenship* and the (specific) logic of *belonging*. Hence, it is inevitable that it is precisely those democratic movements and tendencies that aim to present themselves as the 'party of rights' which have to assume the centrality of this paradox in its entirety. From here stems the paramount question: how can one be the bearer of rights without opposing the logic of belonging? How is one to conjugate *universalism* and *difference*? Two historical examples will suffice to signal the difficulty of the problem.

Already in the revolutionary phase, *fraternité* sought and found a lasting referent in the idea of the *nation*. But it was precisely this idea that would trigger the retaliation of the 'nationalization of the masses'.[6] After the Napoleonic wars, the post-revolutionary European states adopted the national factor as the identifying element of recognition and belonging to contrast the French pretence of imposing, through universalist-revolutionary legitimation, its own nationalist and expansionist interests.

The other thorn in the side of the universalist model is represented by the logic of class. To the same extent but in a different manner from the question of nationality, it too posed the problem of belonging and of a symbolic identification that is not given by the terms of liberty and equality themselves. Both these claims of belonging acted as limit and break to the logic of rights, understood as the expansive dynamic of rules and formal *dispositifs* providing a universally valid insurance. To be schematic, we could say that class, in contrast to nation, involves two types of division. A horizontal one that forms the basis of its transnational (or internationalist, as one used to say) vocation, and a vertical one that sustains the 'strong' (and originally exclusive) character of its criteria of identity and belonging. However, even the historical

---

6   George Lachmann Mosse, *The Nationalization of the Masses*.

projection of 'class' appears marked by a two-sidedness or – if you prefer – by an inextinguishable ambiguity. Consider, on the one hand, the polemic that for a long period the workers' movement conducted, in the name of 'cosmopolitan' enlightenment, against the 'nationalistic revivals' of the bourgeoisie. On the other hand, think of the reiterated calls to 'take up the flags' that had been allowed to fall into the mud by the ineptitude of the ruling elites. As we know, the course of European social democracy has hardly been free from nationalistic (as well as statist) tendencies, even without going as far as the extreme solution represented by Leninism. In Leninism, class and state tend to be so tightly screwed together that they result in a model far from the one originally delineated by Marx and the First International (and, partly, even from that developed – in a much more complex climate and in a more enduring form – by the Second).

B) To grasp the paradoxes inherent to the dynamic and historical experience of the principles of universalism, we must take up again and deepen a theme that was clear to the disenchanted gazes of Tocqueville and Weber but also to the infernal and mercilessly demystifying eye of the old Marx. The process of capitalist modernity constitutes a unique, absolutely exceptional event in the context of human societies, precisely because it is realised through the revolutionising of values and a radical break with the bonds of the community that held together the traditional areas of life. Therefore, the affirmation of modern universalism coincides with the experience of *universal uprooting*. But this experience is nothing other than the effect of the unfolding of the cultural presupposition of universalism, that is, of its irreducibly *individualist* nucleus. It is the 'individualist model' and not (to adopt Louis Dumont's oppositional couple) the 'holistic model' that forms the basis of the very principle of equality. And it is on this basis that one should look for the explanation for its unprecedented expansive force. Tocqueville said that once equality irrupts into history, it can no longer be driven out. Nevertheless, whereas the holistic model has always been *differentiating par excellence* (paradoxically, precisely because of its organic and hierarchical nature), the individualist model (conversely, for its intimately egalitarian vocation) has been *homologating par excellence*. This is a crucial paradox that Tocqueville, Marx and Weber – each in his own way – sharply bring into focus. But, having done so, they infuriatingly, each for different if not completely opposed reasons, leave the paradox unresolved. As disenchanted diagnosticians must, the first and last thinkers proposed an ethics to confront destiny, not a theory to make history. Marx, on the other hand, who wanted instead to make history and unquestionably made an impression on it, outlined a solution but – properly examined – did so in terms of a grand finale of individual realisation and collective fulfilment. Who can forget the 'each' as sender and receiver of 'all' in the propositions of the *Manifesto* or of the *Critique of the Gotha Programme*? Contrary to what is believed today, the proliferation of 'false paths' taken by the Marxist-inspired left have not depended on an excess but on a deficit of prescriptions in Marx's work. It was precisely the absence of medium-term indications concerning 'what is to be done' – compared with the 'irenic' long-term projections and the many analyses of the present and the short term – that left the political organisations of the various Internationals with the challenges of the paradoxes of universal emancipation. On the one hand, the workers' movement declared it was carrying forth the Enlightenment idea of emancipation by immersing it into the materiality of real struggles, while on the other hand, it brandished the logic of class as a weapon against the model individualist homologation. In other words, belonging to a class has always represented an alterity and an insoluble aporia of universalism, coagulating the social link against the fragmentation provoked by the principle of individualism.

Looking back at the dramatic history of the last century, one has the impression that the aporia has doubled, making way for two separate [*divaricati*] but interrelated phenomena. The first historic phenomenon is represented by the flowing of the latent determinism of the idea of 'law of motion' (an aspect that coexists and conspires with the radically individualist premises) into the fetishisation of the Collective. This route has led – with all the 'orthodox' alterations and legitimations of doctrine – to the tragic experience of 'real communism'. The second phenomenon is constituted by the flowering of counter-tendencies and zones of resistance to universalism, which involve the championing of the irreducible autonomy of partial subjects, whether they be real or mythologically constituted: race, ethnicity, *Volk*. It would be extremely interesting to analyse the various manipulations that the concept of 'the people' underwent in the twentieth century. We would no doubt discover some unexpected and unsettling collusions between 'right' and 'left'. But I believe that, once again, an anthropologist such as Louis

Dumont is correct (in contrast to many political scientists) in affirming that contemporary totalitarianism is by no means an 'aberration' or an 'exceptional event' – that would confirm the rule of our 'Splendid, and progressive, destiny'[7] – but a creature born from the viscera of universalist individualism;[8] despite the fact that it completely reverses its polarity, assigning to a collective Identity or Fetish the (individualist) prerogatives of the will to power and dominion over the world. It is certainly no accident that it is precisely through the analysis of the dynamic of the masses in the last century that emerges the need to excavate the 'heart of darkness' of the Occident, to bring its constitutive elements to light. But for the fact that – and I come now to the most subtle point of my argument – to confront the problem in these terms means inevitably running into the limits of a rationalistic and utilitarian-type approach to social phenomena.

Pluralism and Conflicts of Value

To highlight some of these limitations I will introduce a theme that, today, is decisive not only at the level of theory but also with respect to the socio-cultural challenge of the Communitarians: the theme of the *conflict of values*. Not only Western philosophy but Western politics as well has always – except in the case of some significant exceptions – tended to consider the conflict of values to be a pathological accident. This has not, however, only influenced/affected the utilitarian paradigm but the Kantian idea of Man as a moral agent as well. Following the dissolution of causal determinism and substantialism, we have in recent years witnessed the return of ethics on a grand scale. And yet, this return appears to be infected with an old prejudice: the doctrine of rational behaviour. According to this doctrine, whose most celebrated representative is Kant, every person is a transcendent ethical subject able to act in accordance with universal principles and independently from his existential situation and, specifically, from his historical and cultural roots. It is a case now of seeing whether such a doctrine can form an adequate platform to confront the challenges of our time, or whether this extremely noble idea might not contain instead the roots of the ethnocentric paradox of Western universalism, that is to say, of the

---

7   Giacomo Leopardi, 'Broom', in *Selected Poems*, p. 105.
8   Louis Dumont, *Homo aequalis*.

paradox which allows it to be a vehicle of 'colonisation' of other cultures that is the more powerful the more subtle it is. We shall now verify/investigate in what sense the theme of the conflict of values explodes the two principal contemporary versions of the doctrine of rational behaviour.

In the course of this investigation, we shall consider positively, and then critically, two philosophers who develop a particularly mature and sophisticated level of ethical and political argument: Bernard Williams and Isaiah Berlin.[9] They share the belief that the limit of neo-Utilitarianism lies in its pretence to reduce the conflict of values to a case of logical incoherence, and the limit of neo-Contractualism consists in the presupposition of a high level of cultural homogeneity between the subjects and groups that are located in the 'original position'.[10] From this standpoint, the critique that neo-Communitarians direct at Rawls seems to be anything but foundationless. The 'veil of ignorance' that forms the presupposition of the 'original position' of the contract is, in reality, too flimsy. If one wants to include subjects that are also unaware of the facts of the French Revolution or are, at least, unwilling to attribute universal significance to the values that flowed from it, it is necessary to increase the veil's thickness. But this is precisely the problem with which democratic Occidental societies find themselves faced: that of confronting the demands for citizenship of culturally differentiated individuals and groups who, while they instrumentally demand recognition of their rights, are not prepared to acknowledge the universal legitimacy of the democratic formalism. For both Berlin and Williams (despite the difference of their language and theoretical framework), the Western philosophical tradition meets its limit precisely where it considers the conflict of values as a pathology, an obstacle to be removed, a nuisance against which one must defend oneself at the first opportunity. According to Berlin, the dominant philosophical and political tendency of the Occident rests upon three fundamental assertions. 1) For every authentic question there exists one correct answer that excludes all other responses as erroneous, as not-true. As long as it is formulated in a logically clear manner, there is no question of which one can provide two distinct answers both of which would be correct (and equally, there is no correct

---

9   See Isaiah Berlin, *The Crooked Timber of Humanity*; Bernard Williams, *Ethics and the Limits of Philosophy*.

10   John Rawls, *A Theory of Justice*.

answer to an inauthentic question). 2) There exists *one* method to find logically valid answers. 3) All valid answers must be compatible amongst themselves. A tradition structured in this way is, in truth, able to 'tolerate' *only* the conflict of interest. Conversely, the conflict of values is registered – by this tradition – as a pathological *outburst*;[11] i.e., literally separation from the chain of being, collapse of logical coherence, deficit of rationality. But the reality of the social context is one constituted by a plurality of values that can enter into conflict and that are not necessarily reducible one to the other. Therefore, this conflict can also be translated into a *conflict of obligations*, of mutually incompatible imperatives that can in no sense be treated as a case of logical incoherence, or only at the price of thinking in accordance with an ethnocentric and colonial model of Reason. In short, there is a dramatic typology of the cases that we could call 'tragic', in which we find ourselves faced with the Williams idea of the incommensurable exclusivity of a hierarchy of incompatible values. This is not only a confrontation between Western culture and other cultures, but of a conflict of values that traverses the very heart of the *Cosmopolis*, of the Occident's metropolitan life as well.

From the diagnosis of these two philosophers, there emerges the clear awareness that – following the globalisation of the Western model – the problem of cultural alterity does not exist only as a clash with the outside, but as an *aporia internal to the functioning of Western society itself*. It is Berlin, however, who registers the centrality of the problem most acutely. His most recent reflections directly concern the decline of utopias. He indirectly poses the question: why is it that the failure of the idea of the 'new man' and the 'perfect society' does not end with the collapse of real communism but continues to reverberate strikingly from East to West? In attempting to answer this difficult question, he sets out from the link between Western utopia and the idea of a homogeneous and universal (ethical and rational) nature of man. All the variants of utopia, he argues, are anchored to the original universalist vocation of Western culture. The entire arch of their historical development – from colonial utopias to the so-called colonisation of the future – would receive the seal of universal fulfilment, that is, of static perfection, understood as the restoration of a shattered original unity.[12]

---

11   *Translator's note:* In Italian, *scatenamento* means literally unchaining.
12   See Octavio Paz, *Conjunctions and Disjunctions*.

Isaiah Berlin's suggestive historical and doctrinal fresco concludes with the proposal of *pluralism* as the one plausible solution to the symmetrical but inconvenient opposites of universalism and cultural relativism. But in what way and with what arguments is such a solution prospected?

Common Good and Self-Refuting Prophecy

The core of Berlin's argument consists in opposing the universalist model to the other aspect of the Enlightenment (and, *mutatis mutandis*, Hegelian) philosophy of history: namely, the idea of the irreducible autonomy of cultures proposed [*prospettata*] by Herder (and before that, by Vico). In contrast to the utopia of history understood as the progressive (linear or dialectical) transition towards the transparency of Reason, there stands the 'healthy' opacity of cultural *differences* understood in their incommensurable individuality. No ethics or rationality of action is formed independently of the riverbed of tradition and language, i.e., in accordance with a specific *symbolism*. Every culture has its own parameters and its own hierarchy of values that is different from others. Therefore, to postulate a criterion of valuation that presupposes a single standard of measure for 'rational behaviour' is a proof of the blindness towards that which makes humans human: the capacity to differentiate themselves culturally. Berlin's warning is extremely severe. Either democracy sheds its traditional prerogatives of cultural autochthony and abandons the universalist and monist fetish of the substantially homogeneous Subject, or it will find itself ensnared in the critical mass of its paradoxes. It risks being sucked back into the spiral of the self-refuting prophecy.

And yet Berlin's solution to the question is as unsatisfactory as his framing of it is rigorous. Essentially, the inadequacy can be traced back to his way of understanding the democracy of 'difference', which he interprets in terms of pluralist democracy or democracy *of* differences. This is in no sense a 'weak' interpretation of the term. On the contrary, it turns conflict into a *constitutive* moment of the democratic process and the search for the 'common good' into the unstable equilibrium between the aspirations of various groups. But such a reading allows one a merely rhetorical escape from the horizon of ethical relativism of the type represented by Kelsen. At best, it allows one to correct it and integrate it via the anthropological notion of *cultural pluralism* (that is, in any case, not alien from Kelsen's thinking). And this is so because Berlin leaves substantially unanswered two decisive questions that are of vital importance for democratic theory.

First, the question regarding the presupposition of the value of democracy: the inviolability of human rights in terms of individual rights and the inalienable rights of the individual. Kelsen's ethical and philosophical relativism includes such an ultimate value in the rigorously conditional schema: '*if . . . then . . .*'. *If* you choose the principle of the right to life and liberty of each, *then* you can only opt for the democratic form. Conversely, a coherent escape from the swamp of relativism leads to the adoption of this value as an element of challenge and comparison with 'other' cultures that negate it or subordinate it to other values (the Collective, the State, the Nation, the People, etc.). But this compels one to overcome the axiom of the incommensurability of cultures that is part and parcel of a particular anthropology, as well as the adoption of a comparative perspective that is able to contemplate the moment of *symbolic interaction* between cultural contexts. In fact, assigning the symbolic dimension exclusively to the moment of differentiation indicates the inheritance of a burdensome ethnocentric prejudice that is widely present in anthropological studies. On closer examination, the highlighting of differences (that each, in their own domain, acts as though they were irreducible *identities*) is not at all an antithesis but the other side of the coin of homologating universalism.

Therefore, the abandonment of the universalist and substantialist idea of the 'common good' should not necessarily result in an embrace of the Herderian scenario of cultures that relate to one another as insular self-sufficiencies, or monads without doors or windows. The globalisation of the world that took effect with the collapse of the wall between East and West has suddenly projected us against a wall that is so vast that we are unable to see its contours. Those contours are of a problem that is so macroscopic as to pass unobserved: that a confrontation between the great cultures of the planet has not yet happened. At this time, when Western democracies are becoming heir to ever more active and conspicuous elements of other cultural contexts, this confrontation is on the point of imposing itself with an absolute urgency.

All this takes place in the presence of a critical threshold that we have only just begun silently, and almost imperceptibly, to traverse. The crossing of this critical threshold crucially implicates the very idea of 'nature' that we had become accustomed to and upon which we had constituted – since the modern era – our political order and social contracts. To this point, nature had essentially been conceived in two ways by Western culture. First, nature as 'temple', as ordered cosmos and impassable container of events that followed one another cyclically (in accordance with the classical account that spanned from Greek and Roman civilisation to the Middle Ages). Second, nature as 'laboratory': a partitioning of the universe for experimentation (according to the account that spanned the period from the 1600s throughout the industrial epoch). Now we see a new idea emerge, where the very boundaries between nature and artifice begin to fade: nature as code. This is an entirely new idea – postmodern, if you like – but extremely ancient as well. It evokes the traditional, hermetic or cabalistic theme of the cipher and deciphering. It is on this basis that we must rethink the very idea of contract, which originally postulated nature as a 'state', an unmodifiable presupposition upon which the artifice of the state – the 'mortal god', the 'great and omnipotent' Leviathan – would be erected. It is from this standpoint that the challenge of universalism must again be launched by considering a new range of possibilities for the destiny of the species on this planet.

Given this – to say the least – unsettling backdrop, what is the task for democracy? First, it must contend with the radical transformation that has affected some of the key problems against which it has measured itself historically, beginning with the problem of exploitation, which today tends increasingly to turn into that of marginalisation. But the very problem of marginalisation cannot be conceived in classical terms, since it now directly implicates the *critical-cultural* dimension. In his most recent work, Shmuel N. Eisenstadt – a sociologist who has come closer than most to a comparative approach to the cultural problems of 'modernisation' – has provided an illuminating interpretation of contemporary fundamentalisms. He has explained how it is not the exploited or poor classes that are fundamentalist, but rather those strata of the population who feel themselves to be marginalised by the 'centre' of society. This feeling of *marginalisation from the centre* constitutes an essential aspect not only for sociological analysis but for a radical redefinition of the concept of democracy itself. To assume it fully means going to the very root of this concept and initiating a confrontation between the *two halves* of the Occident. In addition, it involves an unprejudiced attempt to verify whether the 'oceanic model' of the common-law countries

is more suited than the 'Continental model' of the civil-law countries to make the two poles of *universalism* and *difference* interact.
But acknowledging this would mean – both for theory and practice – renouncing once and for all the idea of the state as the 'lever'
of emancipation. It would mean . . . *oublier Paris*.

Therefore, the adoption of a comparative perspective on
cultures is essential to the reconstruction of a political concept
adequate to our times. It is of vital importance to establish the
relationship between invariance and mutation in the forms of
power on which are staked the destinies of the 'third phase'[13] of
democracy, i.e., of that transnational democracy that is definitively able to leave behind the obsolete 'referents' of the preceding
phases – from the *demos* to the nation states. But for democratic
culture (in both its liberal-democratic and its social-democratic
variants) to make/satisfy such demands it must measure itself
against a series of unresolved conceptual problems. I will merely
consider the principal ones, which – ideally – should be inserted
into a whole series of others.

The *first* conceptual node to be resolved is that formed by the
confrontation between the two paradigms underlying the different conceptions of order and conflict: the *methodological-
individualism of rational behaviour* (or the *voluntarist theory of
action*) – which sets out from the agent and his/her rationality,
turning on the notions of 'preference', 'intentionality', 'model of
ends', 'project' etc. – and the anti-utilitarian model of *social
normativity*, according to which the individualist dimension of
action is instead overdetermined by symbolic systems that are
experienced and acted upon, above all, *unconsciously*. Are we
certain that the theme of the relation between *common* and *shared*
values – in Jon Elster's words, by the 'cement of society'[14] – is
entirely subsumable under the first paradigm? Are we sure that –
schematically speaking – it is resolvable within Weber's perspective,
without having first attentively evaluated Durkheim's or Mauss'
positions, and, last but not least, Freud's?

The *second* unresolved conceptual theme is that of the 'sacred',
which is the inescapable constant of power and of the social bond
once one adopts the idea of society as a relational-symbolic whole;
that is, as something more than, and other than, the simple sum of
the individuals who compose it. Even to those who are reluctant

---

13   Robert Alan Dahl, *Polyarchy*.
14   Jon Elster, *The Cement of Society*.

to take up the radical notion of 'sacred sociology' that emerged in the 1930s from Georges Bataille and Roger Caillois' Collège de Sociologie, it will be difficult not to agree with Clifford Geertz[15] that a society that is entirely desacralised is one that has been completely depoliticised. If the motif of the sacred is identified with that of the persistence of iterative rituals and models that preside over the mechanisms of symbolic identification – a question the sociologist Alessandro Pizzorno has focused on keenly in relation to democratic theory – then another significant requirement follows: that of a radical revision of the concepts of 'secularisation' and 'Western rationalism' as they were elaborated in Max Weber's great comparative investigation. In other words, secularisation does not connote a linear 'desacralisation', in the same way as the crisis of the so-called centralities (from the People-subject to the State-subject)[16] does not necessarily result in an attenuation or weakening of the mechanisms of symbolic identification. A paradigmatic example of this is Marc Bloch's analysis of the symbolic interchange between religious *auctoritas* and political *potestas* in *Les Rois thaumaturges* of 1924,[17] which constitutes a veritable jewel of historical anthropology. As he argues there, the centuries-long conflict between the two powers does not bring to an end a linear process of differentiation. Rather, it draws to an end a mirror game in which the one tends to assume the prerogatives of the other. The Church takes on the characteristics of a state (assuming the qualities of centralisation and bureaucratic rationalisation) and the state adopts ecclesiastical ones (increasing its sacred features and ritualising its procedures).

The *third* conceptual node we need to consider is that of the mythical-ritualistic pattern of sovereignty. This theme emerged from Samuel Hooke's ethnological investigations at the start of 1930s, which were collected together in *Myth and Ritual* and *The Labyrinth*. The significance of these investigations is not only that they bring to light (some decades before Michel Foucault) the persistence of a mythical-ritualistic complex independent from the existence – or otherwise – of a topologically identifiable and

---

15   Clifford Geertz, *The Interpretation of Cultures*.

16   *Translator's note*: this also includes debates around the centrality, or otherwise, of the working class, of 'the Political', etc. that was so important to the debates within – and without – the Italian Communist Party in the 1970s. See, for example, Giorgio Napolitano, A. Accornero, M. Cacciari, M. Tronti, *operaismo e centralità operaia*.

17   Marc Bloch, *The Royal Touch*.

visible sovereign Centre. Their importance, instead, is in their shattering that 'contempt of ritual' that Mary Douglas saw as one of the negative attributes of contemporary social theory.[18] By demonstrating the *derivation of myth from ritualistic practice* (and not vice-versa, as in the formula that goes back to the German cultural tradition and, in particular, to the phenomenologism of Frobenius' school), those investigations showed the importance of power's spatial framework. But in so doing they ended up rehabilitating the Latin function of *ritus*. It is no coincidence that there is no equivalent for this term in the Greek language. Ritual (in which that system of rules and procedures that we call 'law' is cultivated) is the 'black box' that links up the two key moments of the symbolism of power: *augurium* and *regnum*, *auctoritas* and regal/monarchical *power*. They both derive from the common root *aug-* (from which the verb *augere* stems); *augurium* and *auctoritas* include the meaning of 'augmentation' [*aumento*], of symbolic increment. In relation to these, *regnum* acts as normative operator and *regulator*. In other words, regal *potestas* translates the *augmentum*, the increment of sense (and the conferment of authority) implicit in the augural [*augurale*] function, in a *dispositif* of signs. As has been documented by Benveniste, the etymology of *rex* – from the root *rex* – relates back to the meaning of *regere*, 'marking', tracing a straight line and, hence, delimiting or marking the perimeter of a space.

> *Rex*, which is attested only in Italic, Celtic, and Indic – that is at the Western and Eastern extremities of the Indo-European world, belongs to a very ancient group of terms relating to religion and law.
>   The connexion of Lat. *Rego* with Gr. Orégō 'extend in a straight line' (the o- being phonologically explicable), the examination of the old uses of *reg-* in Latin (e.g. in *regere fines, e regione, rectus, rex sacrorum*) suggests that the rex, properly more of a priest than a king in the modern sense, was the man who had authority to trace out the sites of towns and to determine the rules of law.[19]

Originally, the expression *rex regit regiones* means 'the marker [*segnatore*] marks [*segna*] the marks [*segni*]'. Thus, the couple *augurium/regnum* – indicating a link but an unresolvable tension as well – forms the constant supporting the symbolism of power and of public space, even in its multiple variants and historical

---

18   Mary Douglas, 'The Contempt of Ritual'.
19   Émile Benveniste, *Indo-European Language and Society*, p. 307.

metamorphoses. The dynamics of power perennially pose the problem of an *excess of meaning*, a *surplus of sense* that must each time individually be translated into an intrinsically coherent *system of signs*. It is from the irreducible tension of this polarity that the secret logic presiding over all myths of *foundation* draws its origin: the mythology of a single and 'sovereign' source of power. Consequently, the *crises of legitimacy* of a political order or regime are always produced from the uncoupling of the two poles of the *augurium/augmentum/auctoritas* and the *regnum/ regere* of *potestas*. If it is true to say that, today, such a crisis affects the democratic form, as is attested to by the neo-Communitarian and neo-Populist rebellion against 'procedural liberalism', it follows that there is only one way to confront it: to once again raise the question of its 'essence' or 'value' (from which, in the final analysis, stem its 'rules' and 'techniques' as well), and to verify if it can be said to contain a symbolic reservoir, an 'augural' redundancy of meaning, that its currently codified signs are no longer able to transmit, and, if so, where this may be found. It is doubtful, however, that such a verification can be given without submitting the two poles of the 'individual' and the 'community' to a further investigation that would go well beyond the terms in which their relation had been thought of by the dominant paradigms of liberalism and socialism.

I will conclude by coming to the other – more specifically theoretical – point left out in Isaiah Berlin's diagnosis. It concerns what we could call – following Robert Dahl – the 'shadow concept' of democracy. It consists not so much in 'overcoming' its metaphysical-substantialist status in a relativist or pluralist manner, so much as the activation of its metaphysical implication. If it is true to say that the vocation of democracy, inasmuch as it is the typical political-cultural institution of the Occident, is represented – as Tocqueville, Marx and Weber well knew – by the cipher of uprootedness, its most suitable definition will be that of the *commonplace of uprootedness*. Only on this basis – which is also an alternative rethinking of the potential of the tradition – is there a possibility of a confrontation with cultural 'alterities' that can escape the opposed and specular risks of hegemonic universalism and relativism. Only democracy can truly call itself a *paradoxical community: the community of the without-community*, not despite but precisely because of its formal rules that, limiting the *taxis*, the sphere of the exercise of power, guarantee the autonomous development of the spheres of life. Democracy is always 'to-come' [*ad-venire*], precisely because it does not sacrifice the opacity of friction and conflict to the utopia of absolute transparency. Democracy does not enjoy a temperate climate, nor does it benefit from a perpetual and uniform light. For it is nourished by that *passion of disenchantment* that holds together – in an unresolvable tension – the rigour of the form and the disposition to welcome 'unexpected guests'.

For this reason, it knows that it would go to ruin were it to forget, even for a single instant, the only presupposition that keeps it alive: the *totum* is the totem.

7

THE ORIENTAL MIRROR: VOLTAIRE AND THE ROOTS OF INTOLERANCE

Il y aura toujours des barbares et des
fourbes qui fomenteront l'intolérance . . .
Nous avons été si infectés de cette fureur,
que dans nos voyages de long cours
nous l'avons portée à la Chine, au Tonquin, au Japon.
Nous avons empesté ces beaux climats.
Les plus indulgents des hommes ont appris de nousà être les
*   plus inflexibles.*
Nous leur avons dit d'abord pour prix de leur bon accueil:
'Sachez que nous sommes sur la terre les seuls qui aient raison,
et que nous devons être partout les maîtres.'
Alors on nous a chassés pour jamais;
il en a coûté des flots de sang:
cette leçon a dû nous corriger.
(Voltaire, *Questions sur l'Encyclopédie*, 1772)

After the Earthquake

No one would have guessed that it had been written in the peaceful surroundings of Ferney, a little strip of France at the doors of Geneva. Despite the austerity of its title – *Traité sur la tolérance* – the opening chapter of this blistering little book immerses us straight into the atmosphere of crime fiction. At the core of the plot of the book is a remarkable tale of 'religion, suicide and parricide'.[1] The task is to find out whether the parents strangled their own son; a brother killed his brother; a friend killed his friend; whether the judges were responsible for killing an innocent father on the wheel; or, vice-versa, whether they were responsible for saving a guilty mother, brother or friend.

---

1   Voltaire, *Treatise on Tolerance and Other Writings*, p. 3.

However, the events narrated were not a product of the imagination but had really occurred. And equally real was the scene of
their occurrence: Catholic Toulouse in 1762. Two centuries
earlier, popular fanaticism had resulted in the massacre of four
thousand heretics. This time it threw itself on a Protestant shopkeeper named Jean Calas, exhorting the judges to condemn him to
death for the murder of his son, who had revealed his intention of
converting to Catholicism. But when shortly after the execution
the presumed murder had been proved to have been a suicide, the
violent prejudice to which the Calvinist shopkeeper fell victim was
revealed in all its gravity. The merit for Calas' rehabilitation –
achieved through a hard and tenacious struggle – is to be ascribed
to the narrator of these facts: François-Marie Arouet, who was
already celebrated throughout Europe under the name of Voltaire.
Immediately after the campaign of rehabilitation that ended with
the victory of the *parti philosophique*, the most famous of the
philosophes decided to adopt the episode as an exemplary case of
the 'spirit of intolerance'.

It is the singular fortune of the classics to become universally
recognised at the same time as being unknown. Not even a brief,
tight and dazzling book such as *Traité sur la tolérance* (1763)
appears to have escaped this fate – at least if we rely upon the
regrettable misunderstandings and the frightening simplifications
to which the idea of tolerance is now subject at the hands not only
of its detractors but also of its apologists. Whoever rereads it or
looks at it for the first time today – with all that has passed under
the bridges of history – will be stunned to encounter entirely
different motifs from those imagined or coined by certain current
bagmen of anti-Enlightenment mannerisms. One finds nothing of
the pro-Western supremacism in vogue today. Nothing of the
conceited counterposing of 'us' and 'them', nor of the presumed
championing of the principles of a 'civilised' Europe against the
'barbarians' or the uncivilised non-Europeans. The accusation of
the *philosophe* is such as to leave no margin of ambiguity. It is
rather we Europeans who have sowed discord by transplanting
the seed of intolerance in other cultures.

We are struck by the latitude and longitude of Voltaire's gaze,
and equally by the comparative vision and the diachronic breadth
into which he inserts his discourse, which is never abstractly
moralistic or tediously pedagogical but always prodigious in
examples and case studies ('in the manner of the English', of
whom at the time he was a great admirer). Reading him, we

understand how much we have lost in the course of the last two
centuries with our emphatically Eurocentric idea of Europe and
our narcissistic 'reflection' on the apogee and twilight, the zenith
and nadir of the Old Continent. From the myriad of arguments
and ideas that form the counterpoint of Voltaire's polemic, two
dominant motifs – acting as gravitational centres – stand out. First
of all, the constant reference to 'others'. This is the supreme
distancing technique, where the reference to distant cultures (both
in time and space) acts as a burning glass to turn against ourselves
in order to brand the miseries of Civilisation and denounce the
breakdown and corruption of our present condition. Second, the
insistence on the 'weakness of our reason': an island in an ocean
of conflicts, of troubles and evils that no theodicy, no historical
providence is able to explain. These are typical motifs of Voltaire's
mature thought, which begins immediately after the break with
Frederick of Prussia and, on the basis of the 'crisis of optimism'
triggered by the Lisbon earthquake,[2] will end up situated precariously on the crest of the epoch between the reformist illusions of
the preceding period and the revolutionary results of the subsequent climate. Let us attempt to fix his thinking's salient traits in
relation to the subject of intolerance.

The problem of tolerance for Voltaire – as for his great predecessors Locke and Bayle – was, first of all, a religious one, because
the ultimate roots of intolerance are religious. It would be not
only disingenuous but fatal to skirt around this aspect by relating
it back – in a historicising manner – to the particular conditions of
a now distant epoch that was ignorant of the achievements of our
extremely civilised democratic systems of government. It is sufficient to glance at the world today to understand just how
unjustified and out of place is the edifying optimism rooted in
such a belief. We are forcefully reminded of the need to rethink
the origins of intolerance not despite but precisely because of the
fall of the various walls and ideological blocs which divided the
world until very recently, by the ethnic conflicts that tear apart the
regions of Eastern Europe and of the ever less latent intercultural
tensions that traverse the North American democracies. Alfred
Ayer, a philosopher who is not known for being seduced by ideologies, affirmed that of all the forms of intolerance, religious

---

2 The *Poème sur le désastre de Lisbonne* appeared in 1756, followed in the
same year by the monumental *Essai sur le mœurs et l'esprit des nations* and three
years after the sparkling *Candide*.

intolerance is the one that has caused the most harm; but – he added – it is also the most difficult to explain. It appears equally inexplicable to Voltaire himself, or at least to the Voltaire that we are considering: not the still optimistic and fundamentally providentialist Voltaire author of *Zadig* (1748), but the Voltaire of *Candide* (1759), the post-earthquake Voltaire under whose pessimistic parabola we must reread *Traité sur la tolérance*.

Logically inexplicable, impossible to relate back to any form of 'ground-reason' or *raison d'être*, the sources of intolerance can, however – or rather *must* – become the objects of historical narration and reconstruction. Despite the fact that such a narrative or reconstruction no longer has the prerogatives of the 'law' or of being a privileged key to knowledge, it has instead the eminently practical function of a cathartic representation designed to arouse a feeling of horror and repulsion towards the radical evil that appears to enfold, in a frequently alienating envelope, human events and the world. In what other way could one read the magisterial conclusion to *Candide*: 'we must cultivate our garden'?[3] The now disenchanted student is no longer able to accept the consolation suggested by his teacher Pangloss: 'since Leibniz could not possibly be wrong, and besides, pre-established harmony is the finest notion in the world, like the plenum and the subtle matter'.[4] He is left to ironically withdraw to the edge of the abyss, following the numerous vicissitudes and images of misfortune that he underwent in quick succession, as if in what was – in Italo Calvino's words – 'a great cinematic experience of the world today': 'from the villages destroyed in the Seven Years' War between the Prussians and the French' to the Lisbon earthquake; from the auto-da-fé of the Holy Inquisition to the experiment of the Jesuits in Paraguay; from Constantinople to the mythical riches of the Incas, leaving aside the vignettes 'on Protestantism in Holland, on the expansion of syphilis, on Mediterranean and Atlantic piracy, on the internecine wars of Morocco, the exploitation of black slaves in Guiana, giving some space for reports on literary and high-society Paris, and for interviews with the many dethroned kings who had arrived in Venice at the time'.[5]

This image of a 'world that is going to ruin' – in Calvino's

---

3 Voltaire, *Candide*, p. 75.
4 Ibid., p. 70.
5 Italo Calvino, 'Introduzione', in Voltaire, *Candido ovvero l'ottimismo*, pp. 6–7.

words once again – 'where no one is able to save themselves anywhere, aside from the only wise and happy country, El Dorado', appears to be relegated to the background of the work on tolerance; specifically in the place where its fate is assigned to the destiny of the 'rule of reason, which slowly but infallibly shines a light on men'.[6] Nevertheless, it would be misleading to render this aspect absolute, which – in Voltaire – appears to be counterbalanced and in constant tension with the preceding pole. Far from constituting a stable spotlight, the rational light/light of reason is nothing but a precarious achievement, a feeble spark in the darkness. Even in the *Traité*, the obsessive succession of evils returns – like the unsettling emergence of what has been latent or 'repressed' – as the decisive scene lying behind hard-won civic orderings: the long and torturous period of the civil wars of religion. It is to that scene that Voltaire alludes when he affirms that the men of Europe 'have for long carried with them their own Hell on earth',[7] when they did not hesitate to slaughter one another 'for a parcel of words'.[8] It is from the fear that such a condition of absolute precariousness and uncertainty could present itself again that he draws his decisive argument in favour of tolerance.

Civil Intolerance

The argument is more historical than logical. One should note the distance from the teachers of disenchantment that precede him: from the 'wise Locke'[9] to Pierre Bayle himself, upon whose work of demythologisation he draws at the same time as altering its principal ideas. Voltaire, like Locke, motivates his argument for tolerance with reference to the so-called latitudinarian argument, which had already been used by Ockham and propagated throughout the religious conflicts by the Anabaptists and, in particular, by the Socinians (a group of reformed Italians opposed strongly even by the Calvinists). As in Boccaccio's celebrated tale of the three rings in the (*Decameron*), where three equal chances for salvation are given to Christians, Jews and Mohammedans, so 'latitudinarism' established (in spite of every theological controversy) the necessity of a pacific coexistence of faiths on the nucleus of natural

---

6   Ibid., p. 7.
7   Voltaire, *Treatise on Tolerance and Other Writings*, p. 48.
8   Ibid., p. 28.
9   Ibid., p. 22.

religion common to all of them. In addition, with an analogous reference to natural religion, Jean Bodin (in *Colloquium hepta-plomeres* [1593]) and Hugo Grotius (in *De jure belli ac pacis* [1625]) had established the need of a 'religious peace'. In so doing they deepened and radicalised the arguments in favour of tolerance previously advanced by thinkers such as Marsilio of Padua, Giacomo Aconcio and Michel de Montaigne. However, whereas in Locke's *Epistle on Tolerance* (1689) the latitudinary argument is bent – in a strictly Puritan style – to the rigorous logical principle of the distinction between political and moral religion (between the public sphere of the political body and the private and metapo-litical sphere of interior conscience over which – as Locke argues – the magistrate has no jurisdiction), the consequent limitation of the right to tolerance excluded both atheists and 'Papists' by brand-ing them subjects of a foreign sovereign (with anything but negligible historical effects, *docet* Ireland). In the case of Voltaire, on the other hand, that same argument is transvaluated in the light of concrete historical experience. It is thanks to a historical and practical contextualisation, not to an abstract logical criterion, that Voltaire is able to identify the only possible solution to the problem of tolerance in the promotion and maintenance of an ample, 'pluralistic' framework of beliefs: 'The more sects there are, the less dangerous each one becomes'.[10] The prejudice that affirms the Enlightenment to be obstinately hostile to history is revealed to be entirely empty. But we should be a little more specific.

Voltaire's 'historicisation' shares little with the unitary (linear or cyclical, evolutionary or dialectical) representations of Universal History to which the 1800s has accustomed us. Far from absolut-ising the Reason of the Occident and its magnificent and progressive destinies, Voltaire's *philosophie de l'histoire* is arranged like a framework with multiple entry points, open to comparison between different cultures. Constructed in antithesis to the providential plan outlined in Bossuet's *Discours sur l'histoire universelle*, it is no coincidence that Voltaire begins with a consideration of China, precisely in order to 'challenge the bibli-cal tradition of the creation'.[11] Inverting the theological-historical schema that rests on the Judeo-Christian axis, Voltaire ends up affirming the superiority of Chinese over Jewish history and opposing sober Confucian wisdom to the 'fables' of prophecy.

---

10   Voltaire, *Treatise on Tolerance and Other Writings*, p. 24.
11   Karl Löwith, *Meaning in History*, p. 106.

Not for nothing did he hang in his room an effigy of Confucius with the (ironic, but only up to a point) words *Sancte Confuci ora pro nobis*. It is certainly not difficult – in the light of the documentation produced by a number of studies – to expose the lacunae and limits of Voltaire's 'comparativism', even taking into account the state of knowledge at the time: from the anti-Jewish prejudice to the libertine myth of the 'wise Chinaman' passed down to him by La Mothe le Vayer (who had linked Confucius to Socrates) and Bayle. Nevertheless, it is not by adopting a philological-historical key that we can fully evaluate Voltaire's argument. Instead, we should grasp its critical function – at once polemical and relativisable – in relation to Western culture. After all, was not Montaigne the first to invoke Chinese wisdom to criticise his society?

Only against this background is it possible to grasp – despite the clear forcing of the point – the *dispositifs* of comparison, opposition and distancing that we see at work in the *Traité*, where the supposition of other cultures' (such as China and Japan) or past civilisations' (such as Greece and Rome) tolerance acts as elliptical point of comparison to indicate the unredeemably autochthonous roots of *our own* intolerance; roots that Voltaire detects – and this is perhaps the main novelty and intensity of his thesis – in the (tendentially absolutist) logic of monotheisms. 'I say it with repugnance, but with truth: it is we, we Christians, who have been the persecutors, the executioners, the assassins!'.[12] Here lies the reason why the only cure for this evil – which can never be eradicated once and for all, inasmuch as it is embedded in humanity's natural inclination to credulity and 'fanaticism'[13] – is, as we have already seen, the fragmentation of faiths and the pluralisation of religious beliefs. Despite the emergence, here and there, of more naïvely optimistic tones (such as the belief that the stock market and the generalisation of exchange will favour the attenuation of conflicts), nevertheless, the destiny of tolerance hangs by a slender thread that we cannot allow to fail. It is, therefore, entrusted to the sense of weakness – certainly not strength – of our reason. As he writes in the entry 'Tolerance' in the *Philosophical Dictionary*: 'We are all steeped in weakness and errors: let us forgive one another's follies, it is the first law of nature'.[14]

---

12 Voltaire, *Treatise on Tolerance and Other Writings*, p. 47.
13 Ibid., p. 25.
14 Voltaire, *Philosophical Dictionary*, p. 387.

From Tolerance to Respect

As we approach our conclusion, it is worth reflecting on the rigour and elegance of this statement: *Tolerance is a necessary consequence of our human condition. We are all children of fragility: fallible and inclined to error. We can, therefore, only forgive one another's follies. This is the first law of nature. The principle that lies at the foundation of all human rights.* The fact that in recent years a philosopher such as Karl Popper has recognised the need to rework the concept of tolerance more or less in these terms, assimilating it to his 'falsificationism', is testimony to the extraordinary vitality of Voltaire's definition of tolerance. It continues to display an extraordinary vitality but, at one and the same time, it has a paradoxical flavour inasmuch as it is only fully comprehensible today, *after* the crisis of the ideas of Progress and Directional History which only emerged after the period in which Voltaire lived and worked. And yet Popper is aware that revisiting such a formula must face up to a radically changed reality. In contemporary democratic societies, the problem of religious toleration is accompanied by the problem of political and ideological tolerance. Furthermore, Voltaire could not predict that, in such societies, minorities would arise who accept the principle of intolerance. Setting out from these premises, Popper (and, in his wake, a host of other thinkers) poses a crucial question for the functioning of democratic systems: the question of the *limits of tolerance*.[15] It is a crucial problem but by no means a new one. Locke and Rousseau had already posed it clearly. And what, if not the question of limits, adumbrated the conclusion of the entry 'Tolerance' in the *Encyclopédie*, with its warning not to confuse political and religious tolerance with speculative tolerance, that is, with the 'pernicious indifference' of which Bayle spoke (and that Popper would call 'relativism')?

At this point we must ask a further and more radical question. If it is true to say that the scene has changed in the ways indicated above, can we still maintain the term 'tolerance'? We are all aware of the problem raised at the end of the 1960s by Herbert Marcuse's thesis of 'repressive tolerance'. But few have registered that the core of this thesis had already been raised by Mirabeau in 1789, at the French National Assembly: 'the word tolerance . . . seems

---

15   For a discussion of Popper's notion of the paradox of tolerance, see Raphael Cohen-Almagor, *The Boundaries of Liberty and Tolerance*.

to me in a certain sense tyrannical itself, because the authority that tolerates could just as well not tolerate'.[16]

Another step towards a deeper understanding of the problem is to say that tolerance always presupposes an authority that is not in question. If I tolerate you, I 'bear' you. This means that there is, on my behalf, a tacit condescension behind which lies/hides a radical devaluation of the 'truthfulness' of your position. With this in view, the social groups that operate within Occidental democratic societies have gradually shifted the axis of their demands from the *vertical* plane of the struggle for tolerance to the *horizontal* plane of the *politics of recognition*. In the meantime, the nature of the 'subjects' has radically altered. They are no longer constituted only by religious groups or social and political aggregates of interests. They are collective identities (ethnic, cultural, gender) whose actions put a strain on the traditional liberal-democratic spheres of 'citizenship'. They do not limit themselves to demands for greater participation and inclusion in the procedures of the institutions of democratic universalism. They ask to be recognised in their irreducible autonomy and specific difference. Along this axis, the centre of gravity of the conflict has increasingly shifted (especially in the 'politically correct' United States and Canada) from the theme of tolerance to that of *respect*. It would be a significant acquisition, were it not for the fact that behind the preoccupation with recognition there hides the risk of a *new intolerance*, which this time stems not from an absolute, paternalistic or illiberal power, but from the latent hostility between 'armour-plated' differences that relate to one another like monads with neither doors nor windows.

Following this paradoxical path, the problem of tolerance that had been overcome when understood in relation to the vertical logic of authority becomes current once again in the novel terms of the horizontality of intercultural conflict that threatens to assume the fundamentalist tones of the old wars of religion. In this atmosphere, it is like a breath of fresh air to reread the old Voltaire and become reacclimatised to the supreme irony that nourishes his merciless exposure of power, injustices and the evils of the world.

---

16 Quoted in Preston King, *Toleration*, p. 8.

8

CIPHERS OF DIFFERENCE

Border and Limit

The cipher of the 'glocal' – of the interface-relation or short-circuit global/local – which distinguishes our present sits ill with the traditional descriptions of social and political subjectivity. Entrusted to conceptual nomenclatures still of an industrial stamp, these descriptions not only are unable to escape capture in the vice of state and market but actually strengthen the cogency and voca-tion of totalisation to the highest degree. More than an antithesis, it is an indissoluble binomial. The state/market pincer inevitably tightens each time the presumed opposition of the terms is empha-sised as an alternative between the logic of 'privatisation' and the pure logic of 'defence' of the social state. The factor that, for Hannah Arendt, constituted the peculiar element and the means of subsistence of politics, the public sphere – understood in its autonomy from the institutions of the state, both in the sense of 'civil society' reduced to a system of needs and as mere economic *ratio* – tends to disappear in the pincer of state and market, of 'statism' and 'free competition'. Nevertheless, the search for a new *public space* that is able to escape from the dichotomous pincer that – with the tacit complicity and confusion of roles between 'right' and 'left' – always makes the 'public' coincide with the statist and 'private' demands with the anti-statist, even for it simply to begin, requires an even more radical operation than the one envisioned by Arendt: namely, to problematise the very concept of politics which had turned on the simultaneous and intersecting adoption of the concepts of 'border' [*confine*] and 'difference'.

Accordingly, we will attempt to approach the subject of 'differ-ence' in the contemporary philosophical (and post-philosophical) debate from a specific perspective delimited by the notions of 'border' [*confine*] and 'limit'. To adopt difference as an optical standpoint of displacement and a perspective shift from the traditional metaphysical nomenclatures of 'Subject' and 'Substance' implies a theoretical practice of borders [*confini*] where the logics of identity come to be destructured and redefined by the irruption of new insurgencies. These new insurgencies are no longer characterised by an ontology of 'participation' and 'gender commonality' but, rather, by an anti-essentialist criterion of singularity and symbolic relationality. Such an operation appears, today, not only indispensable for the attempt to 'update' the analysis but literally pre-liminal (precisely, the *limen*) to any discourse on politics that really wants to be adequate to the challenges of the present, of our binding and involving 'global time'.

We shall begin by considering the words 'border' [*confine*] and 'limit'. Every time we speak of the 'border' [*confine*], we should not lose sight of the dual valence of the term. Alongside the meaning of final margin, of terminal line, *con-fine* recalls the sense of a *shared* border [*condivisione*] with alterity or the extraneous. The border [*confine*] is not only the limit, but the shared limit. There is also another meaning of 'confine' [*confine*], linked to the idea of 'to confine' [*confinare*], to relegate to the margins. This is the crucial sense in another discursive context, for example that which invests all the forms of power and the spatial organisation of society modelled on the binomial of centre and periphery, but it is less important for the theme that I am concerned with.

The modern philosophical dispute on the border/limit [*confine/limite*] harks back to the celebrated notion introduced by Kant in the *Critique of Pure Reason*: the notion of *Grenzbegriff*, or limiting concept. The function of the *Grenzbegriff*, which we could also translate by 'marginal concept', is for Kant that of 'limiting'. The German verb used by Kant for this purpose is *einschränken*. There arises here a first problem, inasmuch as *einschränken* refers also to *Schranke*, a term that does not specifically denote the limit or border [*confine*] so much as barrier or obstacle. The Kantian limit-concept (which as we know is the *noumenon*: the key concept of the critique whose philosophical significance we shall not enter into here) also bears with it a dual valence. On the one hand, *Grenzbegriff* delimits in the same way as a margin, an edge. On the other hand, it attaches [*incardina*] the presumption of knowledge to the *Schranken*, to specific architectonic barriers. It goes without saying that, in Kant, the notions of border [*confine*] and limit are presented as negative or inhibiting. This makes way for a field of tensions and subversive potential that will then be translated by Hegel and Marx into the need for a dialectic of *Grenze* and *Schranke*, 'limit' and 'barrier'.

There is no doubt, therefore, that the Kantian tradition defines the limit-concept as a negative, inhibiting, hinging [*incardinante*] notion, one that poses delimitations, barriers to knowledge and to its pretensions. It is also unquestionable that in philosophy, today, we can see a decisive turn, to which I shall try and remain faithful: the turn to a positive declension of the limit. Such a positive declension of the limit means to put in question – as Foucault has acutely noted – not all of Kant, but a certain Kant: the Kant of the 'first *Critique*'. In a renowned lecture at the Collège de France, the later Foucault spoke of two traditions, two trajectories of modern philosophy both of which stem from Kant: first, that of the analytic of finitude, the analytic of true and false propositions; second, the trajectory of the ontology of the present. It is not difficult to detect in the identikit of the two trajectories the physiognomy of the philosophical dualism that has characterised post-Kantian philosophy: the analytic tradition and the hermeneutical one. Nevertheless, we face, today, a different setting from the one that Foucault traced for us in his inimitable style. It is one that demands not only the interaction between the two traditions, but the disruption of the borders [*confini*] between the two traditions: so that the theme of finitude affects that of the ontology of the present; the 'linguistic turn' is absorbed into the notions of action and forms of life; language, insofar as it is an originally practical and culturally situated dimension, becomes the cipher for the limit and radical contingency. The inherence of our practices to an irrepressible and irreducible plurality of forms-of-life and the consequent necessity of relating them through 'passages' confers upon the positive declension of the limit the significance of a passage-to-the-limit, in which the theme of experience and its redefinition become crucial. But let us take one step at a time.

In what does the positive declension of the limit consist and where can it be seen? In contemporary philosophy, the most macroscopic aspect is that represented by the irruption of the concept of 'difference'. This irruption is visible both in the Continental tradition (from the Nietzschean and Heideggerian revival of the 1970s to the first theorisations of 'sexual difference' in feminist thought) and in the Anglo-Saxon tradition (observe the parabola of the 'politics of difference'). Taken in radical form, this concept postulates precisely the transvaluation of the idea of limit.

It is the crux of the thesis that I wish provocatively to articulate here. However, difference is not a simple concept. Its declension takes two forms, which I shall attempt to outline below.

Beyond the Nature-Culture Dualism

Currently, what we may call the two 'canonical' acceptations of the notion of 'difference' tend to be classified in terms of the distinction between 'sex' and 'gender'. Roughly, the alternative is thought to be between an ontological (or, even, naturalistic) version of difference and a cultural one. Such a classification is best ignored, as it fails to do justice to either of the two already internally multifaceted and complex theoretical tendencies. It leaves out the fact that the former is constituted from its very beginnings in contrast to the metaphysical tradition, whereas the second turns upon a lively dispute – as chance would have it – with the anthropological concept of culture.

Therefore, I will define the former version as the *strong* concept of difference (*absit iniuria verbo*: but I cannot think of a more appropriate way to define this line of thought). This concept, developed by the earlier philosophies of sexual difference, picks out the sexualised body as 'the Repressed', the conical shadow that demarcates the originary logocentric limit of Western metaphysics, inasmuch as Western metaphysics is a universalism constructed on indifference and the absence of limit, on the presumption of the self-sufficiency and autochthony of a logic completely entrusted to mythology and to the jurisprudence of the neutral. In this strong concept of difference, the body is configured as the vital and concrete *space* subtracted from the logocentric obsession with time. Thus, a linear and accelerated, homogeneous and undifferentiated temporalisation of events that unfolds fully only in the modern era is said to betray the formally neutral but substantively male inclination for verticality and productive accumulation inscribed from the beginning in the genetic origin of Occidental thought. In the face of this mono-logic and its pretences-presumptions to self-sufficiency, the spatiality of the sexualised body – and, in the case in point, of the feminine body as the source of generation exemplified by the silent persistence of its cycles – erects itself as an intransitive and untraversable place. I am perfectly aware that my rendition sacrifices important variations and distinctions. However, the very theorists of sexual difference maintain that this first, strong – 'inaugural' – version of

the concept had to pay the heavy price of a rigid and heavy localisation of the capacity for representation and narration of the
feminine in order to counter the logocentric plan of Western
philosophy. The critique that second-generation feminism directed
at this version of sexual difference goes, more or less, as follows.
In this strong, heavy postulation of sexual difference that posits
the uncrossable body-space against the logocentric dominion of
the neutral, the feminine risks being construed not as the alternative to the ontological nomenclature but as its specular double.
Having begun as a critique of the metaphysical Subject, the strong
version of difference ends up giving rise to a hypersubject; its radical challenge to the metaphysical foundation and to institutional
orders that stem from it risks issuing in a hyperfoundation, in a
foundation to the second power that presents itself as better than
the former because it promises real stability and real order.

I shall now turn to the second acceptation of the term 'difference'. Once again, I will refer for simplicity's sake to a particularly
explicit and radical version, drawn from the most recent results of
North American thought: the postfeminist thinking of Donna
Haraway and her well-known and provocative formulation of the
feminine cyborg. For Haraway, the dualism sex/gender is nothing
but the reproposition of the nature/culture dichotomy. We must,
therefore, insist on gender as a notion that is increasingly emancipated from the fixity of sex. Briefly, gender understood as sexual
difference is also a constituted difference. We could add here, a
culturally constituted difference. But such a specification would
only be justified had we decided to remain within the nature/
culture dichotomy. Such a dichotomy is – as chance would have it
– what Haraway explodes. Gender is not a mere cultural construct.
Rather, it is the product of a construction that cannot remain
indifferent, for example, to the revolution in the understanding of
the physical world, in the idea of the *bíos*, of life, and so it cannot
be indifferent to the break-up of the logic of identity following the
advent of biotechnologies. Such a technology turns the body, that
body-space from which the previous feminist thought set out, into
a constructable entity: both a scientific but an aesthetic artifice as
well. In Haraway's constructivism, the borders [*confini*] between
the aesthetic and the biological tend to contaminate one another,
or literally become con-fused, revealing a complete *partage*. In
this extreme postfeminist thought, amongst which we can also
place other significant thinkers, such as Judith Butler, that I cannot
discuss here, we have the irreversible crisis of sources of identity.

This crisis projects us decisively in the direction of the post-human, of the hybridisation of the body with the machine. Bodies increasingly appear in the form of *coded texts*.

To grasp the sense of this passage, we must take note of the silent revolution that has invested the concept of nature in the Occident over the last decades. To summarise: in the Western tradition of thought we have, until very recently, worked with two dominant concepts of nature that we can sum up as follows: *nature as temple*, as *kósmos*: a perfectly delimited, perfectly enclosed harmonious space (it is no coincidence that 'cosmos' and 'cosmetics' derive from the same etymological root) within which events occur. All *hybris*, every violation of the sacredness of the confines [*confini*] of the *kósmos* gave way to a reaction, to an equal and contrary violent backlash that would restore the shattered order. This is the dominant idea of nature during the classical age, transmitted from the Greek and Roman eras (with a number of significant amendments that we will not specifiy here) through the Middle Ages to the time of the first scientific revolution of modernity, that of Galileo and Newton.

A new concept of nature takes over after the 'Copernican revolution'. Once again resorting to metaphor, I shall define this concept as 'nature as laboratory': no longer *kósmos*, no longer temple or preconstituted, pre-delimited, sacred 'zero-sum' space but *universum*. This term, which literally means 'one-way unfolding', expresses the homologating power of a uniform, mathematical space that is no longer qualitative (as in antiquity) but quantifiable and measurable. Therefore, nature is transformed into a laboratory; a section of homogeneous universe-space that can be carved out and extrapolated for experimentation, as a necessary step to extract from nature its secrets and formulate its laws. This is the praxis-idea of nature that was widespread until the exhaustion of the era of the Industrial Revolution.

Nature as temple; nature as laboratory. The scenario today is radically different from that of the images of nature mentioned above, which were so influential and so prolonged. Not only because of the rupture produced by events such as Einstein's relativity theory, quantum mechanics and the developments contemporaneous with them (whose philosophical implications I have attempted to tease out in *Minima temporalia* and *Kairós*), but also because of the silent revolution, the subcutaneous overturning of the modern scientific paradigm that has taken place in the last decades and that has now effected its *Durchbruch ins*

Freie, irruption into the open, through the hegemonic function of biology, of the life sciences. The unbridled result of this silent revolution was to introduce a new concept of nature: *nature as code*. In the idea of nature as code we have, when compared to the two preceding intuitions of nature, the upsetting of another traditional dualism that had traversed the entirety of ancient and modern thought: the dualism of subject and object. It is a resounding case of limit-experience and dissolution of the traditional border [*confine*] lines. The current representation of the nature of subject and object no longer views them as an antithesis. They appear formally homologous: isomorphism in the code. The investigating and experimenting subject is informed by a code in exactly the same way as the object of investigation and experimentation. It borders [*con-fina*] with it in the sense of sharing the same border rather than in the sense of estrangement and separation. The limit is posed, in the sense that one cannot observe the code on the basis of what one observes. This type of paradox was consummately prefigured, at least in philosophy, by the early Wittgenstein – in logico-philosophical terms – and then overcome pragmatically by the later Wittgenstein. As for the Wittgenstein of the *Tractatus*, we are unable to escape language, which coincides in every way with the extension of 'our' world – just as we are unable to 'say' the limits of language or, which comes to the same thing, we cannot describe the totality of the language-world but only 'show' its borders. Therefore, the dominant scientific paradigm today is unable to escape the code, but only force its limits from within – manipulating and reproducing it; thereby making nature itself into the product of artifice. Once again, then, we discover violated borders [*confini*]. And the upsetting of the borders [*confini*] evokes another celebrated classical dualism: that of nature and artifice. One should pay heed, however, to the manner in which the dualism is evoked: nature appears, as such, 'artificialised' inasmuch as the artifice itself participates in the code-character of nature. *Biology of artifice*: no formula appears to adapt itself better to the climate of this passage/turn of the millennium. Subject and object are similar insofar as they belong to the same code. Observer and observed are within the 'great code'. The great code overshadows and embraces not only the *bíos*, not only that circular and self-referential *dispositif*, that 'eternal golden braid'[1] that is the DNA code, but the concept of

---

1 Douglas R. Hofstadter, *Gödel, Escher, Bach: An Eternal Golden Braid*.

matter itself. Has not the physics of subatomic particles told us that an informational energy lies at the basis of the matter of bodies?

Although, today, the concept of nature as code presents itself in dramatic colours, at home, apparently in the current postmetaphysical and postmodern climate, in fact it relates back to an extremely ancient idea. It harks back to the old cabalistic and hermetic image of nature as a *ciphered* language susceptible to *deciphering*. The couple ciphering/deciphering or coding/decoding, semiotic couples *par excellence*, are currently used (in a more or less conscious and reflected-upon form) in the applied sciences as well as the theoretical ones.

Returning to the theme of difference, it seems to me that what is at stake in postfeminism becomes clearer in the light of the results of this scientific revolution. If the confines [*confini*] of bodies must be freed from their organic barriers, this liberation is all the more true of the logics of identity. This raises, once again, the relationship of border [*confine*] to barrier. Once the organic barriers are unhinged, the body presents itself as a code in perennial transformation, which incessantly dislocates and redesigns its own borders [*confini*], in the same way as a dynamic whole that is composed, essentially, of three aspects: *sign*, *context* and *time*. These are the coordinates of the body and of identity. Every body is a system of signs, a contingent 'putting-into-form' of signs that exists, situatedly, in determinate contexts or forms-of-life and that is continually remodelled in the course of time. The confines of identity are, therefore, subject to an incessant process of deconstruction–reconstruction. Identity is never given. We are decidedly outside a logic of identity in the shape of a stable, spatial map. Normalised functions are nothing but the relative stability of that map, whose configuration always appears contingent and precarious. Thus, we must leave behind the image of the 'I' as a stable spatial map, whether it is understood in the traditional metaphysical and 'subject-centred' sense, or the postmetaphysical and 'structure-centred' sense of systemic self-referentiality. Once these models are surmounted, the question of subjectivity will be given its most appropriate translation by the image of a map in the process of becoming, in constant deconstruction-reconstruction, in which the transaction occurs between sign, context and time. As Donna Haraway says, in this way bodies become material semiotic and generative modes.

Multiple Self: Difference and Identification

Let us shift our attention to another aspect for a moment, in order to allude rapidly to the revolution in the concept of personal identity that has occurred in recent years within postanalytic philosophy. I am referring to a very important text by Derek Parfit from 1984, *Reasons and Persons*. In this book, we find Parfit taking up again and developing a theme that had already been tackled by the later Wittgenstein (in *Philosophical Investigations*): the subject of identity as the succession of partial and contingent 'I's. Each one of us does not so much 'have' an identity that 'is made' in time (an image that in every way can be reconciled with the dialectical process). Rather, each of us has an identity that 'is' composed of subjectivity part-time. In short, we are all a cluster, a plurality of part-time 'I's that unfold in time. If we wanted to indicate the synchronic aspect of this conception, we would have to refer to the observations of another postanalytic philosopher, Jon Elster. The key notion introduced by Elster is that of 'multiple self': a 'self' that is at once individual but irreducibly multiple. Multiple identity is never a self-referential, unitary and homogenous 'I'. Within the space of identity there coexist or, rather, cohabit a number of identities, which are sometimes in conflict with one another. The decisive point is this: the *inherence of the community within the individual* and the contrasts that this inherence induces. More simply, the 'I' is not a subject-substance nor a homogeneous structure. Rather, it is a space, like the cavity of a theatre in which echo diverse imperatives, values and normative frameworks stemming not only from heterogeneous and 'asynchronic' traditions, but sometimes incompatible and potentially conflicting ones.

It is not illegitimate to note that these postanalytic reflections on the problem of identity reveal some significant points of contact or even convergence with hermeneutic standpoints. However, a hermeneutic approach is able to interact fruitfully with these themes only if it abandons certain apologetic or edifying attitudes, which can be traced back to an excessive faith in the virtues of a 'communication' or 'social conversation' that finds consolation via a historicising reference to the authority of tradition. If one is to take seriously the postanalytic challenge, one will have to critique that accommodating version of hermeneutics for which not only (and not so much) has the subject always been 'thrown' into or 'situated' in a tradition that it must each time interpret, but rather which draws its criterion of truth as interpretation from the fact of finding itself – as Gianni Vattimo has recently suggested – the illegitimate child of that culminating phase of the history of nihilism and the weakening of being (that is to say, our epoch) whose point of arrival would coincide with the idea of truth as interpretation. The question remains whether such a *dispositif* – according to which we are justified by the fact that, not today in the same way as yesterday, but precisely today in contrast to yesterday, the nihilistic trajectory has (supposedly) concluded with the beneficial dissolving of truth into interpretation – is nothing but the repetition in disguise of the philosophy of history.

But beyond these disputes – to which we shall have to return – the challenge of the postanalytic approach to the theme of personal identity poses a question to hermeneutics that is truly subtle and difficult to sidestep. The 'self' immersed in the tradition is problematic, in itself, because it is constitutively multiple. Which of these 'selves' – observing things from *a parte subjecti* – is each time called upon to interpret? And – observing things from *a parte objecti* – which tradition does the 'self' interpret? There are many interpreting 'selves' and many traditions that must be interpreted. Contingency even acts retroactively on the hermeneutic programme of weakening the classical notions of truth and subject, investing the very liberating significance of interpretation understood as the point of arrival of the history of nihilism.

In contrast, one of the implications of the concept of 'multiple self' (Jon Elster) and 'successive selves' (Derek Parfit) does seem to me liberating: the radical destitution of the foundation of a constant of Western thought, which in *Kairós* I called the 'patrimonial conception of the subject', that is, the idea of subject *mit Eigenschaften*, 'with properties' (as Musil would put it). Such a subject is identifiable only insofar as he is the legitimate proprietor of certain qualities and owner of certain attributes. It is only by virtue of this patrimonial logic and grammar that the paradigms of rational action are constituted – so influential in modern economics and politics – which entrust the realisation of the person to the strategies of 'possessive' or 'acquisitive' individualism.

By this route the idea of the 'self' as stable, titular possessor of his or her own identity is put in question. In the most recent developments concerning the mobile frontiers of identity, we encounter the delineation of a no-self theory that tries to push the consequences of the desubstantialised image of the subject as a succession of contingent and partial 'selves' as far as they will go. It is difficult to deny the suggestive force and the descriptive pertinence of these approaches. Each of us will, on occasion, have considered how he or she was ten or twenty years ago and tried to ideally establish a relationship with 'one's self' at that time similar to the one we might establish with a good friend or, occasionally, with a stranger or even an enemy (to the extent that we become aware of a feeling of estrangement or – even – of hostility towards our past 'self'). Naturally, it is also possible that one might perceive one's life, the unfolding of one's personality in time, as a perfectly unitary and coherent process. I would not blame someone for doing so but I most certainly would not envy that person either.

In any case, no one – whatever idea they may have of their life: whether they conceive of it as a series of caesurae or turns, or as a compact and coherent unity – can evade this question: to what extent and under what conditions can we say that the past we have lived is 'ours'? The finest (not only philosophical) thinking of the twentieth century has provided a variety of answers to this nagging question, but it always rejected the atomistic and solipsistic prejudice of the individual as a preconstituted entity. The biography of the individual, like the individual him or herself, describes a problematic process of construction, which is closer to the weaving of a plot – always composite, frequently knotted and contorted – than to the unfolding of an uninterrupted and coherent thread. It is only from taking cognisance of the relational and irredeemably intricate nature of our history that is born the incessant activity of connecting that – following narrative or constructive strategies – throws a bridge between different phases and aspects of our 'selves'. What is true retrospectively, for the elaboration of the link of past and present, is also true prospectively, for the link of present and future. Between my current 'self' and my future 'self', I am able to establish relations like – at the limit – those between the experiences of person A and those of person B. Not, therefore, two existential phases or states but precisely two different 'persons'. Perhaps it will be another person who will develop the results I have arrived at today. As is the case with every decomposition, that of a subject not only determines separations and fractures but also – not despite of but thanks to them – new relational and communicational possibilities. It may be true that my future 'I' will be a person B different from the person A that I am today but, equally, some features of A (of my current state) may be taken up again and developed by another. It is in terms of this double movement of disarticulation and rearticulation – where the decomposition is not only a dissolution or fracture but also the virtuality of new relational interweavings – that we must understand the revolutionising of the classic notion of identity, replaced today by the image of an uninterrupted migration of successive 'selves'. From this perspective, postanalytic thought revisits Hume's federal conception of the mind. In order to overcome the obsession with identity, Hume is a thinker that can be reclaimed by post-metaphysical thinking (as did Gilles Deleuze).

As is well known, the dissociation between the concepts of continuity and identity is an exquisitely Deleuzian motif. To begin to think of what is radically Other to metaphysical custom (and not what is merely a drift away from it) involves, first of all, separating the problem of becoming and the experiential continuum (a continuum furrowed by constant folds and fracture lines) from the logic of identity. Metaphysics told us that continuity was nothing but a variable dependent upon identity. In contrast, we must *learn to think* of continuity as something *other* than identity. The concluding thesis I now wish to propose is the following: continuity (of dynamic contexts, of forms-of-life) can be given from the perspective of difference.

But at this point, what *difference* are we speaking of? Not difference as anti-foundation, which always becomes a hyperfoundation, nor the difference that dissolves into the differences of Donna Haraway and of post-differentialism. The difference that I will discuss now in deliberately drastic and provocative terms develops in a, perhaps, heretical manner some ideas that I have encountered in Deleuze's work.

How is one, then, to understand difference, difference understood not as dialectical negativity, nor as the mere opposite of the logic of identity, but difference as the *cipher of the unidentifiability of being*? Being does not tolerate identifications. It has no identity card. If it is true that the strange complex of events that we call 'world' is, inasmuch as it occurs, made up of differences, then it follows that *differences never identify being but, precisely, they differentiate it*. Precisely because they differentiate it, they produce the phenomenon of the becoming of life. The becoming of life is given insofar as there is no identifiability of being. There can be, obviously, identification and classification of events, but we must be aware that they have nothing to do with the order of the world. Rather, they are a response to a practical need – as Nietzsche saw so well. Only by grasping this passage can we explode the *dispositif* of metaphysics, which is at one with the *dispositif* of power: the idea of the One as the unity of differences. However, we must guard against the all-too-easy – and 'too human' – overcomings of metaphysics that are so commonplace on the cultural market. Metaphysics has thought about difference. It has thought about it as obsessively as it has thought about identity. But – and this is the point – it has done so in the sense that its thought of being has coincided, from Aristotle to Hegel, with the thought of the unity of differences. On this insidious ridge of metaphysical thought nestles the *dispositif* to which I have just alluded: the *dispositif* that is common to both power and to the logic of identity. I am increasingly aware of the fact that the thought of the One as the (functional, structural or even dialectical) unity of differences is born of a fundamental confusion; the confusion between the *stoicheion*, the 'constitutive', the constituting, and the 'identitarian'.

Thus, I am convinced that the future of the concept of 'difference' and the entire future of post-philosophical thought is entrusted to our ability to carry out a symbolic inversion of the logic of identity, keeping the thought of the constituting apart from that of the One. The constitutive is the contrary of the One. Instead, if we insist on the strategic game of foundational logic, wagering on our ability to reabsorb the thought of the *stoicheion* within the self-referential circle of the One, we will do nothing but 'reset' the question of the 'common', of what constitutes us, within the architectonic barriers of the logic of identity. In which case, the metaphysical obsession with identity, having been thrown out the front door, will return through the welcoming windows of the neo-functionalist and systemic models. Once captured by the cogency of these models, we will no longer be able to frame the question of the 'common' as it should be: as the question of the *cum*, of the *infra*, of the relation, of proximity and difference, of the bond and the conflict between irreducible differences that can *never* identify being. Not even the being of subjectivity, from which all differentiation begins.

9

EUROPE AFTER THE LEVIATHAN: TECHNOLOGY, POLITICS, CONSTITUTION

The Future of Europe: from the Protected Society to the 'Risk Society'

Having crossed the threshold of the twenty-first century, what is the 'fate of Europe'? Once the pillars that supported it have fallen, how do we perceive the destiny of the Old Continent within the Occidental passage that marks the course of civilisations in the globalised world?

These are the mandatory questions that force themselves upon us once we arrive at the last station in our circular journey around the nerve centres of the global era. We shall attempt to answer them by drawing upon the results of an interdisciplinary, Europe-wide working group launched by the Fondazione Basso in 1998, which culminated in the International Convention on the Public Sphere and the European Constitution held in Rome on 15–16 December 2000. The meeting (which brought together a number of jurists, political scientists, philosophers and social scientists) took place in a moment that was propitious for two reasons: that is, soon after the proclamation of the Charter of Fundamental Rights of the European Union at the Nice summit on 7 December 2000 and of the resolution to open up to the countries of Eastern Europe, and at the end of a century – 'short', perhaps, but certainly great and tragic – that coincides with the taking leave of the second millennium of the Christian era. The symbolic value of this coincidence and of the welding of structure and conjuncture, short wave and long wave of European historical and cultural development that it represents, had been accurately signalled by Jürgen Habermas – the mentor and instigator of the initiative – in his book *Die postnationale Konstellation*.

The threshold of the twenty-first century exerts such a strong grip on our imagination because it also leads us into a new millennium. This calendrical turning point is itself the product of a construction of religious history, whose starting point, the birth of Christ, marked what we recognize in hindsight as a break in world history.[1]

The general significance of this passage should be clear to anyone who considers the decisive function Christianity has played in the constitution of historical time and of the identities of the modern Occident, not least in defining the 'indivisible, universal values of human dignity, freedom, equality and solidarity' that the Charter of Rights itself places in the Preamble to the foundational 'spiritual and moral heritage' of the Union.

Nevertheless, if we want to grasp – beyond the 'wall of time' [*Zeitmauer*][2] – the measure of the persistences and changes, of the continuities and discontinuities of the problems, we must free ourselves from the cage of chronology. Rarely do the round figures of the calendar coincide with the actual temporal nodes of salient historical events.

Years like 1900 or 2000 are meaningless in comparison to dates such as 1914, 1945, or 1989. What's more, these calendrical blocs can have the effect of concealing the very continuity of far-reaching social trends, many of which have origins well before the beginning of the twentieth century and will continue well into the new millennium.[3]

Habermas' admonition will be particularly valuable in helping us focus on the current political conjuncture of Europe, whose *constitutional present* is literally inconceivable without reference to the long-term tendencies that have crossed its history, high and low, and marked, with often violent and bloody conflicts, the troubled course of its cultural identity.

In commenting on the Nice summit, the president of the Italian Republic, Carlo Azeglio Ciampi, affirmed that the decisions taken there represent a 'good compromise in order to march on more quickly towards a more integrated and enlarged Europe'. Along this path – which now is 'enlarged' – the first step to be taken should be, according to Ciampi, that of turning the Charter of Rights into a genuine European Constitution. However, in adopting this demand for ourselves, we think it necessary to

---

1 Jürgen Habermas, *The Postnational Constellation*, p. 38.
2 Ernst Jünger, *An der Zeitmauer*.
3 Habermas, *The Postnational Constellation*, p. 38.

pose two essential and unavoidable questions. First, what are the necessary conditions and intermediate stages for the actualisation of this passage? Second, what should the distinctive political and constitutional characteristics of Europe be? We should note that the future of Europe proposed by the different European partners currently appears not only very different but sometimes even divergent. This is an acknowledgement of fact that in no way authorises us to embrace those diffuse objections that continue to nourish the arguments of the Eurosceptics. While it is true that the Nice compromise is hardly a cause for facile optimism, we must recognise that – after the proclamation of the Charter of Fundamental Rights and the decision to open up the Union to the countries of the East – the European question has taken a step forward. This step forward potentially projects Europe towards a new horizon: passing from a 'necessary', eminently economic-monetary phase marked by the categorical imperative of 'stability' to a phase of 'normative' integration of a constitutional character.

The result of this new phase will depend on Europe's ability to a) put itself in play in the world of global interdependency, shifting from the current dominant paradigm of the 'protected society' to that of the 'risk society'; and b), to characterise itself, on the basis of choices and decisions, as a real political entity. However, the points of view within the Union are divided precisely with respect to the 'normative' political and constitutional plane, not only and not so much vertically, from country to country, but – as demonstrated by the European working group of the Fondazione Basso – also horizontally, along the borders [*linee di confine*] that transversally cut across the different national areas. The perceptible complication of the set of problems that follow inevitably from this should not necessarily be considered negatively. For despite the persistence of what are in many respects heterogeneous traditions and languages, the fact that there can exist a commonality of outlooks between intellectuals of different nationalities and – conversely – a divergence between intellectuals of the same country, could be seen as the symptom, if not the embryo, of an incipient process of formation of a European public sphere.

State and Constitution: The Controversy Between
Dieter Grimm and Jürgen Habermas

For these very reasons, far from constituting a *querelle* internal to German political-juridical culture, the alternative that emerged from the congress between Dieter Grimm's standpoint and Jürgen Habermas' – itself the continuation of the celebrated debate that they led in the pages of the *European Law Journal* in 1995 – invests a field of forces that crosses all the principal European countries. In his intervention 'Does Europe Need a Constitution?',[4] Grimm had set out from the classical distinction between constitution, understood as the juridical foundation of the state, and treaty, understood as the juridical foundation of international institutions. He then indicated the core of the institutional identity of Europe in the separability of the constitution from the state. However, although the European Union is composed of states, it is not itself a state. Even if it is endowed with sovereign prerogatives by the member states, the European community utilises powers that are not disciplined by constitutional law. Consequently, the institutional status of the Union is marked by a structural contradiction. On the one hand, the European Union is a supernational organisation founded upon treaties, which is the reason it is not a sovereign state in the modern sense of the term (one that maintains a 'monopoly of legitimate physical violence', in Weber's celebrated phrase[5]). On the other hand, the Union – although it is not a state – has at its disposal a capacity for domination that once belonged to states, producing legal norms that are binding on member states. Therefore, the gap that opens up between the ever-wider authority of the decision-making organs of the Union (Commission, Council of Ministers, Court of European Justice) and the processes of legitimation, which are still contained within the areas of sovereignty of the single member states, generates a democratic deficit as its ineluctable consequence.

A process of constitutionalisation, with the aim of conferring on the European Union the characteristics of a federal state, does not appear a realistic objective given the lack of a European people.

---

4   This is the English version of a lecture given in January 1994 at the Carl Friedrich von Siemens Stiftung. See Dieter Grimm, 'Does Europe Need a Constitution?'.

5   Max Weber, 'Politics as a Vocation', p. 33.

[I]t is inherent in a constitution in the full sense of the term that it goes back to an act taken by or at least attributed to the people, in which they attribute political capacity to themselves. There is no such source for primary Community law. It goes back not to a European people but to the individual member states, and remains dependent on them even after its entry into force. While nations give themselves a constitution, the European Union is given a constitution by third parties. It consequently does not have the disposal of its own constitution. The 'masters of the treaties', as it is sometimes put, are still member states, who have not been, as it were, absorbed into the Union.[6]

Certainly, at the basis of such an argument there lies the classic – linear – equation of the modern public-law doctrine, which relates the state constitution back to popular sovereignty. It would, however, be disingenuous to delude oneself that the hypothesis of such a sophisticated and competent jurist could be discounted by ascribing it to a substantialist conception of the *Volksgemeinschaft*. Indeed, Grimm is perfectly aware of the lack of foundation to the idea of a homogeneous popular community and of the 'divergences of opinions and interests'[7] that characterise the notion of 'the people'. The presupposition of democratic legitimation – that Europe is supposed to lack – need not be that of a homogeneous ethnicity but, rather, that of a society able to make way for a 'collective identity'[8] and to an 'awareness of belonging together that can support majority decisions and solidarity efforts'.[9] In contrast to the United States of America, Europe lacks a unitary party system or unitary groups and civil movements (just as it lacks a common language and – consequently – a European media network in publishing or radio and television). As things stand – Grimm concludes – '[c]onverting the European Union into a federal state can in these circumstances not be an immediately desirable end', for the simple but decisive reason that its degree of legitimacy would be 'lower than a nation-state's, also lessening its capacity to solve problems, something that has not just technical but also legitimatory prerequisites'.[10]

The argument put forth by Habermas in response (and then included in his *Die Einbeziehung des Anderen*) is equally well known and – in our opinion – decisive. If we take seriously the

---

6   Grimm, 'Does Europe Need a Constitution?', p. 248.
7   Ibid., p. 250.
8   Ibid., p. 254.
9   Ibid., pp. 254–55.
10 Ibid. , p. 255.

'deconstruction' of the concept of 'the people' postulated by Grimm – understanding it in opposition to the homogenising *völkisch à la* Carl Schmitt – should we, then, not grasp 'collective identity' as a consequence rather than as a premise of the constitution and of democratic citizenship? Once we have left the metaphysical-substantialist conceptions behind, identity is never given *a priori*, independently of the democratic process, but, rather, it is the result of the relational and communicative dynamic between citizens. Soldering together the paradigm of communicative action and the procedural method of legitimation, Habermas can claim the need for a European constitution as the condition for the formation of a European society and a citizenship marked by the model of a 'solidarity among strangers'[11] that is mediated legally – in the same way, incidentally, as national identities have been formed historically.

> The ethical-political self-understanding of citizens in a democratic community must not be taken as a historical-cultural a priori that makes democratic will-formation possible, but rather as the fluid content of a circulatory process that is generated through the legal institutionalization of citizen's communication. This is precisely how national identities were formed in modern Europe. Therefore it is to be expected that the political institutions that would be created by a European constitution would have a catalytic effect.[12]

We have already underlined the significance of this framework. It is equally important to note, however, the tension between two unresolved nodes at the heart of Habermas' theoretical-political proposal. On the one hand, he affirms that the American model of a nation of citizens held together by 'constitutional patriotism'[13] represents the most adequate solution to confront the challenges of the cultural and ideological pluralism of an increasingly complex and differentiated society. In contrast to the 'culturally assimilationist French model', this solution can enable the coexistence and cooperation of various 'cultural, religious and ethnic forms'.[14] On the other hand, the most suitable model for realising European identity, in the form of a unity in plurality of nations, is German federalism in Gerhard Schröder and Joschka Fischer's version (the inheritors of that project of a federal state auspicated

---

11 Habermas, *The Postnational Constellation*, p. 102.
12 Jürgen Habermas, *The Inclusion of the Other*, p. 161.
13 Habermas, *The Postnational Constellation*, p. 74.
14 Habermas, *The Inclusion of the Other*, p. 160.

by Altiero Spinelli). But can we be certain that the two assertions are compatible and capable of converging on a single objective? And to what extent can the solution of a federal European state be considered an adequate response to the theoretical need – rightly advanced by Habermas – for a flexible, pluralistic and differentiated legal order capable of confronting the challenges of the 'post-national constellation'?

   In working out our strategic response to these questions, we will adopt two distinct – but strictly complementary and interdependent – registers of argument. One will be theoretical and political; the other historical and comparative. With the help of the former we will attempt to gauge the degree to which the categories of public law endure or become obsolete. With the aid of the latter we will seek to situate the process of European constitutionalisation within the dynamic of so-called globalisation and so attempt to overcome the risks of a 'Eurocentric' perspective.

The Perils of Constituent Power

If we observe the ongoing process from the perspective of political and constitutional doctrine, the question of the 'identity' of Europe seems to demand setting aside the oscillation between legality and legitimacy: procedural normativism and the mythology of constitutive power. In reality, the poles of this supposed dilemma have never arranged themselves along a one-way axis but – rather – in circular fashion. Besides, from Hegel onwards we should know how difficult it is to identify the beginning, the commencement, the *fiat* of a constituent process. Nevertheless, the modern doctrine of sovereignty, which centres on the legal fiction of the *Person-State*, has never – from Bodin to Hobbes, from the Rousseauist and Jacobin idea of the 'General Will' to the German dogmatics of public law as in Jellinek or even Carl Schmitt – ceased basing itself on two postulates: a) the distinction between *pouvoir constituant* and *pouvoir constitué*; and b) the counterfactual hypothesis of the *homogeneity of the People-Subject*. Insofar as it is a *limit question* of constitutional law, the theme of constituent power is still considered by an authoritative heir and prosecutor of this tradition such as Ernst-Wolfgang Böckenförde from four standpoints.

1) From the *historico-genetic* angle, the notion of constituent power aims to identify the eminently political origin of the

constitution: its formative dynamic and the forces that come together to determine it.

2) From the standpoint of the *theory of law*, the concept of constituent power concerns the philosophical and legal problem of the substantive foundation of the constitutional norm. That is, to the normative presuppositions from which is derived the *presumption of validity* of the constitution (understood as 'legal arrangement fundamental to the community').[15]

3) From the perspective of the *theory of the constitution*, this notion is concerned with the petition [*istanza*] or subject that is able to confer *legitimacy* (or democratic legitimacy) on the constitution.

4) From the viewpoint of the *doctrine of constitutional law*, it aims to fix the procedures of revision of the constitution anticipated by the constitution itself, right up to and including the transformation or suppression of its very core: 'acts no longer reserved for the legislator of constitutional revision but to the very constitutor (*pouvoir constituant*)'.

The theory of constituent power contests, at its very roots, the normative conceptions that – like Kelsen's pure doctrine of law – posit a 'fundamental norm' (*Grundnorm*) as the axiom of opening/ closure of the ordering/regulation. Such a 'hypothetical assumption' – argues Böckenförde, repeating Schmitt's famous critique almost word for word – merely serves to 'pose the question of *legitimacy* without actually resolving it'.[16] Consequently, it subtracts the moment of *pouvoir constituant* from 'the sphere of the political to which it, nevertheless, belongs'. In short, the force that produces and legitimates the constitution cannot be reduced to 'a point of ideal-normative imputation' but, rather, must be a '*real political entity* that founds the normative validity of the constitution'.

The logical cogency of the argument set out by the German constitutional theorist results in a definition that is as concise as it is conclusive: 'Constituent power is that (political) force and authority that is able to *create, sustain and overcome* the

---

15   Ernst-Wolfgang Böckenförde, *Staat, Verfassung, Demokratie*, p. 92.
16   Ibid., p. 93.

constitution's presumption to normative validity'.[17] As such, it cannot subsist within or on the basis of the constitution, as does an 'organ'[18] created by it, but must pre-exist the constitution and the '*pouvoir constitué*'[19] that it delimits and regulates. However, a corollary follows from this pre- and over-determination of the *pouvoir constitué* that is decisive to the definition of constitutive power: it is never identical to constituted state power but, on the contrary, precedes it. The bluntly revolutionary imprint of constituent power resides here, argues Böckenförde. It stands in relation to the state as the dynamic does to the static, as 'life' to 'form'. Such a quality reveals itself even more forcefully if we take into consideration the other postulate upon which the concept is constructed: the fiction of the People as a homogeneous subject.

With respect to origin and content, *pouvoir constituant* is a 'democratic and revolutionary concept' that is legitimately situated 'only within a *democratic* theory of the constitution'. Coined by the Abbé Sieyès on the eve of the French Revolution, it represents a significant example of 'political theology', in the sense of a transference to the People-Subject (understood politically) of the typically theological attributes of divine *maiestas*: *creation ex nihilo, norma Normans, potestas constituens*. In virtue of this 'transposition', the People becomes – in the height of the revolutionary climate – the exclusive subject of sovereignty and the authentic possessor of *pouvoir constituent*. The sovereign centrality and indivisibility of the new subject should not, however, be understood in the fully metaphysical or substantialist sense. In the same way as Grimm, Böckenförde rapidly qualifies the category of 'the people' by saying that although it cannot be resolved into that of 'the citizenship', 'neither does it coincide with the people conceived in the natural or ethnic sense, as a group united by a language, by descent or by a common civilisation'.[20] *The People* is, rather, a political and legal notion. In the *political sense*, by people we understand a group of men and women that 'has become conscious of itself as a political entity and that, as such, intervenes as an agent in history'. In the *legal sense*, the 'sovereign people' – the legitimate possessor of constituent power – is a 'concept of public law' that plays a decisive role 'not only in

---

17 Ibid., p. 94 – our italicisation.
18 Ibid., p. 93.
19 Ibid., p. 94.
20 Ibid., p. 96.

France but also in German constitutional development'.[21]

An axis is delineated through the limit-notion (*Grenzbegriff*) of constituent power, which links the model of the French Revolution directly to the German dogmatics of the *ius publicum* that turns on the towering notion of 'sovereign decision' – instituting an ideal continuum between Sieyès *Qu'est-ce que le tiers état?* and Schmitt's *Verfassungslehre* – and that ends with this drastic conclusion:

> The constituent power of the people, understood as the *pouvoir constituent* that *precedes* the legal constitution, cannot be legally regulated by the constitution itself, nor can it be regulated in the forms in which it manifests itself. It has preserved its original, immediate and even elementary character; consequently it is able to procure and create – precisely inasmuch as it is a political entity – its very forms of appearing.[22]

However, the Continental dogmatics of the *ius publicum europæum* misses the decisive element of the historical period of the constitutions; namely, that the inheritance of the French Revolution does not consist only in the people-sovereignty-state axis (with the paradoxical exchange of roles between the 'revolutionary' appeal and 'reactionary' appeal to the constituent power of the People-Subject that follows from it), but also in that phenomenon of *deterritorialisation of law* that – according to Arendt – represents the extraordinary historical significance of the revolutionary processes that took hold in America and France at the end of the eighteenth century. Carefully examined, it is clear that the political theology of constituent power hides the fact that the constitutions resulting from those revolutionary processes are preceded by declarations of universal rights and principles that should be valid extra-territorially and not only within the space of a single sovereign nation state. Hence, democracy does not coincide *sic et simpliciter* with popular sovereignty. It counter-balances this principle with constitutional guarantees advanced to protect the citizen. The source of democratic legitimacy is, in other words, neither exclusive nor unique but dual. It is properly constituted by the binomial – or by the bipolar interaction – of popular sovereignty and fundamental rights.

The tragic course of the twentieth century should have proven

---

21   Ibid., p. 97.
22   Ibid., p. 99.

sufficiently that the plebiscitary drift and the direct appeal to the popular will represent the typical features of totalitarianism. To take up a theme of Arendt's, once again, it is more the offspring of Napoleon than of Louis XIV; more the perverse by-product of equality and 'mass politics' than of *ancien régime* absolutism. The theoretical implication of this line of argument is that what really counts is not the *single act* of constituent power, but the dynamic unfolding of the process of constitutionalisation, that is to say, the concrete passages that lead to the assertion of a table of universally valid values and principles and, through them, to the fundamental rights that lie at the basis of a constitutional charter. Jon Elster has correctly observed that, to this very day, a 'comparative study of constitution-making is practically non-existent'.[23] Although comparative constitutional law has been for some time an established discipline; although the comparative study of ordinary legislations constitutes a central part of political science; although the comparative analysis of the revolutions now has a long history; despite this, we are still missing works that discuss 'the process of constitution-making in a general comparative perspective'.

If, within a relatively short time, we could be presented with the synoptic tables requested by Elster, we would certainly have a further tool to help us orientate ourselves in relation to that phenomenon of 'synchrony of the asynchronic' (*Gleichzeitigkeit des Ungleichzeitigen*), in the suggestive expression introduced in the mid-1930s by Ernst Bloch in *Heritage of Our Times*, from which stem the forest of different and, at times, contrasting points of view on the political and institutional identity of Europe. It is enough to bear in mind, just to widen the range of examples, the British position – expressed baldly by Anthony Giddens in an interview with Nina zu Fürstenberg, published in *Focus* – in which Europe cannot constitute itself in a super-state of either the centralised, French type or of the federal, German type. Or, think of the recent and instructive encounter between two European political personages of the highest order, Jacques Delors and Václav Havel, in which the former proposes the transformation of the Union into a federal state as a constitutional solution and the latter responds that 'what is emerging in

---

23   Jon Elster, 'Constitution-Making in Eastern Europe: Rebuilding the Boat in the Open Sea', p. 174.

Europe is not a federation in the classic sense of the term'[24] but something new, for which political scientists will have to 'invent a new category'. From this game of counterpoints and dissonances there emerges a common recognition that the political unity that must be constructed will be all the more effective and credible the more it is fully able to valorise the plurality of traditions, languages and cultures that constitutes the richness of our inexpugnable continent. Not for nothing does the Preamble of the Charter of Fundamental Rights of the European Union decline the People-Subject in the plural rather than the singular: 'The peoples of Europe, in creating an ever closer union among them, are resolved to share a peaceful future based on common values.' As if to say, the conditions authorising the adoption of a formula of the type 'We the people of the United States . . .' are lacking. And the common values, defined at the start of the second paragraph as the 'indivisible, universal values of human dignity, freedom, equality and solidarity', are placed, at the start of the third paragraph, in a two-way relation in 'respecting the diversity of the cultures and traditions of the peoples of Europe'. So, if it is true that the choice which lies before Europe today is well expressed – as Jacques Derrida and Étienne Balibar have lucidly observed – by the alternative between the fortress and the open space of liberty and democracy, it follows that its common identity will be unable to possess the exclusive (and, in the final analysis, ethnocentric) character of the *demos*. Rather, it must have the inclusive character of the *civitas*. The 'Roman way' – the *voie romaine*, as Rémi Brague called it – clearly still has much to teach us in view of the twenty-first century.[25]

However, the reference to the value of plurality must avoid the perils of a 'patrimonial' rhetoric and logic. The new form can be born neither of a mechanical summation nor of a simple convergence – or worse still, by a compromise – between the constitutional traditions of the member countries. In other words, it is necessary that the Union is able to express 'added value' with respect to the significant (and historically hypercelebrated) 'European constitutional heritage'. From this point of view, the Charter – at least in the light of some of its formulas – appears somewhat ungenerous to itself in its forceful underlining of continuity, of its

---

24   Jacqueline Henard and Daniel Vernet, 'La Grande Europe vue par Jacques Delors et Vaclav Havel'.

25   *Translator's note*: For a translation, see Rémi Brague, *Eccentric Culture*.

'patrimonial' links with the past and in the faint markings of novelty that it brings to all the preceding constitutional traditions on crucial themes such as life and the body, the new horizons of bioethics (art. 3) and the problem – which should, perhaps, have been made more explicit – of gender differences (art. 23). It is thanks to this spirit of cultural openness that the Charter 'deconstructs' the other benchmark of the Continental legal dogmatic: the counterfactual assumption of the homogeneity of the people. The critique of the concept of 'the People' in terms of a 'totemic mask' that hides the multiplicity of differences that constitute the social community had, as is well known, already been widely discussed by Hans Kelsen – long ago in 1920 – in *Vom Wesen und Wert der Demokratie*. The 'unity of the people' – the great Austrian jurist had underlined, in the spirit of the most unadulterated Hobbesian tradition – was not to be understood in a sociological sense, but in a legal and constitutional sense. The text of the Charter goes even further. It is not limited to the destructuring of the unitary idea of the People understood as a 'substance-concept' (*Substanzbegriff* in Kelsen's terminology) but as a 'function-concept' (*Funktionsbegriff*), and as a political fiction. The instance of plurality and difference no longer invests only the metaphysical-substantialist presuppositions underlying the classical doctrine of the *ius publicum europæum*, but irrupts into legal language itself, permeating its syntax and semantics. The homogeneous postulate of 'identity' is also left behind on the 'fictional' plane of legal and constitutional science.

'Behind', as it were, the formulations adopted by the Charter, we can detect the pressure exerted by the complex (and currently discontinuous) dynamic of the formation of a European 'civil society' and 'public sphere', whose phases and modes of realisation must still reckon with an epochal passage of traumatic proportions. In this dynamic, the old coupling of civil society and state appears to be traversed by a dual process of integration and disarticulation: the integration of social contexts and the disarticulation of traditional functions of the territorially enclosed sovereign nation states. From this ongoing process new powers and new subjects, new discriminants and new dimensions of existence are generated. These are mutations of civilisation that invest, as Habermas would say, the *Lebenswelte*, the lifeworlds, but appear, to this day, to have been unable to scratch the self-reproducing political oligarchies. In this passage, European legal space risks situating itself in a no-man's-land, in a sort of interlude or time suspended between a 'democracy of identity' and a 'democracy of differences'. Despite Habermas' hopes, we are still far from a theory and a praxis able to legitimise itself through the 'inclusion of the Other'.

The European Union and the 'Post-Hobbesian Order': The Multilevel System of Government

The crucial question that still awaits an answer concerns the political nature of that mysterious object called the European Union within the 'postnational constellation'. In some recent interventions, Giuliano Amato has defined Europe as an 'unidentified flying object the nature of which is not yet ascertainable and that flies, nevertheless'. The European Union, the outlines of which have emerged in the course of the postwar years, represents an absolutely novel institutional model in political and constitutional history. 'It is the model of an authority above the states, which adopts rules that will increasingly become effective within the states themselves'.[26] From the theoretical standpoint, for Amato – in a way similar to Havel or Giddens – it is 'entirely unrealistic to view our future as that of a mega-sovereignty'.[27] The national states have certainly lost much of their sovereignty. However, sovereignty has not been transferred elsewhere. In other words, there has been a 'dispersal of sovereignty' or, rather – to return to the socio-institutional interpretation of Alessandro Pizzorno – a *dispersal of powers*. Certainly no one could define the member countries of the Union as 'sovereign states' in the same way they were half a century ago. 'They lack monetary sovereignty . . . ; in many areas the laws that judges apply are laws that come from above and not from them, so they can no longer be said to have the *jus superiorem non recognoscens* over their territory'.[28] But that by no means entails that the European Union is a sovereign organisation. Not even in the sense of a federal state *in fieri*. Strictly speaking, it is 'not a state; it does not even have a legal character and the Maastricht Treaty was careful not to give it'. So, how are we to define this mysterious object? The Union, says Amato, constitutes

---

26 Giuliano Amato, 'L'originalità istituzionale dell'Unione Europea', p. 82.
27 Ibid., p. 81.
28 Ibid., p. 84.

perhaps the analytically most clearly identifiable and explanatory example of that phenomenon of our time that some of our thinkers define as the 'multilevel system of government'. This corresponds to a phase when human interrelations have left the confines of the nation, but whose regulations are found at different levels.

The 'novelty' that the European institutional model represents in comparison to all the preceding, classical and modern, typologies of the forms of government belongs, then, to the new dimension that Philippe Schmitter has called the 'post-Hobbesian order'. On the one hand, this order is open to the future, to an outlook of the *after-Leviathan*. On the other hand, at least some of its features reveal not insignificant analogies with the phase that precedes the 'Westphalian model' and the formation of the modern sovereign states. Indeed, European society has already experienced non-state-like orders. It 'experienced the multilevel system of government before it closed itself within the nation-state', in the form of an 'untying of law from the state'.[29] Without question, new and important perspectives open up, not only on the theoretical plane but also on the political. Only on the condition, however, that we heed a warning concerning the discourse on the 'multilevel system of government'. The historical and structural analogy between the 'before' and 'after' should not be taken literally, nor should it become absolute. Whereas the forms can be considered analogous, the nature of the subjects is different. The differences that follow the Leviathan, or the modern state, are not the same differences that preceded it, for the wedge of equal rights and political universalism (unknown to the medieval legal order, where differences necessarily implied hierarchy) inserted itself dynamically between these differences, the before and after.

At this point a further question arises. How can Europe, on the basis of a plural and multilevel framework, play a united, autonomous and clearly recognisable political role? We cannot disguise the fact that one of the crucial questions today is that of the absence of Europe as an active and authoritative subject in the final phases of international politics. Once again – as is always the case – the internal aspect and the external aspect of politics appear intimately connected. This is the reason the problem of the institutional form of the Union coincides with the problem of its role in a globalised world. An analogous problem is forcefully raised

---

29   Ibid.

by Habermas: Europe's economic unity risks imploding if the
question of its political nature is not put on the agenda. Not,
however, for ethical reasons – because of a rejection of the
presumption that the economic market should expand to the
point of becoming a market society – but for a realistic, rigorously
structural and functional reason: a purely economic/market society is – theoretically speaking – a contradiction in terms. From the
perspective of political ideology, it is the most illusory of utopias.

Europe and the "Postnational Constellation": The Glocal Pincer and the New Tendencies to Universalisation

What characterises the 'post-Hobbesian order' or, if you prefer,
the 'postnational constellation'? The inescapable first step to
respond to this question is to note that the new situation is determined by factors that pass over – and through – the horizons of
Europe and escape Europe's current capacities for control. They
are the factors that give rise to that set of phenomena that are
customarily summarised in the *passe-partout* term 'globalisation'.
The antecedents to this process stretch far back in time: from the
opening of markets in the first phase of modernity following the
discovery of the New World and the scientific revolution, through
to the internationalisation of commodities and capital produced
by the Industrial Revolution at the turn of the seventeenth and
eighteenth centuries. However, the current phase of *mondialisation*, symbolically inaugurated by the fall of the Berlin Wall and
the collapse of 'real socialism', is characterised by an ambivalent
structure, signalled by the paradoxical coexistence of two aspects:
technical-scientific uniformity and *ethical-cultural differentiation*.
These do not coexist harmoniously or peacefully. Instead, there is
an apparently conflictual cohabitation of two vectors that are in
reality complementary and that imply one another: *deterritorialisation* and *reterritorialisation*, 'uprooting' and 'habituation'. The
technological-mercantile *mondialisation*, which imposes standardised laws and models of consumption, is accompanied by a
localisation of identities and values of belonging. The true frontier
and point of contrast does not, however, pass through the global
and the local, but on the one hand through the *glocal* block – or
perverse short-circuit – and on the other hand through the search
for new universalising practices that burst out from the contexts

of experience of the *Lebenswelte*. In short, today there is a –
tendentially antagonistic – conflict between *globalisation* and
universalisation. Whereas the former exemplifies a mechanics of
uniformisation and separation, the latter displays an interactive
and communicational dynamic of the forms of life. In this conflict,
the local does not constitute itself as an alternative to the global,
but rather as its 'interface', its specular double. The logic of localisms belongs entirely to the logic of globalisation. Localisms are
nourished by it even as they affect irreducible hostility to it, to the
point that they demand compensation for the migratory flows
towards the rich regions that are an inevitable consequence of
globalisation. The technocratic self-referentiality of the global
logic and populist drift of the local contexts of symbolic identification relate to one another as to two sides of the same coin.
Together they describe an axis that is in conflict with the politics
of universalisation.

In addition, the European Union in its exhausting process of
institutionalisation appears to be conditioned, not only exter-
nally but internally as well, by the antagonistic structure that
marks the relationship between economics and politics, globalisation and universalisation (or, in the terms of Stefano Rodotà,
market and rights). In this way we can explain the questions and
pessimistic warnings of those who – from Claus Offe to Gian
Enrico Rusconi – have invited us to take note, with the required
level of disenchantment, of the situation of deadlock in Nice.
Indeed, the necessary push that led to monetary unification (to
the Europe of the euro and of financial technocracy) has not met
with an equally powerful imperative towards constitutionalisation. Despite this and in spite of all manners of paralysing
scepticism, we must also accept these undeniable difficulties as an
opportunity and challenge. The construction of an institutional
identity of the Union cannot be given spontaneously, as the natural outlet of a process of economic integration, but it invests – as
Habermas has vigorously underlined – the normative plan of the
political choice and will.

The imbalance in the intensity of investment on the monetary
plane when compared to the institutional one leads back, in
turn, to an even deeper problem, that is, to that symbolic deficit
of politics which is particularly evident in the younger generations; this deficit is rooted in the fact that the processes of
identification are today produced principally at the local dimension of belonging. In this way, the processes of identification

remain caught in the pincer of the *glocal* (which sociologists such as Ulrich Beck tend to understand with overly rose-tinted lenses). After the nationalistic racism of the twentieth century, the twenty-first century is opening before us under the sign of regionalistic xenophobia. The new phenomenon of regionalisms makes the relationship between the global and local dangerously close to a short-circuit, due to the falling away – this is the *punctum quæstionis* – of the intermediate ring between the two dimensions that was traditionally formed by nation states. One of the crucial knots that the European Union will have to increasingly face up to is the transformation of the symbolic dimension of belonging. Not only does one feel more Scottish than British or more Catalan and Basque than Spanish (this is old news), but also more Lombard or Venetian than Italian.

The crisis of the nation state means not only – as we have seen – crisis of the 'Westphalian model', of a system of international relations resting on closed territorial sovereign centres. It also means a decline in the way of understanding and practising the law through an undisputable monopoly over its sources – by whose means one was able to govern the processes of symbolic inclusion and identification of social subjects. There is but one road to take to resolve the logic of this crisis and draw the appropriate political consequences from it. One must look back over the process of the genesis of the modern state as though one were projecting a film backwards. Only by projecting the film in reverse will we be able to identify the building blocks, the multiple components that have come together to establish the 'Great Leviathan'. We will then begin to see the emergence of the modern-day physiognomy of Europe in the guise of a *policraticus*, of a polycentric structure far more similar to the *respublica Christiana* than to the scaffolding of a super-state in becoming. We will find a proliferation of autonomistic and localistic pressures: mayors who presume to act as princes; regional presidents that adopt the manner and severe, frowning demeanour of governors; and, as though that were not enough, the reawakening of the *potestates indirectæ*, represented today by the 'Soldiers [*cavalieri*] of Fortune' of media power,[30] financial lobbies and religious authorities that interfere

---

30   *Translator's note:* In Italy, Silvio Berlusconi – media mogul and, at the time of writing, Italian president – goes by the nickname of 'il Cavaliere', the Knight. There is more than a passing reference to Berlusconi, although Marramao is speaking of the power of the media more broadly, even beyond the very specific Italian situation.

directly in politics and the workings of institutions, attempting to condition or even hegemonise them.

In this situation, the Old Continent figures on the scene of the global world without a precise political physiognomy. It is not a case of a transition but of a suspended time, pregnant with uncertainties that threatens to disarticulate and even inhibit the formation of a civil society and of a European public sphere. The challenge of globalisation presents Europe with three fundamental unresolved problems.

Europe, in its tripartite economic, political and cultural aspects, is caught in the vice of two other colossi of the global age: the American colossus and the Asiatic colossus. America – which is not only synonymous with political and military hegemony, technological leadership and the new economy, but also with the crisis of acquisitive individualism, the politics of difference and struggles for recognition – provides a striking example of a phenomenon that is destined to mark the future of Western society in the coming years: the gap between the stalling of a democratic system that has become simply a self-referential machine for the reproduction of oligarchies, and the pluriverse of languages and experiences of groups of people caught up in a mutation of civilisation – which is also anthropological – that invests the hierarchy of values, the structure of desire and the dimension of the *bíos*, of corporeality and of life in a planetary world-environment. Asia is not only synonymous with the 'economic miracle' and the 'Pacific tiger'. It bears the challenge of 'Asian values' as well, that is, of those 'Asian values' that – as Amartya Sen has explained – presume to break the Western equation of capitalism with the ethics of individualism, founding, instead, development and productivity on associative structures of a hierarchical and communitarian type. That is, on the subordination of the objectives (and rights, of course) of individuals to those of collective entities (from the family to the business, from the group to the state). Caught in this pincer, Europe must formulate its own autonomous response; its own alternative ethical and cultural model that cannot be pierced by either horn of the dilemma, nor attempt a compromissory mediation.

Another crucial problem for the Union is the enlargement to Eastern Europe. It is certainly an important decision, which should by no means be placed in competition with the vector of the Mediterranean (which, more correctly, should be seen as complementary). But it would be foolish to hide the significant problems that such a choice bears with it. The indisputable fact that those countries have, for centuries, been constitutive components of great importance for 'Europe's cultural heritage' should not lead us into facile optimism. If it is true that Budapest and Prague, St. Petersburg and Kaliningrad belong to the 'spirit of Europe' as much as Paris and London, Berlin and Rome, it is equally certain that the social and institutional contexts from which they emerge appear, in the medium term, difficult to 'synchronise'. The inclusion of these areas, were it to occur according to the logic of annexation of an *Anschluss*, is destined to bring with it enormous problems and difficulties, equal to those that the integration of *Ostländer* have for Germany. Such a risk can be avoided only on three conditions: a) by not underestimating the economic, cultural and socio-psychological fractures that the 'contemporaneity of the non-contemporaneous' necessarily bears with it; b) of not conceiving (or putting into practice) Europe as a 'fortress', that is, as a geometrically closed space of integration but as a space of variable geometry with elastic and dynamically open borders [*confini*]; and c) of not postulating the opening to the East as an alternative to another vector, constituted by the pluriverse of Mediterranean cultures that formed the original vector of Europe.

The final problem is constituted by the British variant. From the standpoint of the legal and institutional culture, with its common law, it represents a true alterity with respect to the tradition of civil law that is dominant on the continent. It is no accident that during the convention at the Fondazione Basso, the comparativist Mads Andenas warned against the undifferentiated usage of words such as 'state', 'constitution' and 'civil society' that have a different meaning in Britain than in Continental debates that are characterised by the *ius publicum*. The British resistance to full participation in the institutional destiny of the European Union is certainly not of an economic or generically political order. In the final analysis, it is of a cultural nature. To overcome this, it will be necessary not to effect a mere *contamination* but a hard and intense labour of 'translation' and confrontation of the two traditions of common law and civil law, specifically in relation to rights and their constitutional translation.

Political Pluriverse and 'Constitution without a State' (Provisional Conclusions)

Continuing along this line of argument, I propose to decline Habermas' well-known proposal of a third normative model of democracy – alternative to procedural liberalism and to communitarianism – in post-state terms, by emptying it of what I believe are the persistent classical elements inherent to the Continental tradition of the *Rechtstaat*. In order to construct a constitutional form that is able to confront adequately the challenges of the 'post-Hobbesian order', we must become accustomed to thinking and practising politics by projecting it beyond the modern dimension of the Leviathan state. The political *forma mentis* of Europe must shift from the paradigm of the *universum* to that of the *multiversum*, imagining a model of political association that turns on a plurality of pillars, of 'sovereign powers' in equilibrium. It must delineate a dynamic field of tensions between nation states (in decline, but nevertheless persisting) and Union (a novel institutional form that is, nevertheless, still in formation). In other words, we must think of a *constitution without a state*, founded on a balanced plurality of demands, in which – as Maurizio Fioravanti has rightly argued – the role of constitutional jurisdiction is accompanied by the representative and legislative process (without, therefore, situating itself hierarchically above or below).

Equally correctly, Eligio Resta has observed that the Charter of Rights voted on in Nice acts already as a source of political legitimation in virtue of its inclusive character. But this does not mean that the elaboration of a constitution, to which the Charter itself would be prefaced, would be useless or redundant. Every declaration of *rights* ideally refers back to a constitution that, in its organisational section, determines the articulation of *powers* with their respective areas of reciprocal autonomy, and – at the same time – defining the *dispositifs* of limitation of control over their exercise. Behind this requirement there lies a fundamental theoretical question. If it is true that, on the one hand, rights are not the notary's or stenographer's registration of subjects but, on the contrary, constitute them and simultaneously change the actual power relations, it is also true to say that they are not, in themselves, a sufficient condition for the production of a process of symbolic identification. For that to occur, it is necessary that rights become connected to the dimension of belonging. Not in the traditional sense of the 'community of destinies' but in that of the set of experiences and practices expressed by the 'life-worlds'.

To conclude, the labour of 'reconstruction of the ship on the open sea' that we find in the process of the constitutionalisation of Europe will have to delineate itself – as Erhard Denninger has shown in his writings – less in terms of sovereignty and increasingly in terms of a dynamic equilibrium and of reciprocal limitation between a plurality of demands and of powers, not so much in accordance with the classical models of the transfer of sovereignty, and increasingly the shift towards a Union not only of technical (or technocratic) capabilities, so much as by means of effective procedures of legitimation. From this perspective, the form of the pact and of the treaty will be able to and will have to act as the essential stage for the constitutionalisation of fundamental rights (as was already the case with the birth of the first Occidental democracy, the American one). Only the trinomial formed by a Parliament endowed with real powers, by a Commission transformed into an effective executive and by a Court of Justice as a truly Constitutional Court will we be able to assure that the European ship – like Plato's ship of the Republic – keeps equidistant from the contrasting risks of technocratic proceduralism and from the mythological or populist appeal to sovereignty and to the constituent power of the People, and thereby safeguard fundamental rights and guarantees from the prevarications of the majority.

Only by keeping to this course will it be possible to solder rights onto the forms-of-life and experiences of social subjects, of concrete women and men who will contribute, through their practices, to the construction of a Europe-wide public political sphere that is able to situate itself – in accordance with Hannah Arendt's indication – beyond the state and the market, beyond any obsession with identity and without any nostalgia for *reductio ad unum*. But, above all, without ever forgetting the warning – which is at once post-liberal and anti-totalitarian – from the old teachers of Frankfurt Critical Theory: only limited power is good power. The *totum* is the totem.

10

AFTER BABEL: TOWARDS A COSMOPOLITANISM OF DIFFERENCE[1]

A Multiple Universal

It is a daunting task, certainly, to try to grasp the intrinsic character of the present: to identify its logic and structure beyond the hubbub of contemporary events and to conceptualise this logic and structure in an adequate and appropriate fashion. It has always been a daunting task, whether in the time of Hegel and Marx or in the time of Weber and Lenin. If possible, it appears even more daunting today: in the 'finite world' [*mondo finito*] of our present, one that is spatially compressed and temporally accelerated, it remains increasingly difficult to reduce it to a mono-logic. It is a world that seems in reality to be dominated by the disconcerting effects of a *bi-logic* in which the standardising structure of the techno-economy and the global market finds itself confronted by an increasing diaspora of values, identities and forms-of-life. In order to describe this state of things, I have often turned in the past to evocative metaphors drawn from great literature, such as the Kakania of Robert Musil, for can we not perhaps regard our own world as a globalised version of Kakania? Or to images drawn from those crucial scenes (rather in the sense of Freud's 'primal scene') that belong to the mythico-religious heritage of our civilisation, such as the tale of Babel: does not our standardised world, like the Tower of Babel, also increasingly resemble a cacophonous recapitulation of proliferating and untranslatable languages? Yet it is difficult today to find a literary text or essay (apart, perhaps, from George Steiner's splendid collection of essays *After Babel*, which was published back in 1975)

---

1 *Translator's note:* Chapter 10 was added in the second edition of the book, in 2009.

that would be capable of capturing the bewitching bi-logic of our global Babel with the same intensity and symbolic power as certain films, or perhaps we should say certain cinematographic texts. For films too are texts – or, according to the inimitable contribution of Roland Barthes, *textures* – which have little cause to envy written texts with respect to expressive dignity or thought-provoking depth.

Babel is the title of a suggestive film by the Mexican director Alejandro Gonzáles Iñárritu made in 2006. It presents the globalised world as a Babel-like space, as a mosaic composed of multiple dispersed forms of life – at once materially heterogeneous and culturally differentiated – that are connected and brought together by the flux of events that traverse them. These events are either macroscopic, such as major financial crises, or microscopic, such as that which furnishes the starting point for the plot of the film: a stray bullet discharged from a highly sophisticated rifle, inexpertly handled by a young boy who got it from his father, a shepherd in the desert mountains of Morocco, that ends up hitting a tourist bus and critically injuring a young American woman (Cate Blanchett) who is travelling abroad with her husband (Brad Pitt). The repercussions of this random event make themselves felt, through a chain reaction, in different contexts and parts of the world which suddenly become interdependent through the explosive immediacy of the initial event: from a still largely archaic country like Morocco to the opulent environs of California where the tourist couple live; from the combination of modernity and tradition in a Mexican village (the original home of the nanny who looks after the couple's children) to the existential and intergenerational problems of teenage communities in the metropolitan reality of contemporary Tokyo (the home of the Japanese 'global hunter', a widower whose wife has committed suicide, who has an ambiguous relationship with his own deaf-mute adolescent daughter, and who, before returning to Japan, had given the rifle to the Moroccan shepherd in the first place.)

It is difficult to deny that the richly suggestive character of the film depends on its paradoxical, descriptive topicality: on the effectiveness with which it recognises the enigmatic interdependence of what has been called the 'glocalised' world, a world where differentiation unfolds hand in hand with unification, where centrifugal, independent and idiosyncratic tendencies are inextricably entwined with the technological-economic homogenisation of styles of life and patterns of consumption.[2] Nonetheless, something essential seems to escape this otherwise relevant and perspicuous snapshot of our global era. The true issue at stake in the dramatic transition which we are living through today, namely the transition from the modernity of the nation state to the modernity of the global world; from the no-longer of the old order between states that was dominated by the West to the not-yet of a new supra-national order which can only be constructed multilaterally, can neither be reduced to the alternatives of liberalism and communitarianism – or, rather, of *liberal* individualism and *communitarian* holism – nor resolved by some compromise or synthesis between a redistributive universalism and an ultimately identitarian conception of differentiation. As Seyla Benhabib has perspicaciously pointed out in her more recent writings,[3] the task now is not merely that of resolving the false dilemma between universalism and relativism, but that of addressing the impasse produced by a normative political philosophy which tends to objectify 'cultural identities' and 'struggles for recognition' by treating them as givens rather than regarding them as problems. But this situation of stalemate (which fatefully affects the force of liberal contractualist theories as well as the Rawlsian notion of 'overlapping consensus') can be overcome only on two conditions: 1) by challenging the equation between culture and identity; 2) by liberating the universal – despite the etymology of the word – from the logic of homogeneous unification, from the *reductio ad unum*, and applying it instead to the realm of multiplicity and difference.

This is equivalent, in short, to breaking the mirror, to rupturing the specular relation that we tend to set up between 'ourselves' and the 'others'. Such a rupture cannot consist in a simple reversal of perspective (understanding how the others see us rather than how we see the others can be extremely instructive, but this alone will not suffice to dismantle our various forms of 'Orientalism'), but must rather involve an ability to discover *an autonomous and original universalising perspective* at work amongst the others themselves. The important thing, in the light of the problem posed by the Babel of the present, is not so much to understand how so-called cultural differences or outlooks see

---

2   Peter Sloterdijk, *Im Weltinnenraum des Kapitals: Für eine philosophische Theorie der Globalisierung*.

3   Seyla Benhabib, *The Claims of Culture* and *Another Cosmopolitanism*.

one another (in the double sense of reflexivity and reciprocity), but to understand how each of these different outlooks thinks and imagines the universal. And not only, I would add, how each outlook thinks or imagines the latter, but how, collectively, it has transcribed and codified the universal in terms of its own judgements of value and its own declarations of principles and fundamental rights.

Other Constitutions, Constitutions of the Other

It is for this decisive reason that the debate surrounding multicul-turalism – a debate that is currently replete with ambiguities – can become genuinely fruitful and relevant to the future only if we are prepared to extend the comparative spectrum to embrace the different conceptions of rights and values that serve to ground different constitutional arrangements. The founding texts and documents for such arrangements – whether they be charters or declarations of fundamental rights or constitutions in the narrower sense – always represent, more or less closely, a certain concentra-tion or condensation of specific socio-cultural dynamics. Far from constituting an abstract ideal dimension or a merely ideological superstructure, such texts and documents, if the most recent approaches to legal and constitutional history are to be believed, furnish the traces of real processes: of the attainments and devel-opments of new values which have been acquired, depending on the particular cases, through bitter conflicts or attempted compro-mises. It is particularly instructive, for example, to consider the dynamics of constitutional development in Africa precisely because these dynamics seem to suggest an alternative to the European model of authoritative codified law based on a rigid hierarchy of relevant sources, pointing instead to a different kind of logic that is based on the infra-systemic circulation of a plural-ity of 'issues'.

Once we have abandoned the old nineteenth- and twentieth-century approaches that are predicated on the binomial schema of base and superstructure, many of the processes now unfolding in different parts of the world will appear to us as so many mani-festations of the phenomenon of the 'contemporaneity of the non-contemporaneous'; as different ways in which the most fundamental rights strive for expression within a constitutional framework that is capable of legitimising and consolidating them. The tendency that we see emerging in various quarters to suggest the outlines of a post-state conception of rights is nothing but an expression – on the juridical plane – of the way in which the synchronicity of the asynchronous, or the all-pervasive character of global interdependence, exercises its effects in local contexts. At this point, the argument would naturally become very detailed and highly technical if one were to attempt to furnish specific and differentiated analyses. But limiting ourselves simply to general comparative considerations, it is possible to argue, albeit only in extremely abbreviated form, that we are confronted with a very serious problem here: the problem regarding the network of rights and therefore the constitutional dynamic itself (where the latter is understood as the search for a bridge between morality and law, a way of translating axiological principles into the positive form of fundamental rights). In short: the different sources and foundations of rights enter into relation with one another and thereby generate an entire complex of reciprocal implications. This question presents a number of analogies with the issues that have arisen from the attempts to develop a constitution for the European Union. But from this point of view, it is also highly instructive to consider the results of some of the more innovative research which has been conducted with reference to Africa for some years now – and specifically in the context of an extended comparison between Western declarations of rights and the 'declarations of the others'. In the light of these analyses, the entire area of that great (and neglected) continent turns out to be far more complex in character than has generally been believed: it reveals itself, in fact, as a true and authentic space with variable geometries of its own. I believe that it is necessary to examine this question in greater depth for the decisive reason that the African continent can no longer be treated as an object of undifferentiated neglect or of populist demagogy – and both approaches are basically two sides of the same coin. The demand for a more differentiated analysis appears to me to be particularly important. In this sense, the approach pursued by recent research with regard, on the one hand, to the role of the two 'superpowers', South Africa and Nigeria, and with regard, on the other, to the 'shadowy line' – to employ a well-worn literary expression – between Islamic Africa and Black Africa (and it is no accident if this question has hitherto attracted the special and hardly disinterested attention of the United States), provides us with a number of emphatic hints and pointers.

However, it is also necessary to underline some of the decisive theoretical implications of these precise and differentiated analyses of the Arab-African context (having to hide, for what it is worth, behind this hyphenated expression) that are less inclined to exploit the current journalistic themes of radical Islam, 'jihad' or the 'clash of civilisations', and that encourage us instead to stop conflating deep-seated social dynamics with the more immediately striking and dramatic expressions of change, or identifying the transformations of the Muslim masses that are internally linked to certain material and symbolic conditions with a transnational network of individual subjects (largely equivalent to certain educated and 'Westernised' strata of the Islamic diaspora). Some of these analyses have even suggested the necessity of interpreting the codes and charters of the Arab-Islamic area with a comparative approach that draws on the idea of secularisation. On the other hand, we must also recognise that the process of secularisation, if in Europe it facilitated the creation of the sovereign secular state, *superiorem non recognoscens*, along with the concept of the separation of powers, also gave rise to a further and equally important development: the progressive (though by no means simply linear) tendency towards the deterritorialisation of right which can be tracked in the trajectory that leads from the American Declaration of Independence and the Declaration of the Rights of Man in 1789 to the Universal Declaration of Human Rights in 1948.

The other aspect which clearly emerges from the contributions that we have just mentioned is that we can no longer conceptualise the universalising processes in question by reference to a simple model of modernity as a standard. In other words: universalism can no longer be understood in a merely uniform manner but must be reformulated in the knowledge – to adapt Hamlet's famous remark – that there are more roads to liberty and democracy than have been dreamt of in our poor philosophy. But in addition to the poverty of philosophy we must recognise other forms of poverty today as well, such as the poverty of sociology itself. And we are not speaking merely of the worst sociology either.

Exception and Contingency

Several recent contributions in the field of Oriental studies (from the comparative philosophy of Amina Crisma, François Jullien

and Giangiorgio Pasqualotto to the investigations of Renzo
Cavalieri and Luigi Moccia concerning the evolution of Chinese
law, not to mention the pioneering works of Jürgen Osterhammel
on the 'disenchantment' of Asia and of Heiner Roetz on the
Chinese ethics of the axial era) have now convinced me, confirm-
ing the claims I advanced in the first edition of this book, of the
necessity of attempting a serious and detailed revision of the
most extensive (and conceptually most suggestive) comparative
examination of civilisations still available to us, namely the
Religionssoziologie of Max Weber. The section of this work that
dealt with Confucianism and Taoism contained an analysis of
the Confucian model which was in many respects very careful
and precise. Yet the conclusion which Weber drew was an
extreme one: the Confucian model was presented as the polar
opposite of ascetic Puritanism and interpreted as entirely antipa-
thetic to the emergence of a productive and dynamic capitalist
society. The history of the last few decades has shown us just
how erroneous and premature this judgement actually was. It is
particularly relevant, in this connection, that one of the most
authoritative Italian commentators on Weber's work has recently
claimed that now, almost a hundred years on, 'the Weberian
approach must be significantly re-examined and corrected' in the
light of our radically transformed 'image of the European societies on the basis of which Weber proclaimed the exclusive
connection between rational capitalism and the Protestant ethic,
and thus the distinctive character of the development of the
modern West'.[4] In contrast to the proponents of the *exceptional-
ist thesis*, we must accept that the so-called European miracle is
not a presupposition from which to begin, but rather the *contingent result* of a specific complex of historical circumstances
(within which techno-scientific rationalism and the potential of
what Carlo Cipolla has called the combination of 'sails' and
'guns' has certainly played a considerable role) which has
allowed a relatively limited and marginal area of the globe to
assume a hegemonic position in relation to other civilisations.[5]

It seems to me plausible to claim today that the judgement
regarding Asian civilisations has been framed, not only by
Weber but also by Marx, on the fateful presumption of what I
have formerly defined as the standard model of modernity: a

---

4 Pietro Rossi, *L'identità dell'Europa*, p. 172.
5 Carlo Cipolla, *Vele e cannoni*.

model that is ultimately dependent on a linear theory of the stages of socio-economic development which declares that the 'Asiatic mode of production', on account of its intrinsically despotic structural logic, effectively lacked the internal dynamic factors capable of encouraging an eventual 'transition' to modern capitalism. But how, on these paradigmatic assumptions, are we to explain the Asian economic miracle that is currently unfolding before our eyes? It is true that this miracle – in which the demand of productivity is coupled with that of technological innovation – is accompanied by an apparently conservative vindication of the communitarian and paternalistic values typical of the Asian tradition. It is also true that the appeal to *Asian values* represents a kind of propaganda manifesto developed by the governing elites of the South-East Asian countries in response to the 'Orientalising' Western stereotype.[6] Yet we are also dealing with a strategic response here, and not merely with a purely reactive mechanism. From this perspective, the well-known critical observations of Jürgen Habermas and Amartya Sen with regard to the Bangkok Declaration of 1993 (drawn up in the preparatory Asian meeting of the World Conference on Human Rights held in Vienna), while they may be entirely relevant and legitimate in a theoretical context, appear less well directed when considered in the political context. The problem posed by a strategy based on 'Asian values' cannot be resolved simply by pointing out – incontestably enough – that it provides an ideological legitimation for the 'dictatorial authoritarianism – more or less "soft" – of the developing countries';[7] nor again by justifiably stigmatising the instrumental character of an undifferentiated approach which ignores the specific character of different experiences, histories and cultures, and 'utilizes the political force of anti-colonialism to strengthen the attack on fundamental civil and political rights in post-colonial Asia'.[8]

The question we must answer is whether, and to what extent, the 'Asian values' slogan has proved politically effective, helping to build a broad consensus and promoting economic growth in a very different context. The Bangkok Declaration attempted to square

6   Emanuela Fornari, *Modernity out of Joint: Global Democracy and 'Asian Values' in Jürgen Habermas and Amartya K. Sen*.

7   Jürgen Habermas, *The Inclusion of the Other*, p. 227.

8   Amartya Sen, 'Human Rights and Asian Values', p. 163.

this circle in a very singular manner by combining universalism and contextualism, the principle of globality and the principle of territoriality, cosmopolitanism and national sovereignty, and including a denunciation of the strategic-instrumental exploitation of 'human rights' on the part of the West. The text of article 8 of the Declaration is particularly instructive in this respect: '*We recognize* that while human rights are universal in nature, they must be considered in the context of a dynamic and evolving process of international norm-setting, bearing in mind the significance of national and regional particularities and various historical, cultural, and religious backgrounds'.[9] The underlying reasons and motivations for this declaration are anything but merely 'occasional' in character. As many different informed observers have noted, they are ultimately rooted in an ethical-cultural hinterland which has – not since yesterday but since the sixth century B.C. (and especially in China) – been particularly concerned with two crucial issues: 1) the question of the connection between individual autonomy and the 'network' of communal relations (*guanxi wang*) in which the individual is embedded; 2) the question of the bi-univocal relation between 'law' and 'rite' (*li*), between explicitly codified norms and that complex of social and behavioural rituals which we are accustomed in the West, in a long philosophical tradition that stretches from the three *Ethics* of Aristotle to the *Essays* of Montaigne, to associate with the practical efficacy of 'custom' and 'habit'. It is at this point of intersection between the situation of the present and the *longue durée* of the past that we must reconsider the problem of the contemporary relevance and continuing efficacy of Confucian ethics in the context of an encounter between the 'Occidental' and the 'Asiatic' model of rights: 'when we speak today of the minimal common denominators in terms of which we may pursue a universal reflection on human rights, we must recognise that the world possesses narratives and experiences which are significantly different from our own, but which must also be taken into account, and that we can no longer simply content ourselves with claiming that East Asia is a world where despots exploit traditional Confucian thought, and contrasting this with a more mature position which we insist on regarding as natural and progressive in relation to the individual rights and liberties of the citizens'.[10]

---

9 'The Bangkok Declaration', Final Declaration of the Regional Meeting for Asia of the World Conference on Human Rights.

10 Renzo Cavalieri, 'La Carta asiatica e la Cina', pp. 74–75.

Therefore, if we examine the matter more closely, we find ourselves confronted by a project which, far from being merely 'reactive', begins to reveal the outlines of an alternative notion of globalisation that is no longer based on the primacy of competitive individualism but, instead, shows a commitment to the productive efficacy of a more hierarchical community where the goal, the objective, is not so much the singular individual as a 'collective individual', understood as a true and genuine expanded family, whether it be the company, the municipality, the region or the state. We are thus witnessing the emergence of a model of modernity which is radically different from the Occidental model. This is a model that breaks the ideal-typical nexus of rationalisation and disenchantment, modernisation and deracination, and is generating economic growth of awesome proportions, and that is destined, in the course of the next two or three decades, to turn China into the major world economy. This process will undoubtedly be encouraged by the specific character of the Confucian ethos. For while its conception of order is indeed hierarchical, unlike the Indian conception of karma it is not immutable, for it clearly envisages the possibility of change and social advancement.

Cartographies of World-Modernity: From the 'Fact of Pluralism' to the 'Reality of the Hybrid'

One of the most pernicious effects the identitarian strategy of appealing to 'Asian values' has had upon theoretical debate in Europe and the United States is the way in which it has so often provoked an undifferentiated account of the West itself. This risks lending succour to those positions of an ideological (rather than genuinely geocultural and geopolitical) kind that invoke the so-called clash of civilisations and that see themselves reflected in a world that is ever more interdependent and intimately hybrid in character. It is this that motivated the critique of the paired terms of 'us' and 'the others'. This critique springs from the fundamental recognition that – despite the specular antithesis of identitarian logics which underlies our contemporary global disorder – we are actually confronted not with a *single* Orient or a *single* Occident, but with an irrepressible (or as Hannah Arendt would say, an 'unrepresentable') plurality that is internal to both poles of the distinction. And if we are right to accept Edward Said's invitation

(as formulated back in 1978) to abandon the stereotype of
'Orientalism', it is just as necessary to apply the same treatment
to the stereotype of 'Occidentalism'. For the 'Orient' and the
'Occident' must be read as cartographical labels that in each case
embrace an internal plurality of phenomena. It has rightly been
pointed out before that Asia does not exist as a unity, that there
is no such thing as a *single* Asiatic culture. When I had the opportunity of delivering a number of lectures in Hong Kong in 1997,
my colleagues at the Hong Kong Baptist University never tired of
reminding me that it was we, the Westerners, who appeared to
the Chinese in terms of standardised sameness, while they
perceived themselves as extremely diverse and internally differentiated. And when, some time later, I was invited by Marc Augé to
present a paper at an international conference under the title of
Dynamiques culturelles et mondialisation (held in Avignon in
October 2003), I was able to hear from the comparative analyst
Wang Bin how Chinese cultural identity, far from being homogeneous in character, is actually a historical construct which has
been elaborated over centuries as a collage of various different
experiences, histories and forms-of-life. Confucianism itself must
thus be understood not as some sort of static basis or original
invariable, but rather as a practical and ethical attitude which has
been subjected over the centuries to innumerable adaptations and
reinterpretations. We must speak therefore of several 'Orients'
and several 'Occidents'; and not only of synchronic plurality, but
also of diachronic mutation.

Whenever we find ourselves confronted with 'the others', with
forms of culture that are different from 'our' civilisation, we
must never lose sight of the fact that many of the prerogatives of
which we are rightly proud – the constitutional state, liberty,
equality, suffrage extended to all, including women, and so forth
– are in fact extremely recent achievements of the West (and are
never simply achieved once and for all). And leading representatives of the Anglo-Indian intelligentsia, such as Amartya Sen or
Homi Bhabha, will also rightly continue to remind us that at a
time when we still countenanced witch-hunts, the Inquisition,
the burning of heretics, etc., in Europe, enlightened principles
were prevailing in India. And a Muslim could likewise remind us
that, in twelfth-century Spain, the Caliphate of Cordoba was
tolerant enough to accommodate individuals such as Mosheh
Ben Maimon, commonly known as Maimonides, and Ibn 'Arabi,
that it is to say, the greatest Jewish philosopher and the greatest

Islamic philosopher of the medieval period. It seems to me, therefore, that we must constantly bear in mind the double synchronic/diachronic character of the plurality presented by our global Babel: for diachrony harbours not only the possibility of evolution, but also the risk of involution. From this point of view, a decisive example of such an involution with regard to the process of secularisation can be recognised in that indigenous fundamentalism of the West that is represented by *neo-con* ideology in the United States.

The cartography of problems exhibited by the modern world confirms that the only way of comprehending what is transpiring today is to acknowledge that we inhabit a sort of *double movement of contamination and differentiation*. All the examples we have mentioned clearly reveal, on the one hand, the all-pervasive phenomenon of interdependence and contamination (and Islamic charters and constitutions – as the investigations we have already cited remind us – have also been affected in their own way by Western values), and on the other, the transverse character of the specular-oppositional phenomenon of the diaspora. I believe that both of these aspects must be incorporated, not independently but contextually, into any genuine analysis. In other words, we must take the *reality of the hybrid* as our point of departure, rather than simply appealing to the 'fact of pluralism', as many political philosophies variously inspired by the neo-contractualist model of Rawls propose. For the plurality in question is not only a plurality of the between, of the *infra*, but a plurality of the within, of the *intra*: it is not only inter-cultural, but also infra-cultural, not only inter-subjective, but also intra-subjective, not only between identities, but also internal to the symbolic constitution of each and every identity – whether it be individual or collective in character. This is the decisive reason why I have been driven, in the course of my reflections over the last few years, to formulate a *cosmopolitanism of difference*, understood as a way of escaping the paralysing theoretical and practical dilemma posed between identitarian universalism (as defended by assimilationist conceptions of citizenship) and anti-universalistic differentialism (as defended by emphatic versions of multiculturalism); or, to simplify matters drastically, between the model of the République and the model of what has been dubbed Londonistan. A number of important interdisciplinary studies appear to me to move in the same general direction insofar as they relate the insights of comparative law and cultural anthropology, and suggest possible ways of codifying an intercultural democracy based upon a multiple and 'hybrid' conception of law.[11] For my own part, I have been convinced for some time that the subterranean tendencies leading towards a hybrid cultural and institutional reality have long been active and that the dominant form of the conflict of our time can be traced back to a symbolic mechanism of reaction to the phenomena of growing hybridisation and to what a pioneering scholar such as Ernest Gellner,[12] adopting a celebrated expression of Quine's, has described as the experience of 'cosmic exile' (or 'universal deracination'), which has affected all cultures to varying degrees. The nature of this mechanism appeals to the logic of identity and identification: in other words, it exhibits markedly identitarian features. In the first edition of this book, I argued, before Amartya Sen propounded the same thesis in his outstanding book *Identity and Violence*,[13] that the conflicts of the global era present certain characteristics that are more reminiscent of the fundamental conflicts which marked the civil and religious wars in Europe in the era that preceded the Peace of Westphalia than they are of the conflicts of interest which were typical of the industrial era. The dramatic character which is beginning to attach to the nexus of identity and violence today can only be explained in the light of a detailed and careful diagnosis of the mechanisms which have generated the emergence of the *dominant identitarian structure of conflict*.

Beyond Recognition

How then are we to throw some kind of bridge between the 'Occidents', the different variations of the Occident, and 'the others', others that are already diverse within themselves? Over the last few years I have often had the opportunity to discuss with Jürgen Habermas what he has described as the 'divided West'.[14] I think that this formula can properly be employed only on behalf of the self-diagnosis of our own cultural context. But it risks becoming little more than an edifying phrase if we understand this talk of the 'divided West' – as I fear Habermas does in part – to mean that a kind of recomposed or reconstituted West is already

---

11 Mario Ricca, *Oltre Babele*.
12 Ernest Gellner, *Culture, Identity and Politics*.
13 Amartya Sen, *Identity and Violence*.
14 Jürgen Habermas, *Der gespaltene Westen*.

capable, in terms of its own cultural tradition and drawing on its own resources, of resolving all of the problems of a potential global democracy. I do not believe that this is possible, for I am convinced – as I have already attempted to argue with my thesis concerning a necessary *passage* from West to East – that the Occident cannot be regarded as self-sufficient in this sense. In this regard, I find myself in 'conflicted agreement' with those contemporary writers who have attempted to rehabilitate the ingenious structure of 'Western rationalism' represented by the tradition of normative law. I do not believe that the tradition of modern rationalism – even in the noblest forms that it has assumed in the West, such as the moral universalism of Kantian philosophy, or the principle of legally guaranteed rights – is ultimately self-sufficient; that is, that it is capable on its own of offering a solution to the conflicts of our time, of enabling us to build a truly 'cosmopolitan republic'. Or to put the point in the language of Raimon Panikkar: the house of the universal is not already there, waiting to be occupied, but must be constructed in a genuinely multilateral manner. We cannot simply say to the others: come, and you will be accommodated in our house; integrate, and you will be included within our civilisation that is based on the concept of right. On the contrary, what we need to do is precisely to negotiate a new common space, to construct together a new house of the universal. If we are capable of looking at other forms and contexts of experience in a way that is less clouded by prejudice, we will be able to recognise the existence, in other parts of the world, of conceptions of freedom and notions of human dignity which are just as noble as our own (or in any case no less respectable than our own). So it is that when Martha Nussbaum felt obliged to re-emphasise the idea of happiness as human 'flourishing' or *fulfilment*, she could draw both upon the noble tradition of Aristotelian ethics, so important to the history of Western culture, and upon a specifically Indian cultural tradition.[15] It clearly emerges from such considerations that 'freedom' remains an empty word if it is merely taken to mean 'freedom of choice'. The category of 'choice', understood as an expression of a 'preference', already seems to have been seriously prejudiced by its ever more pervasive economic and commercial meaning. We are thus increasingly encouraged to believe that the choice of one's own 'lifestyle' or 'life plan' is entirely analogous to the way in which we choose a particular

---

15   Martha Nussbaum, *Cultivating Humanity*.

article of clothing or a particular type of hamburger in the global
emporium. Yet the deliberate decision – the free and responsible
decision – which permits an individual man or woman to develop
his or her own possibilities is qualitatively different in character.
This cannot merely be a *rational choice* for the simple but decisive
reason that it intrinsically involves the relational dimension of our
affects and emotions. And that is why we must place the idea of
happiness as human flourishing at the centre of our understanding
of human action and political endeavour: namely, the unfolding
of human talents, abilities and emotions, of the personality of
each and every man or woman.

Before bringing these reflections to a conclusion, I should
simply like to offer a few further considerations. I believe that
we should endorse the criticisms which Seyla Benhabib has
raised with regard to the monolithic conception of culture: for
the idea of multicultural tolerance, insofar as it simultaneously
postulates a reified image of different civilisations conceived as
monolithic entities, itself prepares a particularly fertile ground
for the growth of various forms of fundamentalism. But I am
equally convinced that we must go further than this, and
acknowledge the radical crisis which today afflicts both of the
models of democratic inclusion which have been attempted in
the modern world: the assimilationist republican model and the
'strong' multiculturalist model (or what Benhabib describes as
the 'mosaic' model). The French case has clearly shown us how
the emphatically assimilationist approach only encourages the
growth of clandestine identities which organise themselves in a
subterranean manner and can suddenly explode into violence. It
is no accident that the thematic of recognition, of conflicts of
recognition, of the relationship between redistributive conflicts
– I am referring to the now famous pair of terms *recognition/
redistribution* – is the crucial question that agitates current political theory in Europe and the United States. In this regard, the
confrontation between the binary approach defended by Nancy
Fraser (distinction/cohabitation between redistributive conflicts
and conflicts of recognition) and the monistic perspective advocated by Axel Honneth (subordination of redistributive conflicts
to the struggle for recognition) represents an important attempt
to address the two aporiae which have been clearly identified by
the legal theorist Amy Gutmann, one of the most perceptive
participants in the recent international debate. According to
Gutmann, the notion of multicultural 'recognition', when it is

applied to groups rather than to individuals, already implies a double danger: in the first place, public authority becomes powerless to exercise any influence upon the criteria by which each group selects those who govern or represent it or upon the ways in which it responds to its own internal disagreements; and in the second place – and this is an even more important consequence – individuals who cannot gain self-recognition by belonging to any specific group enjoy little chance of seeing their own rights respected and guaranteed. This approach thus tends to produce a kind of delegated or abrogated relation to the norm of universality. In order to counter this tendency, it is necessary to draw a clear and precise distinction between the right to difference and a difference of right. We must never forget that the first difference is the difference of the single individual, that the first and fundamental right is the right of singularity. Naturally, this immediately opens up a whole range of delicate questions: we must be very careful, when we enter into relation to 'others', to see that they are effectively 'represented' by those who put themselves forward as such representatives in a 'self-appointed' manner. It is often the case that the most active and well-organised elements of a given cultural or religious group are those that are accepted as its effective representatives, whereas in reality, in most cases they represent only a limited minority of the group in question. But this phenomenon does not merely concern the different groups of immigrants within the Western democracies, but also concerns the very countries from which they have come. A number of years ago – on 13 November 2002, to be precise – I participated at the University of Rome in a seminar led by Rima Khalaf Hunaidi, Assistant Secretary-General and Regional Director of the Regional Bureau for Arab States in the United Nations Development Program. On that occasion, when she presented the Arab Human Development Report, Hunaidi drew our attention to the fact that the majority of the population of the Arab countries was substantially in favour of the process of modernisation and democracy – albeit understood in a way rather different from that which prevails in the West – while only a limited minority declared themselves in favour of 'fundamentalist' positions, and an even more limited minority claimed to support the violent methods of terrorist or jihadist groups. This implies that we must proceed maieutically here, helping the voices that emerge from the civil society in these countries to make themselves heard in their full significance. But to this end we must remember, once again, Hamlet's advice to Horatio: there are more things in heaven and earth than are dreamt of in our poor philosophy; for there are more paths to freedom and democracy than Western rationalism has ever dreamt of. A politics that is genuinely capable of engaging with 'the others' must appeal, therefore, not to the notion of 'exporting freedom', but to that of encouraging processes that promote rights and democracy on the basis of methods and approaches which are themselves wholly autonomous. The global dynamics that have unfolded since 1989, the watershed year of the fall of the Berlin Wall, is beginning to show us that any attempt to impose a standardised, ethnocentric and supremacist model of modernisation can only lead to a further extension and intensification of conflicts. And here is the crux of the matter. It is here that the West courts the danger of failure, of precipitating the entire world into a state of endemic civil war.

Signa prognostica

Last but not least, I come to the vexed question of the validity and significance of the proceduralist interpretation of democracy. The proceduralist model constitutes the presupposition or, if one prefers, the *conditio sine qua non*, of a conception of democracy which permits a profound form of self-recognition: without specific procedures, without the certainty of guaranteed right, without the dimension of juridical formalism, not a single one of us could claim to be truly free. Nonetheless, democracy is not simply a matter of procedure; not simply a matter of rights. For this decisive reason, in a modern world that is marked by a close confrontation between great planetary civilisations, it is more imperative than ever to redefine basic principles in a way that expressly acknowledges the different visions of the world, the religious conceptions and the 'key forms of metaphysics' which underlie those principles. We cannot gloss over the fact that the attempt to establish an axiologically univocal definition of terms, far from producing a state of peace, has always produced a state of war. It was Thomas Hobbes himself who reminded us, in *Leviathan*, that moral philosophers, exactly when they have attempted, armed with the best of universalistic intentions, to define the good and the nature of peace in a purely univocal manner, have produced wars. And for his part, Voltaire

– looking back in his *Traité sur la tolérance* on the previous confessional conflicts between the Catholics and Huguenots – felt compelled to recall that we Europeans have almost 'exterminated one another over a parcel of words'.[16] If it is indeed the case that the formal rigour of specifically defined procedures is essential, it is equally true that the obsessive concern with univocal definitions has frequently generated fatal struggles and conflicts in turn. I believe that we should open ourselves instead to what an old and noble anthropology used to describe as 'functional equivalents', adopting an ultimate and decisive theoretical task for our programme: the transition from the *method of comparison* to the *politics of translation*.[17] We ought to be capable of retracing, in other cultures, normative principles, values and criteria which are equally valid, even if they are defined differently from our own – without yielding to the temptation to impose our definitions on these principles, without surreptitiously reintroducing the ancient Manichaean distinction between the good and the evil. We should not forget that the categories of good and evil must be handled with extreme care. For this reason, I feel just as distant towards the sort of political philosophy which takes the good as its starting point as I do towards that which is primarily motivated by the normative significance of evil. I am thinking rather of a political approach which, from a perspective 'beyond good and evil', is capable of drawing instead on the influential scene that is represented by the experience of pain or suffering. Perhaps we ought to begin by thinking of democracy as a paradoxical sort of community, as a community without community, one whose constitutive princi-ples derive directly from the *normative priority of suffering*, or, to adopt the formulation of a radically revisited political theol-ogy, from the 'authority of those who suffer'.

One may legitimately object that, when we consider the emphatic and dramatic character of the various conflicts and hostilities which afflict our globalised world, a proposal such as this still clearly belongs to the domain of the purely counter-factual. Yet the refusal to acknowledge just how much this demand is already rooted in our global Babel, and just how much it already pervades the dynamic character of the subjects who

---

16 Voltaire, *Treatise on Tolerance and Other Writings*, p. 28.
17 Giacomo Marramao, *La passione del presente. Breve lessico della modernità-mondo*.

inhabit this space, is simply a refusal to grasp the 'signs of the times': those prognostic signs of our present which indicate a possible change of course, one which might help to guide the different historical dynamics along an alternative anti-identitarian trajectory. That is to say, in the direction of a *cosmopolitanism of difference*.

AFTERWORD: CONFLICTED TIES

As Giacomo Marramao warns, *The Passage West* is a book organised radially. What this means is that, after defining in the first chapter the radical mutation that globalisation imposes on the forms of government and on the definition of the political; after announcing the thesis of the 'passage to the Occident'; he goes on to develop another series of approaches, setting out from peripheral conditions that nevertheless converge within the constitutive dynamic of the 'passage'. What, then, is this 'passage'? Marramao writes: 'my philosophical reading of globalisation [is] as a *passage to the Occident*, where "passage" draws together the continuous and the discontinuous, the process and the turning point'. In other words, the passage to the Occident is a 'passage to modernity destined to produce profound transformations in the economy, society, lifestyles and codes of behaviour not only of "other" civilisations but of Western civilisation itself. . . . Never before the advent of the stereoscopic optic of world-society had the *pluriversal nature of the process of civilisation* and the *plurality of the possible paths towards modernity* been so evident'. *Mundus* and *Globus* establish between one another (like a syntagma of different linguistic perspectives that form the abstractions *'mondialisation'* and 'globalisation') a paradox that leads one to focus at once on the expansion of the world [*mondo*] and the closure of the globe. This is the discovery of the 'passage'. There is no unilateral image, no dialectic between outside and inside, but an opening to a new paradigm that is also the key of a constitutive dynamic: well burrowed, old mole! But one is immediately confronted with the problem of why this phenomenological description of the passage does not bend the perception of mutation to that ontological transformation that most probably underlies it. That is to say, why not interpret the future as 'to-come' [*a-venire*] and then unfold or transform the archaeological method into a genealogical one?

Marramao grasps the problem and immediately gives it an interpretation that excavates it from within: Occident and secularisation, globalisation and secularisation – in line with his previous important and incisive works. His thinking situates itself in the intersection of these dualities. Once again, it is a case of continuity and discontinuity; here lies also the preference for a term like 'second modernity', rather than 'postmodernity', and the insistence on the historical *phylum* as well as the slightly paradoxical idea of a conjunction that contains a disjunction, repeating Ulrich Beck. But *nota bene*: it is not that the *radical* novelty of the passage is denied! If we want to remain faithful to the direction of Marramao's argument, we must recognise that he emphatically insists on this novelty, both from the standpoint of the relationship between space and the processes of singularisation, and from that of the relationship between the political Leviathan and other models of political constitution. In each of these cases it is a case of seeing the *new* arise against the original global horizon: there is no inner analogy between national and global but rather a production of locality, the *glocal*, and in general the interpenetration of the local and the global; and there is an overcoming of all identitarian models and, consequently, of all the traditional mediations of the political. There is instead the opening towards the constitution of new models and a plurality of levels of the definition of government . . . We could continue. As we were saying: through the refusal of all dichotomous optics, by exalting the social practice of the imagination, Marramao internalises the passage.

But to what extent can it be said that this internalisation of the passage blocks and empties the passage itself? The continual reprise of the *phylum* of continuity posits the difference of living as articulation rather than as rupture. And the subjectivity that moves within these passages finds itself consigned to the function of formal organisation; it risks being reduced to an empty transcendental continuity rather than being able to wager itself on the alterity of the processes. There is no longer a subject here. The polyphony of globalisation can certainly open itself to anthropological *métissage*: but what moves this passage? What are the struggles that determine the development? To put this in the same terms as Weber: what is the passage from the emancipation of instrumental reason to that of the liberation from command? The *Angelus novus* that rises up at the heart of the passage can only see the to-come [*a-venire*] when, looking back, he confronts a horizon of struggles, and sees the production of the subject in struggle. So, for example, once again situating itself at the level of empire, the theme of sovereignty may appear incorrect; but only if, with the passage, one ignores a multitude capable of producing new subjectivity and if one fails to oppose the rhizome to the *phylum*. The problem is not that of the theoretical disproportion of the conceptual relationship, but the ontological immeasurableness [*dismisura*] of the insurrection of the multitude.

Marramao is intensely aware of this set of problems, as he shows in some beautiful pages where he contrasts Jaspers with Heidegger and turns the analysis of the spiritual situation of the age into the determination of the incompleteness of the project of modernity. In an increasingly forceful way he attacks every identitarian illusion, all religious identifications; he confronts and conjoins opposed models of representation and modelling of reality: difference is also contingency, and is also relativity, and is even the discovery of a true, effective *dialogical place* that makes the passage real. The critique that Marramao carries out here, in the concluding pages of the first chapter of this book, against Rawls' and Habermas' 'false' relativisations of the socio-political context, is exemplary: to realise the passage it is necessary that there be a *place of conflict*.

Our query arises here: who are the subjects of this conflict? What are the directions from which the conflict emanates and what is its genealogy? What is left over from the double injunction of universalism and difference? For what reason (other than banally sceptical ones) must the hands that write and conjoin these words always be wrong?

Marramao's book is beautiful, and the rhetorical strategy that unfolds the themes raised in the first chapter is powerful. But Marramao is a wise man and hence, before confronting the solution to the problem, he zealously advances its critical exposition. One should approach in this way chapters 3 ('*Dämmerung* – The Twilight of Sovereignty: State, Subjects and Fundamental Rights'), 4 ('The Exile of the *Nomos*: Carl Schmitt and the *globale Zeit*') and 5 ('Gift, Exchange, Obligation: Karl Polanyi and Social Philosophy'). The analyses in these chapters are tied to those of *Dopo il Leviatano. Individuo e comunità*, a book that we can say in many ways merges with the one discussed here. In all the works that we have cited, there are cues for the construction of the theory of the passage, as is clear from the very titles of those chapters. But I believe that there is something more. In particular, in the chapter 'The Twilight of Sovereignty' there is a formidable reprise

of Italian constitutional theory. (This work of recovery of juridical thinkers and texts in philosophical terms is extremely
important. Italian constitutional literature is of global value, as
has been demonstrated by the success of certain Italian books.
The dull emptiness of Italian academic containers, the inability of
Italian publishers to test themselves on the world stage, should
not therefore worry us in the face of the originality and strength
of some works and discourses invented by Italian constitutional-
ists and jurists). The chapter on Carl Schmitt is excellent.
Unfortunately, Schmitt, unlike Marramao, gave a conclusive
direction to his political solution (which, alas, was Nazism) to all
the contradictions of his thought, both virtual and possible, and
that were in this sense extremely productive. The chapter on
Polanyi is a superb, although paradoxical (in accordance with the
radial procedure prescribed by Marramao), introduction to the
analysis and definition of an ethical concept and normative project
of the idea of 'common', against all the privatising and public law
definitions. (This really is a topic that should be launched across
the globe in political discussions.)

Chapters 2, 6 and 7 throw themselves into a thematic development of the hypothesis of the 'passage'. The concept of passage is
advanced in terms of the border [*confine*] zone, as a fan of possibilities, as a self-reflection and assumption of responsibility in the
face of all the violent operations aimed at realising the virtual –
although the problem is, rather, the opposite one, that of
continually virtualising the real. From the standpoint of politics,
what will 'democracy' mean when it breaks with the abstract
universalism of its historical premises? Democracy: a paradoxical
community, a community of those without community, democracy as the opening to the to-come [*a-venire*], as the passion of the
disenchanted, as the acceptance of unexpected guests ... The
thread of the argument is taken up again here, as it is in the subsequent chapter on Voltaire and tolerance ... Here the radial form
of the book is again problematised, sometimes only slightly, at
others with severe determination. The definition of democracy as
a paradoxical community is in reality a forceful interpretation of
the democratic process: one can in effect glimpse here 'communities of *sans-*', subjects who suffer, flesh that wants to become
body ... Marramao does not skirt around the problem: the radial
organisation becomes a political net, and he declares the side on
which he stands.

The final two chapters of the book (chapter 8, 'Ciphers of

Difference'; chapter 9, 'Europe after the Leviathan: Technology, Politics, Constitution')[1] are very important. They offer some ciphers for an effective reconstruction following the problematic that was posed at the start of the book. Chapter 8 sets out from the critique that second-generation feminism directed to the ontological nomenclature of gender that was fixed by that of the first generation. It finds in Donna Haraway and Judith Butler the principle of a generative logic, and more generally a constructivism that enables one to pose the problem of the production of subjectivity in its own terms. Deleuze's advancement of the constitutive concept of difference is contemporaneous to this development. The constitutive is the opposite of the identical; and if we insist on games of strategy, we will once again tie the question of the common, of what constitutes us, to the architectonic barriers of the logic of identity. In contrast, we will move constructively only when we traverse relationships, proximities, distances, ties and conflicts: irreducible differences that never identify being but always produce it. Here the production of subjectivity is a veritable production of bodies.

And to conclude: with regard to the final chapter [of the first edition of the book, chapter 9] and the *Multiversum* that a possible European constitution could bring about, we do not wish to insist on the topic of political federalism (which is nonetheless extremely important). We are more interested in the content of the *Multiversum*, since it is a matter that spreads everywhere. Each subject, in its singularity, constitutes a multitude. But if the multitude constitutes the subject, every world is a world of worlds; and every subject is a multitude of multitudes. This is probably the key to the crossing, that is, the plot of the passage that we must accomplish or, better still, that we are accomplishing.

Who knows if, looking back on this passage, a man from the year 3000 will still be able to speak of the Occident? He will certainly speak of himself in terms of the passage and struggles that have destroyed the Occident as the matrix of the common and of the transformation of his own body; because this man (or woman) of the year 3000 will be a multiversal body and a common passage.

Antonio Negri

---

1 *Translator's note*: This afterword was written following the first edition of this book in 2003.

BIBLIOGRAPHY

Albrow, Martin, *The Global Age*, Cambridge: Polity Press, 1996.

Ales Bello, Angela, and Francesca Brezzi, *Il filo(sofare) di Arianna. Percorsi del pensiero femminile nel Novecento*, Milan: Mimesis, 2001.

Amato, Giuliano, 'L'originalità istituzionale dell'Unione Europea', in *Un Passato che Passa? Germania e Italia tra memoria e prospettiva*, Rome: Fahrenheit 451, 2000.

Anders, Günther, *Die Antiquiertheit des Menschen*, Munich: C. H. Beck, 2002.

Anderson, Benedict, *Imagined Communities*, London: Verso, 1983.

Apel, Karl Otto, *The Transformation of Philosophy*, London: Routledge & Kegan Paul, 1980.

Appadurai, Arjun, *Modernità in polvere*, Rome: Meltemi, 2001.

Appadurai, Arjun, *Modernity at Large*, Minneapolis: University of Minnesota Press, 1996.

Augé, Marc, *Journal de guerre*, Paris: Galilée, 2002.

Ayer, Alfred, 'Sources of Intolerance', in S. Mendus and D. Edwards (eds.), *On Toleration*, Oxford: Clarendon Press, 1987.

'The Bangkok Declaration', Final Declaration of the Regional Meeting for Asia of the World Conference on Human Rights, 29 March–2 April 1993, UN Doc. A/Conf.157/ASRM/.

Barber, Benjamin, 'Jihad vs. McWorld', *The Atlantic* (March 1992).

Barber, Benjamin, *Jihad vs. McWorld: How Globalism and Tribalism Are Reshaping the World*, New York: Random House, 1996.

Bataille, Georges, and Roger Caillois, 'Sacred Sociology and the Relationships between "Society", "Organism", and "Being"', in Denis Hollier (ed.), *The College of Sociology 1937–39*, Minneapolis: University of Minnesota Press, 1988.

Bauman, Zygmunt, *Globalization: The Human Consequences*, New York: Columbia University Press, 1998.

Beck, Ulrich (ed.), *Politik der Globalisierung*, Frankfurt: Suhrkamp, 1998.

Beck, Ulrich, *What Is Globalization?*, Cambridge: Polity Press, 1999.

Beck, Ulrich, 'Wie wird Demokratie im Zeitalter der Globalisierung möglich? Eine Einleitung', in Ulrich Beck (ed.), *Politik der Globalisierung*, Frankfurt: Suhrkamp, 1998.

Ben Néfissa, Sarah (ed.), *Pouvoirs et associations dans le monde arabe*, Paris: CNRS, 2002.

Benhabib, Seyla, *Another Cosmopolitanism*, Oxford: Oxford University Press, 2008.

Benhabib, Seyla, *The Claims of Culture*, Princeton, NJ: Princeton University Press, 2002.

Benhabib, Seyla, *Situating the Self*, New York: Routledge, 1992.

Benhabib, Seyla, and Drucilla Cornell (eds.), *Feminism as Critique*, Minneapolis: University of Minnesota Press, 1987.

Benveniste, Émile, *Indo-European Language and Society*, London: Faber & Faber, 1973.

Berlin, Isaiah, *The Crooked Timber of Humanity*, ed. Henry Harding, London: John Murray, 1990.

Bhabha, Homi K., *The Location of Culture*, London: Routledge & Kegan Paul, 1994.

Bhabha, Homi K., *Nation and Narration*, New York: Routledge, 1990.

Bhabha, Homi K., 'Sul dubbio globale', in A. Martinengo (ed.), *Figure del conflitto. Studi in onore di Giacomo Marramao*, Rome: Valter Casini Editore, 2006.

Blanchot, Maurice, *The Writing of the Disaster*, Lincoln: University of Nebraska Press, 1995.

Bloch, Ernst, *Heritage of Our Times*, Oxford: Polity, 1991.

Bloch, Marc, *The Royal Touch*, London: Routledge & Kegan Paul, 1973.

Bobbio, Norberto, *Which Socialism?*, Worcester: Polity, 1987.

Boccia, Maria Luisa, *La differenza politica*, Milan: Il Saggiatore, 2002.

Böckenförde, Ernst-Wolfgang, *Staat, Verfassung, Demokratie*, Frankfurt: Suhrkamp Verlag, 1991.

Bolaffi, Angelo, and Giacomo Marramao, *Frammento e sistema*, Rome: Donzelli, 2001.

Bonacchi, Gabriella, and Angela Groppi (eds.), *Il dilemma della cittadinanza*, Rome-Bari: Laterza, 1993.

Brague, Rémi, *Eccentric Culture*, South Bend, IN: St. Augustine's Press, 2002.

Braidotti, Rosi, *Patterns of Dissonance*, Cambridge: Polity Press, 1991.

Brunner, Otto, *Land und Herrschaft*, Vienna: Rudolf M. Rohr, 1939.

Brunner, Otto, *Land and Lordship*, Philadelphia: University of Pennsylvania Press, 1992.

Butler, Judith, *Bodies that Matter*, New York: Routledge, 1993.

Butler, Judith, *Gender Trouble*, New York: Routledge, 1993.

Butler, Judith, and Joan W. Scott (eds.), *Feminists Theorize the Political*, New York: Routledge, 1992.

Cacciari, Massimo, 'Ancora sull'idea di Impero', *MicroMega* 4 (2002), pp. 185–96.

Cacciari, Massimo, 'Digressioni su Impero e tre Rome', *MicroMega* 5 (2001), pp. 43–63.

Caillois, Roger, *Man and the Sacred*, Westport, CT: Greenwood Press, 1980.

Calchi Novati, G., and L. Quartapelle (eds.), *Terzo mondo addio*, Rome: Carocci, 2007.

Calvino, Italo, 'Introduzione', in Voltaire, *Candido ovvero l'ottimismo*, Milan: Rizzoli, 1974.

Cardini, Franco, *Europa e Islam*, Rome: Laterza, 2001.

Cassirer, Ernst, 'Zur Logik der Kulturwissenschaften', in *Gesammelte Werke*, vol. 24, Hamburg: Meiner Verlag, 1941–46.

Cavalieri, Renzo, 'La Carta asiatica e la Cina', *Parolechiave* 37 (2007), pp. 73–81.

Cavalieri, Renzo, *La legge e il rito: Lineamenti di storia del diritto cinese*, Milan: Angeli, 1999.

Cavarero, Adriana, *Nonostante Platone*, Rome: Editori Riuniti, 1990.

Cheng, Anne, 'Confucianisme, postmodernisme et valeurs asiatiques', in *Géopolitique et Mondialisation*, Paris: Odile Jacob, 2002.

Cipolla, Carlo, *Vele e cannoni*, Bologna: Il Mulino, 1983.

Cohen-Almagor, Raphael, *The Boundaries of Liberty and Tolerance*, Gainesville: University Press of Florida, 1994.

Collin, Françoise, *Le différend des sexes*, Nantes: Éditions Pleins Feux, 1999.

Colombo, Valentina, and Gustavo Gozzi (eds.), *Tradizioni culturali, sistemi giuridici e diritti umani nell'area del Mediterraneo*, Bologna: Il Mulino, 2003.

Crisma, Amina, *Il Cielo, gli uomini. Percorso attraverso i testi confuciani dell'età classica*, Venice: Libreria Editrice Cafoscarina, 2000.

Dahl, Robert Alan, *Polyarchy*, New Haven: Yale University Press, 1971.

De Bary, William Theodore, *Asian Values and Human Rights: A Confucian Communitarian Perspective*, Cambridge, MA: Harvard University Press, 1998.

De Lauretis, Teresa, 'The Essence of the Triangle or, Taking the Risk of Essentialism Seriously', *Differences: A Journal of Feminist Cultural Studies* 1 (Summer 1989), pp. 3–37.

Dee, John, *General and Rare Memorials Pertaining to the Perfect Art of Navigation*, London: John Daye, 1577.

Deleuze, Gilles, and Félix Guattari, *A Thousand Plateaus*, Minneapolis: University of Minnesota Press, 1987.

d'Entrèves, Alexander Passerin, *The Notion of the State*, Oxford: Clarendon Press, 1967.

Derrida, Jacques, 'The University Without Condition', in *Without Alibi*, Stanford, CA: Stanford University Press, 2002.

Diotima, *Il pensiero della differenza sessuale*, Milan: La Tartaruga, 1987.

Diotima, *Oltre l'uguaglianza*, Naples: Liguori, 1995.

Dominijanni, Ida, 'Il desiderio di politica', in L. Cigarini, *La Politica del desiderio*, Parma: Nuove Pratiche, 1995.

Douglas, Mary, 'The Contempt of Ritual', in *In the Active Voice*, London: Routledge & Kegan Paul, 1982.

Dumont, Louis, *Homo aequalis*, Paris: Gallimard, 1977.

Eisenstadt, Samuel N., *Fondamentalismo e modernitá*, Rome: Laterza, 1994.

Eisenstadt, Shmuel N., 'Innerweltliche Transzendenz und die Strukturierung der Welt: Max Webers Studie über China und die Gestalt der chinesischen Zivilisation', in W. Schluchter (ed.), *Max Webers Studie über Konfuzianismus und Taoismus: Interpretation und Kritik*, Frankfurt: Suhrkamp, 1983.

Elster, Jon, *The Cement of Society*, Cambridge: Cambridge University Press, 1989.

Elster, Jon, 'Constitution-Making in Eastern Europe: Rebuilding the Boat in the Open Sea', *Public Administration 71:1* (Spring–Summer 1993), pp. 169–217.

Elster, Jon (ed.), *The Multiple Self*, Cambridge: Cambridge University Press, 1985.

Esposito, Roberto, *Communitas: Origine e destino della comunità*, Turin: Einaudi, 1998.

Ferrajoli, Luigi, *La sovranità nel mondo moderno*, Milan: Anabasi, 1995.

Fornari, Emanuela, *Modernity out of Joint: Global Democracy and Asian Values in Jürgen Habermas and Amartya K. Sen*, Aurora, CO: Davies Group, 2007.

Foucault, Michel, 'Un Cours Inédit (05/01/1983)', *Magazine Littéraire* 207 (1984).

Fox Keller, Evelyn, *Secrets of Life*, London: New Haven, 1992.

Fraisse, Geneviève, *La Raison des femmes*, Paris: Plon, 1992.

Frankel, Ernst, 'Kollective Demokratie', in *Die Gesellschaft* 6 (8 August 1929).

Fraser, Nancy, and Axel Honneth, *Redistribution or Recognition? A Political-Philosophical Exchange*, London: Verso, 2003.

Fukuyama, Francis, *The End of History and the Last Man*, New York: Penguin, 1992.

Galeotti, Anna Elisabetta, 'La Differenza: politica, non metafisica', in Sebastiano Maffettone e Salvatore Veca (eds.), *Filosofia, politica, società*, Rome: Donzelli, 1995.

Galimberti, Umberto, *Psiche e techne. L'Uomo nell'età della tecnica*, Milan: Feltrinelli, 1999.

Geertz, Clifford, *The Interpretation of Cultures*, New York: Basic Books, 1973.

Gellner, Ernst, *Culture, Identity and Politics*, Cambridge: Cambridge University Press, 1987.

Giannini, Massimo Severo, 'La concezione giuridica di Carl Schmitt: un politologo datato?', *Quaderni costituzionali*, VI, 1986.

Giardini, Federica, 'Identità / Differenza', *Paradigmi* XX, no. 59 (2002), pp. 303–18.

Giddens, Anthony, *The Consequences of Modernity*, Cambridge: Polity Press, 1990.

Giddens, Anthony, *Modernity and Self-Identity*, Cambridge: Polity Press, 1991.

Ginzburg, Carlo, *Rapporti di forza. Storia, retorica, prova*, Milan: Feltrinelli, 2000.

Gnoli, Antonio, and Franco Volpi, *I prossimi Titani. Conversazioni con Ernst Jünger*, Milan: Adelphi, 1997.

Grimm, Dieter, 'Does Europe Need a Constitution?', in Peter Gowan and Perry Anderson (eds.), *The Question of Europe*, London: Verso, 1997.

Grossi, Paolo, *L'ordine giuridico medievale*, Rome-Bari: Laterza, 1995.

Guéhenno, Jean-Marie, *The End of the Nation-State*, Minneapolis: University of Minnesota Press, 1995.

Habermas, Jürgen, *Der gespaltene Westen*, Frankfurt: Suhrkamp, 2004.

Habermas, Jürgen, *Glauben und Wissen: Rede zum Friedenspreis der Deutschen Buchhandels*, Frankfurt: Suhrkamp, 2001.

Habermas, Jürgen, *The Inclusion of the Other*, Cambridge, MA: MIT Press, 1998.

Habermas, Jürgen (ed.), *Observations on 'The Spiritual Situation of the Age'*, Cambridge, MA: MIT Press, 1985.

Habermas, Jürgen, *The Postnational Constellation*, Cambridge: Polity, 2001.

Habermas, Jürgen, 'Reconciliation Through the Public Use of Reason: Remarks on John Rawls's *Political Liberalism*', *The Journal of Philosophy* 92:2 (February 1995), pp. 109–31.

Haraway, Donna, *Simians, Cyborgs, and Women*, New York: Routledge, 1991.

Hardt, Michael, and Antonio Negri, *Empire*, Cambridge, MA: Harvard University Press, 2000.

Harvey, David, *The Condition of Postmodernity*, Blackwell: Oxford, 1989.

Hegel, Georg Wilhelm Friedrich, *Vorlesungen über die Philosophie der Weltgeschichte*, ed. Karl Heinz Ilting, Karl Brehmer, and Hoo Nam Seelmann, in *Vorlesungen: Ausgewählte Nachschriften und Manuskripte*, vol. 12, Hamburg: Felix Meiner Verlag, 1996.

Heidegger, Martin, *Identity and Difference*, Chicago: University of Chicago Press, 2002.

Heller, Herman, *Die Souveränität*, Berlin: W. de Gruyter, 1927.

Henard, Jacqueline, and Daniel Vernet, 'La Grande Europe vue par Jacques Delors et Vaclav Havel', *Le Monde*, 1 February 2001, p. 16.

Hintze, Otto, 'Wesen und Wandlung des modernen Staats', in *Staat und Verfassung*, Göttingen: Gerhard Oestreich, 1931.

Hobsbawm, Eric, and Terence Ranger (eds.), *The Invention of Tradition*, Cambridge: Cambridge University Press, 1983.

Hofstadter, Douglas R., *Gödel, Escher, Bach: An Eternal Golden Braid*, Brighton: Harvester Press, 1979.

Hooke, Samuel (ed.), *The Labyrinth*, London: S.P.C.K., 1935.

Hooke, Samuel (ed.), *Myth and Ritual*, London: Oxford University Press, 1933.

Huntington, Samuel P., *The Clash of Civilizations and the Remaking of World Order*, New York: Simon & Schuster, 1996.

Ianni, Octavio, *A sociedade global*, Rio de Janeiro: Civilizaçã Brasileira, 1992.

Ianni, Octavio, *Teorias da globalização*, Rio de Janeiro: Civilizaçã Brasileira, 1995.

Irigaray, Luce, *An Ethics of Sexual Difference*, London: Continuum, 2004.

Irigaray, Luce, *Speculum of the Other Woman*, New York: Cornell University Press, 1985.

Jaspers, Karl, *The Origin and Goal of History*, New Haven: Yale University Press, 1953.

Jellinek, Georg, *System der subjektiven öffentlichen Rechte*, Freiburg: J.C.B. Mohr, 1892.

Jonas, Hans, *The Imperative of Responsibility*, Chicago: The University of Chicago Press, 1984.

Jullien, F., *Traité de l'efficacité*, Paris: Grasset, 1996.

Jünger, Ernst, *An der Zeitmauer*, Stuttgart: Klett, 1959.

Jünger, Ernst, 'Total Mobilization', in Richard Wolin (ed.), *The Heidegger Controversy: A Critical Reader*, Cambridge, MA: MIT Press, 1993.

Jünger, Friedrich Georg, *Die Perfektion der Technik*, Frankfurt: V. Klostermann, 1993.

Kant, Immanuel, *Critique of Pure Reason*, Cambridge: Cambridge University Press, 1998.

Kelsen, Hans, *General Theory of Law and State*, Clark, NJ: Lawbook Exchange, 2009.

Kelsen, Hans, *Pure Theory of Law*, Clark, NJ: Lawbook Exchange, 2002.

Kelsen, Hans, *Vom Wesen und Wert der Demokratie*, Tübingen: J.C.B. Mohr, 1929.

King, Preston, *Toleration*, London: Allen and Unwin, 1976.

Kirchheimer, Otto, 'Weimar – and What Then? An Analysis of a Constitution', in *Politics, Law and Social Change*, New York: Columbia University Press, 1969, pp. 33–74.

Kristeva, Julia, *Strangers to Ourselves*, New York: Columbia University Press, 1994.

Krockow, Christian von, *Die Entscheidung: Eine Untersuchung über Ernst Jünger, Carl Schmitt, Martin Heidegger*, Stuttgart: F. Enke Verlag, 1958.

Kurtz, Lester R., *Gods in the Global Village: The World's Religions in Sociological Perspective*, Thousand Oaks, CA: Pine Forge Press, 1995.

Latouche, Serge, *The Westernization of the World*, Cambridge: Polity Press, 1996.

Leopardi, Giacomo, 'Broom', in *Selected Poems*, Dublin: Dedalus Press, 1995.

Lonzi, Carla, *Manifesto di Rivolta Femminile*, Milan: Rivolta, 1971.

Löwith, Karl, *Meaning in History*, Chicago: University of Chicago, 1949.

Löwith, Karl, 'The Occasional Decisionism of Carl Schmitt', in Richard Wolin (ed.), *The Heidegger Controversy*, Cambridge, MA: MIT Press, 1935.

Luhmann, Niklas, 'Europa als Problem der Weltgesellschaft', *Berliner Debatte* 2 (1994); also in Beck (ed.), *Politik der Globalisierung*.

Luhmann, Niklas, 'Globalization or World Society: How to Conceive of Modern Society?', *International Review of Sociology* 7:1 (March 1997).

Luhmann, Niklas, 'Die Weltgessellschaft', *Archiv für Rechts- und Sozialphilosophie* 57 (1971).

Lukes, Steven, 'What Is Left?', *Times Literary Supplement*, 27 March 1992.

MacKinnon, Catherine, *Towards a Feminist Theory of the State*, Cambridge: Harvard University Press, 1989.

Maier, Charles S., *Recasting Bourgeois Europe*, Princeton, NJ: Princeton University Press, 1975.

Marramao, Giacomo, 'Apologie des Möglichen. Technik und Ethik an der Jahrtausendwende', in *Insel-Almanach auf das Jahr 2000*, Frankfurt: Insel Verlag, 1999.

Marramao, Giacomo, *Cielo e terra*, Rome: Laterza, 1994.

Marramao, Giacomo, *Dopo il Leviatano. Individuo e comunità*, Turin: Bollati Boringhieri, 2000.

Marramao, Giacomo, 'El crepúsculo de los soberanos', in *Pensar en el siglo*, Madrid: Taurus, 1999.

Marramao, Giacomo, 'Globalization, Conflict of Values and Contingent Identity', in *Normativity and Legitimacy*, Münster: Lit Verlag, 2001.

Marramao, Giacomo, *La passione del presente. Breve lessico della modernità-mondo*, Turin: Bollati Boringhieri, 2008.

Marramao, Giacomo, *Il politico e le trasformazioni*, Bari: De Donato, 1979.

Marramao, Giacomo, *Potere e secolarizzazione*, Turin: Bollati Boringhieri, 2005.

Marramao, Giacomo, *Die Säkularisierung der westlichen Welt*, Insel: Frankfurt am Main, 1996.

Massarenti, Armando, 'Introduzione' to Amartya Sen, *Laicismo indiano*, Milan: Feltrinelli, 1998.

Matz, Ulrich, 'Staat', in *Handbuch philosophischer Grundbegriffe*, vol. 5, Munich: Kosel Verlag, 1974, pp. 1403–19.

Mayer, Hans, *Ein Deutscher auf Widerruf: Erinnerungen*, Frankfurt: Suhrkamp, 1982.

McLuhan, Marshall, *The Gutenberg Galaxy*, Toronto: University of Toronto Press, 1962.

Merleau-Ponty, Maurice, *Signs*, Evanston, IL: Northwestern University Press, 1964.

Mishra, Laxman Prasad, 'Le implicazioni antieconomiche della fuga dal mondo', in *Max Weber e l'India*, Turin: CESMEO, 1986.

Moccia, Luigi, *Il diritto in Cina. Tra ritualismo e modernizzazione*, Turin: Bollati Boringhieri, 2009.

Morin, Edgar, *Pour sortir du XXᵉ siècle*, Paris: Nathan, 1981.

Mosse, George Lachmann, *The Nationalization of the Masses*, New York: H. Fertig, 1975.

Muraro, Luisa, *L'ordine simbolico della madre*, Rome: Editori Riuniti, 1991.

Nancy, Jean-Luc, *The Gravity of Thought*, Atlantic Highlands, NJ: Humanities Press, 1997.

Nancy, Jean-Luc, *The Sense of the World*, Minneapolis: University of Minnesota Press, 1997.

Napolitano, Giorgio, A. Accornero, M. Cacciari, M. Tronti, *Operaismo e centralità operaia*, Rome: Editori Riunti, 1978.

Neumann, Franz, *Behemoth*, London: Victor Gollancz, 1942.

Norton, A. R. (ed.), *Civil Society in the Middle East*, New York: Brill, 1995–96.

Nussbaum, Martha, *Cultivating Humanity*, Cambridge, MA: Harvard University Press, 1997.

Ohmae, Kenichi, *The Borderless World*, London: Collins, 1990.

Ohmae, Kenichi, *The End of the Nation State*, London: HarperCollins, 1995.

Okin, Susam Moller, *Justice, Gender and the Family*, New York: Basic Books, 1989.

Ortiz, Renato, *Mundialização e cultura*, São Paolo: Editora Brasiliense, 1994.

Ortiz, Renato, *Um outro território*, Buenos Aires: Universidad Nacional de Quilmes, 1996.

Osterhammel, J., *Entzauberung Asiens*, Munich: C. H. Beck, 1998.

Panikkar, R., *Mito, simbolo, culto I. Mistero ed ermeneutica* (*Opera Omnia*, vol. IX), Milan: Jaca Book, 2008.

Parfit, Derek, *Reasons and Persons*, Oxford: Oxford University Press, 1984.

Pasqualotto, G., *East & West. Identità e dialogo interculturale*, Venice: Marsilio, 2003.

Paz, Octavio, *Conjunctions and Disjunctions*, London: Wildwood House, 1975.

Perniola, Mario, *Transiti*, Bologna: Cappelli, 1985.

Polanyi, Karl, *Primitive, Archaic and Modern Economies*, Garden City, NY: Anchor Books, 1968.

Prodi, Paolo, *Il sacramento del potere*, Bologna: Il Mulino, 1992.

Prodi, Paolo, *Il sovrano pontefice*, Bologna: Il Mulino, 1982.

Prodi, Paolo, *Una storia della giustizia*, Bologna: Il Mulino, 2000.

Pulcini, E., *L'individuo senza passioni*, Turin: Bollati Borringhieri, 2001.

Rawls, John, *Political Liberalism*, New York: Columbia University Press, 1993.

Rawls, John, 'Political Liberalism: A Reply to Habermas', in *The Journal of Philosophy* 92:3 (March 1995), pp. 132–80.

Rawls, John, *A Theory of Justice*, Oxford: Clarendon Press, 1972.

Remotti, F., *Contro l'identità*, Rome-Bari: Laterza, 1996.

Ricca, Mario, *Oltre Babele*, Bari: Dedalo, 2008.

Rifkin, Jeremy, *The End of Work*, New York: Penguin, 1995.

Robertson, Roland, *Globalization: Social Theory and Global Culture*, Sage: London, 1992.

Robertson, Roland, 'Glocalization Revisited and Elaborated', 2002 (unpublished).

Rodotà, Stefano, *Tecnopolitica*, Rome: Laterza, 2004.

Roetz, Heiner, *Die chinesische Ethik der Achsenzeit*, Frankfurt: Suhrkamp, 1992.

Romano, Santi, *L'ordinamento giuridico*, Florence: Sansoni, 1946.

Rosenau, J. N., *Turbulence in World Politics: A Theory of Change and Continuity*, Princeton, NJ: Princeton University Press, 1990.

Rossi, Pietro, *L'identità dell'Europa*, Bologna: Il Mulino, 2007.

Said, Edward, *Orientalism*, New York: Vintage Books, 1978.

Sanna, Gabriella and Antonella Capasso (eds.), *Orienti e Occidenti*, Roma: Fahrenheit 451, 1997.

Sassen, Saskia, *The Global City*, Princeton, NJ: Princeton University Press, 1991.

Sassen, Saskia, *Losing Control? Sovereignty in an Age of Globalization*, New York: Columbia University Press, 1996.

Schiera, Pierangelo, 'Seicento e Novecento. Le categorie moderne della politica', *Scienza e Politica* 26 (2002).

Schluchter, Wolfgang, *Die Entwicklung des okzidentalen Rationalismus*, Tübingen: J.C.B. Mohr, 1979.

Schmitt, Carl, *The Concept of the Political*, Chicago: University of Chicago Press, 1986.

Schmitt, Carl, *Constitutional Theory*, Durham: Duke University Press, 2008.

Schmitt, Carl, *The Crisis of Parliamentary Democracy*, Cambridge, MA: MIT Press, 1985.

Schmitt, Carl, *Der Begriff des Politischen*, Berlin: Duncker & Humblot, 1933.

Schmitt, Carl, *Die Diktatur: Von den Anfängen des modernen Souveränitätsgedankens bis zum proletarischen Klassenkampf*, Berlin: Duncker & Humblot, 1921.

Schmitt, Carl, *Ex Captivitate Salus: Erfahrungen der Zeit 1945/47*, Cologne: Greven Verlag, 1950.

Schmitt, Carl, *Die geistesgeschichtliche Lage des heutigen Parlamentarismus*, Berlin: Duncker & Humblot, 1923.

Schmitt, Carl, 'Die geschichtliche Struktur des heutigen Welt-Gegensatzes von Ost und West', in Armin Mohler (ed.), *Freundschaftliche Begegnungen: Festschrift für Ernst Jünger zum 60. Geburtstag*, Frankfurt: V. Klostermann, 1955.

Schmitt, Carl, 'Der Hüter der Verfassung', *Archiv des öffentlichen Rechts* 16 (1929), pp. 161–237.

Schmitt, Carl, *Der Hüter der Verfassung*, Tübingen: J.C.B. Mohr, 1931.

Schmitt, Carl, *Land und Meer*, Leipzig: Philipp Reclam, 1942.

Schmitt, Carl, *Legality and Legitimacy*, Durham: Duke University Press, 2004.

Schmitt, Carl, *Der Leviathan in der Staatslehre des Thomas*

Hobbes: Sinn und Fehlschlag eines politischen Symbols, Hamburg: Hanseatische Verlagsanstalt, 1938.

Schmitt, Carl, *The Leviathan in the State Theory of Thomas Hobbes*, Westport, CT: Greenwood Press, 1996.

Schmitt, Carl, *Der Nomos der Erde im Völkerrecht des Jus Publicum Europæum*, Cologne: Greven Verlag, 1950.

Schmitt, Carl, 'Nomos Nahme Name', in *Der Beständige Aufbruch: Festschrift für Erich Przywara*, Nuremberg: Glock & Lutz, 1959, pp. 92–105.

Schmitt, Carl, *The Nomos of the Earth*, New York: Telos Press, 2003.

Schmitt, Carl, *On the Three Types of Juristic Thought*, Westport, CT: Praeger, 2004.

Schmitt, Carl, *Political Romanticism*, Cambridge, MA: MIT Press, 1986.

Schmitt, Carl, *Political Theology*, Cambridge, MA: MIT Press, 1985.

Schmitt, Carl, *Political Theology II*, Cambridge: Polity Press, 2008.

Schmitt, Carl, *Politische Romantik*, Berlin: Duncker & Humblot, 1919.

Schmitt, Carl, *Positionen und Begriffe*, Berlin: Duncker & Humblot, 1940.

Schmitt, Carl, *Roman Catholicism and Political Form*, Westport, CT: Greenwood Press, 1996.

Schmitt, Carl, *Staat, Bewegung, Volk*, Hamburg: HAVA, 1933.

Schmitt, Carl, *Theorie des Partisanen: Zwischenbemerkung zum Begriff des Politischen*, Berlin: Duncker & Humblot, 1963.

Schmitt, Carl, *Theory of the Partisan*, East Lansing, MI: Michigan State University Press, 2004.

Schmitt, Carl, *Theory of the Partisan*, New York: Telos Press, 2007.

Schmitt, Carl, 'Die Tyrannei der Werte', in *Säkularisation und Utopie – Ebracher Studien: Ernst Forsthoff zum 65. Geburtstag*, Stuttgart: Kohlhammer, 1967.

Schmitt, Carl, *Über die drei Arten des rechtswissenschaftlichen Denkens*, Hamburg: Hanseatische Verlagsanstalt, 1934.

Schmitt, Carl, 'Das Zeitalter der Neutralisierungen und Entpolitisierungen', in *Begriff des Politischen: Text von 1932 mit eimen Vorwart und drei Corollarien*, Berlin: Duncker & Humblot, 1963.

Schwitter, Philippe, *The Conditions for Post-Hobbesian Order*,

Madrid: Centro de Estudios avanzadios en Ciencas sociales, 1993.

Scott, Joan Wallach, *Gender and the Politics of History*, New York: Columbia University Press, 1988.

Sen, Amartya, 'Does Globalization Equal Westernization?', *The Globalist*, March 25, 2002, at theglobalist.com.

Sen, Amartya, 'Human Rights and Asian Values', Sixteenth Morgenthau Memorial Lecture, New York: Carnegie Council on Ethics and Foreign Affairs, 1997.

Sen, Amartya, *Identity and Violence*, New York: W.W. Norton, 2006.

Sen, Amartya, 'Indian Traditions and the Western Imagination', *Daedalus* 134:4 (Fall 2005).

Sen, Amartya, 'Values and Economic Success', lecture given for the ninth International Prize of Catalonia, Barcelona, May 14, 1997 (unpublished).

Serres, Michel, *Detachment*, Athens: Ohio University Press, 1989.

Serres, Michel, *Hermès V. Le Passage du Nord-Ouest*, Paris: Minuit, 1980.

Severino, Emanuele, *Il destino della tecnica*, Milan: Rizzoli, 1998.

Sloterdijk, Peter, *Sphären*, Frankfurt: Suhrkamp, 1998–99.

Sloterdijk, Peter, *Im Weltinnenraum des Kapitals: Für eine philosophische Theorie der Globalisierung*, Frankfurt: Suhrkamp, 2005.

Soros, George, *The Crisis of Global Capitalism*, London: Little, Brown, 1998.

Steiner, George, *After Babel: Aspects of Language and Translation*, Oxford: Oxford University Press, 1975.

Taylor, Charles, *The Ethics of Authenticity*, Cambridge, MA: Harvard University Press, 1991.

Taylor, Charles, *Multiculturalism*, ed. Amy Gutmann, Princeton, NJ: Princeton University Press, 1994.

Todorov, Tzvetan, *On Human Diversity*, Cambridge, MA: Harvard University Press, 1993.

Touraine, Alain, *Critique of Modernity*, Oxford: Blackwell, 1995.

Tullio-Altan, Carlo, *Le grandi religioni a confronto*, Milan: Feltrinelli, 2002.

Tulloch, Sara (ed.), *The Oxford Dictionary of New Words*, Oxford: Oxford University Press, 1991.

Valéry, Paul, 'Avant-Propos', in *Oeuvres II*, Paris: Gallimard (Bibliothèque de la Pléiade), 1960.

Valéry, Paul, 'On History', in *History and Politics*, London: Routledge & Kegan Paul, 1963.

Vattimo, Gianni, *The Adventure of Difference*, Cambridge: Polity Press, 1993.

Vattimo, Gianni, *Beyond Interpretation*, Cambridge: Polity Press, 1997.

Veca, Salvatore, *Dell'Incertezza: Tre meditazioni filosofiche*, Milan: Feltrinelli, 1997.

Voltaire, *Candide*, New York: W.W. Norton, 1991.

Voltaire, *Philosophical Dictionary*, London: Penguin, 1972.

Voltaire, *Treatise on Tolerance and Other Writings*, Cambridge: Cambridge University Press, 2000.

Wallerstein, Immanuel, *The Modern World-System*, vols. 1–4, New York: Academic Press, 1974–2001.

Walzer, Michael, *Spheres of Justice*, Oxford: Oxford University Press, 1983.

Weber, Max, *Gesammelte Aufsätze zur Religionssoziologie*, vol. 1, Tübingen: J.C.B. Mohr, 1920.

Weber, Max, *Gesamtausgabe*, vol. I/19, Tübingen: J.C.B. Mohr, 1989.

Weber, Max, 'Politics as a Vocation', in *The Vocation Lectures*, Indianapolis: Hackett Publishers, 2004.

Weber, Max, *The Protestant Ethic and the Spirit of Capitalism*, London: Unwin University Books, 1976.

Weber, Max, *The Religion of China: Confucianism and Taoism*, New York: Macmillan, 1964.

Weber, Max, 'Science as a Vocation', in *The Vocation Lectures*, Indianapolis: Hackett Publishers, 2004.

Weininger, Otto, *The Clinical Psychology of Melanie Klein*, Springfield, IL: Charles C. Thomas, 1984, pp. 65 and 66.

Williams, Bernard, *Ethics and the Limits of Philosophy*, London: Fontana, 1985.

Williams, Bernard, *Moral Luck*, Cambridge: Cambridge University Press, 1981.

Wittgenstein, Ludwig, *Philosophical Investigations*, Oxford: Blackwell, 1973.

Wittgenstein, Ludwig, *Tractatus Logico-Philosophicus*, New York: Routledge & Kegan Paul, 1961.

Wright, Georg Henrik von, *Practical Reason*, Oxford: Oxford University Press, 1983.

Yates, Frances A., *Astraea: The Imperial Theme in the Sixteenth Century*, London: Routledge & Kegan Paul, 1975.

Yates, Frances A., *Theatre of the World*, Chicago: University of Chicago Press, 1969.

Young, I. M., *Justice and the Politics of Difference*, Princeton, NJ: Princeton University Press, 1990.

INDEX

Orientalism, 62, 231
Origin and Goal of History (Jaspers), 47
Ortiz, Renato, 16
Osterhammel, Jürgen, 227
other, 82, 196, 231
    and Occident, 50–52, 233–34
    and politics, 237
outside/inside, 18–19, 241

Panikkar, Raimon, 234
Panofsky, Erwin, 9
Parfit, Derek, 83, 194
    Reasons and Persons, 193
Parsons, Talcott, *Structure of Social Action*, 13
Pasqualotto, Giangiorgio, 227
Pasquino, Gianfranco, 160
Passerin d'Entrèves, Alessandro, 89
    Notion of the State, 89
    the people, 121, 163, 203–4, 207, 211
persona ficta, 90–91
persuasion, 159
Philoctetes (Sophocles), 82
Philosophical Dictionary (Voltaire), 181
Pizzorno, Alessandro, 171, 212
pluralism, 42–43, 62, 68, 167, 204, 232
    corporate, 42, 103, 133, 136
Polanyi, Karl, 129–53
    on capitalism, 136, 138
    and economic, 138–39
    on economy and society, 134, 136, 138
    'Economy as Instituted Process', 139
    and gift, 147–48
    The Great Transformation, 129, 133, 137
    on individualism, 60, 143–44
    'Our Obsolete Market Mentality', 134, 152
    Primitive, Archaic and Modern Economies,
        145
    on rationalism, 130
    on sacred and society, 149–50
    state and market, 129–32
    themes in, 134–35
    and unproductive expenditure, 145–47
    and Weber, 134, 138–41, 150–51
the political, 40–41, 123, 126–27
    crisis of, 2, 65
    and decisionism, 122
    defined, 118–20
    justice, 75
    and nomos, 125
    vs political theology, 121
    and state, 117, 119
    terms, 90
Political Liberalism (Rawls), 44, 74–75
Political Romanticism (Schmitt), 108, 116
Political Theology (Schmitt), 111
political theology, 111–17
    vs political, 121
politics, 68
    bio-, 24–25, 39, 97, 189, 191, 217
    and conflict of values, 67
    deficit of, 215
    friend/enemy, 118–19, 121, 126
    and other, 237

and perspective, 170
and public sphere, 185
and religion, 13, 36
techno-, 98
and technology, 2
of translation, 238
without state, 219
Polybius, 6, 40
Popper, Karl, 182
postmodernism, 20–21
The Postnational Constellation (Habermas),
    199
Potere e Secolarizzazione (Marramao), 20,
    110
power, 70, 93, 100–101, 172–73
    constituent, 205–9
Primitive, Archaic and Modern Economies
    (Polanyi), 145
primitive culture, 134, 136, 148
Prison Notebooks (Gramsci), 143
privatisation, 130
Prodi, Paolo, 87, 91
Protestantism, 56, 58, 60
public sphere, 66–67, 201
    and politics, 185
Pufendorf, Samuel von, 89
Puritanism, 57, 60

rational behavior, 164–65, 167, 170
rational dialogue, 159
rationalism, 64, 67, 166–67
    and crisis of state, 131
    and economic, 139
    Enlightenment, 112
    and excess, 141
    and norm, 138, 142, 150–51
    Polanyi on, 130
    polycentric development of, 54
    vs religion, 47
    vs tradition, 56
    and unproductive expenditure, 147
    utilitarian, 73–74, 142
    Western, 45–48, 50, 55, 59, 110, 119,
        123–24, 134, 140–41, 151, 157, 160,
        171, 234, 237
        and domination, 151
        and jurisprudence, 124
        liberty, equality, fraternity, 157, 160–61
Rawls, John, 42, 44, 66, 165, 232, 243
    Political Liberalism, 44, 74–75
    A Theory of Justice, 74
Reasons and Persons (Parfit), 193
Recasting Bourgeois Europe (Maier), 137
recognition, 44–45, 151, 159, 165, 183, 217,
    223, 235–37
    indifference towards, 159
    and tolerance, 183
Reflections on the World Today (Valéry), 1–3,
    12, 53
Relectiones (Vitoria), 102
religion:
    and civilisations, 15
    of market, 142